MARKETING HOTELS AND RESTAURANTS INTO THE 90s

MARKETING HOTELS AND RESTAURANTS INTO THE 90s

A SYSTEMATIC APPROACH TO INCREASING SALES

SECOND EDITION

MELVYN GREENE

VNR VAN NOSTRAND REINHOLD
New York

First published in 1987 by
William Heinemann Ltd
London, England

ISBN 0-442-20509-0

Published in the U.S. and Canada by
Van Nostrand Reinhold
115 Fifth Avenue
New York, New York 10003

Distributed in Canada by
Macmillan of Canada
Division of Canada Publishing Corporation
164 Commander Boulevard
Agincourt, Ontario M1S 3C7, Canada

16 15 14 13 12 11 10 9 8 7 6 5 4 3

Printed in Great Britain

PREFACE

This book is a revised, expanded edition based on my past experience of marketing hotels and restaurants, and on my thoughts about the future. It is aimed at a larger readership and it is also essential reading for those who purchased the first edition, since markets have changed even if marketing principles have not.

A number of people spoke to me after the first edition of this book was published in 1983. There is no doubt that the hotels and hotel groups who obtained maximum benefit from the book in increased sales were those who gave a personal copy to every department head and key executive so that they could read it at their own pace. They then listed all the points they could introduce and agreed these action points at a meeting after the relevant management had all read the book. The publication of this book should help hoteliers to follow such a procedure.

My consultants have worked in most countries in the Western world, and I have visited most of them. Countries in which I have actually worked, rather than just visited, are:

- Belgium
- Britain
- Canada
- Cyprus
- France
- Holland
- India
- Ireland
- Israel
- Italy
- Jamaica
- Kenya
- Malta
- Mauritius
- Nigeria
- Portugal
- Spain, Majorca, Ibiza
- Swaziland
- Tanzania
- Tunisia
- USA

I am therefore familiar with the problems of hoteliers and restaurateurs in many countries and have written the book with this in mind. The principles contained in it can be applied internationally, not just in my native country, Britain, or in America where I have had many years of experience.

Although the book is about hotels, a major proportion of it is also intended for restaurateurs and executives in all forms of commercial catering and food service, where the principles of marketing are equally applicable. There is a completely new chapter on increasing restaurant sales.

I have deliberately avoided including a mass of statistics in this book. What I am more interested in is inspiring you, the person reading these words at this moment, to make sure that if there is growth you obtain your share of it. That you pick the segments where there will be growth. And if there is no growth that you stay profitable by beating the average.

Melvyn Greene

CONTENTS

ACKNOWLEDGEMENTS

There are various people who urged me to write this book. Unfortunately, there are too many to name them all. But there were a few people who gave me specific help and I would like to acknowledge this with my sincere thanks.

Firstly, Sir Maxwell Joseph who died before publication. He wrote the Foreword and I will never forget how he helped me many times in my career.

There was Robin Henderson, financial controller of Thistle Hotels and a consultant and company secretary to Gleneagles Hotel Limited until his retirement. Robin checked my arithmetic and the figures and calculations generally. Professor Rik Medlik of Horwath and Horwath was very helpful and gave me some constructive suggestions. And I would like to thank Miles Quest, managing director of Wordsmith and Company, for his honest but constructive criticism when he edited the first edition of this book for me.

But there was one person who helped me when I felt like giving up, and put up with my moods and frustrations as I gradually wrote both editions of the book and I would like to thank her. She urged me to start, and constantly encouraged me. This is my wife, Helen.

I

INTRODUCTION

The first edition of this book published in 1983 was very successful. In the UK market it was reprinted three times and a considerable number of copies were exported. Many major companies bought copies for each hotel. The book is being published in America by AVI Publishing and has become an immediate success. Many American universities and colleges with hospitality courses are buying copies for every student. It has also been translated into French and is being published by Editions Delta e Spes of Switzerland to be marketed in France, Belgium, Switzerland, French-speaking Canada, Morocco and Tunisia. As far as we can ascertain this is the first time a hotel management book written in English has ever been translated into French.

The publishers, William Heinemann, have decided to publish this paperback edition, and at the same time I have taken the opportunity to revise and update the book where appropriate. This edition has fifty additional pages.

Markets are changing constantly and it is necessary to update a book on the subject. But marketing principles do not change and therefore the main part of the book requires little revision.

Chapter 7 on market segmentation has been revised completely. A number of social changes covered in the first edition are still occurring – but more so, particularly on active leisure and eating habits. Predictions in this chapter of social developments like 'non-smoker' bedrooms have come true. The new chapter deals with my experience on why sometimes they work and other times appear to be unsuccessful. The pitfalls of marketing to some of the newer segments are covered. Unfortunately a new market situation has developed which must be covered by most hoteliers from an operating and marketing viewpoint, namely security.

During the last twenty years I have worked in many countries but primarily in America and Europe. This book has been written to benefit hoteliers from most countries. In writing for a number of different countries I am aware that markets vary. Americans may ask you to dine with them at 6 p.m. (or earlier), Britons at 8 p.m., and I have been invited to dinner in Spain at 10 p.m. History, religion and tradition cause marketing differences. Most sensible people like to sit down and relax over a drink. We 'crazy' Britons prefer to stand up when we drink our pints in a pub. On the Continent of Europe good service is a leisurely meal, in America slow service is often considered bad service. Some countries start a meal with coffee, others never have coffee till the end of the meal. Even so, after working in numerous different countries I believe that while the circumstances are different, the problems, and in particular the future marketing problems, are very similar.

In writing a book for hoteliers from various countries there was a potential communication problem, even if we all speak English. I apologize if at times my words, jargon or spelling are different from your own. I decided early on (unless it was totally inappropriate) to use dollars as a currency throughout the book. I could not keep chopping and changing from sterling to dollars to rupees. And dollars are still the most widely-used international currency in tourism. I make no apology for being wrong on some of the things predicted. If you are paid, as I often am, to look ahead, then there are many times when you are going to be wrong. Better to take a risk and say something than play safe and say nothing.

Many restaurateurs (and hoteliers) who read the first edition asked me to write a book on marketing restaurants. Frankly, this is an enormous task. However, a completely new chapter on this subject is included in this edition, condensing as much as I could incorporate of my practical experience into one chapter.

When you are a management consultant it is very easy to spend most of your time on hotels and restaurants with marketing and cost problems. From an early age when I first started working in hotels in Florida and Jamaica I sought after success stories. I wanted to find hotels that did better than anyone else – better than the average. I actively sought out hotels which achieved profits which were above the inter-hotel comparative figures.

Whenever I found one with higher sales *and* profits I would ask whether I could examine their operation and talk to the management, at their convenience, and at my own expense. I never received a refusal in America where owners would usually show me all their facts and figures except once with McDonalds, who politely refused. I rarely received a refusal outside America. In fact, many of these hotels and restaurants became clients over the years when I started my own consultancy. I found, to my surprise, that successful profitable companies used and paid for my consultancy services more often than unprofitable hotels, who often were complacent and did not realize they had a problem.

A common theme began to appear with the success stories. The owners and management tended to be more inclined towards marketing and sales rather than cost control. Further, wherever they were constantly seeking to maximize room, double and bed occupancies at all costs they would experience a major profit problem on a cyclic basis which sometimes drove them into liquidation or forced them to sell. But where they were seeking a balance between achieving high occupances *and* high average room rates earned, these managers appeared to experience much higher *long-term* profits.

Another common link I found between the successful hoteliers was an ability to think and plan ahead. It is in my experience that the very nature of the hotel and restaurant business pressures management to think short-term – about today's problems or the next meal period. Most managers end in a trap of rarely thinking ahead more than the coming season, or year. But I found the highly profitable managers often thought two or three years ahead.

A few years ago something started to happen. I was always being asked to speak to the Board of Directors, or the top management team, of hotel companies and to professional associations. But suddenly the requested topics all had a similar theme. 'Melvyn, we would like you to brainstorm ahead about markets and marketing in the next ten years.'

More and more people asked me to talk about titles like:

'Marketing trends in the 80s'
or
'Social and technological trends in the 80s'.

They also all had one common worry and this was 'adequate room rates'. In the three years prior to writing this book I gave twenty speeches, all on similar themes, to nine major hotel groups, two universities and three professional and trade associations. Five other speeches were given to groups of pension funds and institutions in the City of London. I went to India to give a similar talk there to thirty top Indian hoteliers in Bombay and Delhi – spoke to Israeli hoteliers in Jerusalem, Herzlia, Elat, and Cypriot hoteliers in Lanarca. The themes of all the talks were not just occupancies but Average Room Rates and The Future.

Suddenly everyone was aware that the world and the hotel industry were changing rapidly and this change could accelerate in the future. It was not that I was becoming the guru of the hotel industry, only as some managing directors said, 'You have time to think about the future, we are bogged down with the current problems'. What worried me was finding more and more people talking about the 'hotel of the future', showing lovely drawings and models, when we should have been talking about the markets of the future first, and we were getting it the wrong way round. Some hotels were being built which were monuments to the architects, but were dwarfing the personality of the guests. People might try them once but not stay in them regularly. I feel that the building of Megahotels in the last decade – however spectacular and magnificent – has ended, because this is not what an hotel guest really wants. Many hoteliers disagree and claim that the spectacular lobbies and public areas overcome the problem of size. But I have noticed that these same breathtaking lobbies are jammed with sightseers and non-paying guests. Paying guests complain it is like living in Grand Central Station or Waterloo Station.

More hoteliers will realize in the future that it is very difficult to sustain a high average occupancy *and* a high average room rate in a huge hotel, except where the hotel is an adjunct to some other money making source like gambling, or gaming as it is called in Britain. It is interesting to note that the first three hotels listed in last summer's issue of *Hotel and Travel Index*'s league table of largest hotels are all in Las Vegas, Nevada – The Las Vegas Hilton with 3174 rooms, MGM Grand with 2900 rooms and The Flamingo Hilton third with 2250 rooms.

I was also becoming increasingly worried that the hotel industry might follow the fate of the airline industry which has only recently returned to profits after some years of huge losses running into billions. Many airlines can be supported by their governments. The hotel industry is, by and large, owned by commercial interests with a large number of private shareholders who could never carry this level of loss. I have watched, with growing dismay over the years, the airlines' obsession with 'bottoms on seats' and being the cheapest rather than the best or the best value for money.

I do not want this to happen to the hotel industry.

In the last year or two I wanted to write a book on the next decade and this became a burning ambition. So I deliberately made the time available. In a later Section you will see that, in my opinion, even after spending a long time in the hotel industry many top executives still do not fully understand marketing hotels. Many do. Others are good at operating hotels but tend to be product orientated and do not really understand the constantly changing market. Because of the nature of the hotel industry, particularly where management and staff live in or spend long hours on the premises, it is very easy and understandable to become product orientated rather than market orientated. This is not meant as a destructive criticism of the hotel industry as a whole. But competition is going to be much more intense over the next decade. By competition I do not necessarily mean other hotels or countries competing for international tourism or conferences. I am thinking rather of manufacturing industries and retailers selling a whole range of products. It will be a battle for the consumers' disposable spending power. The question in the future may well be whether the consumer buys a video tape recorder, changes his silent movie camera for a sound camera, buys a new home dishwasher – or takes that holiday in an hotel.

In the next decade we appear to be facing a period of continuous rising costs. After the growth decades of the 50s and 60s up to 1973, and a decade of mixed fortunes since, we could face a decade into the 90s where there is slow expansion, or even no growth, together with growing competition. The increased competition could arise from:

up-market self catering
time sharing
home entertainment

and other trends, as well as the competition from producers of a whole variety of consumer products and services.

Many of the producers and retailers of other consumer products are very sophisticated in their marketing. We in the hotel industry must ensure that we obtain our share of future market spending. In order to do so we must recognize the full and changing marketing scene, and spread this 'gospel' to every member of the staff. We must also develop more systematic and dynamic sales action plans. More systematic sales action plans need not stifle flair, but can help develop it. In fact, with the total involvement of all employees advocated in later chapters it is my firm belief that the systematic approach will encourage flair and initiative by creating a more sales-orientated approach. Hence the reason why this book has the subtitle *A systematic approach to increasing sales*.

No book can ever supply all of the answers. And a book tends by its nature to be generalized rather than specific. I would far sooner be sitting in your office, in your hotel at this moment talking about your specific problems. However good your marketing has been in the past, this book is a genuine attempt to help improve it in the future. Apart from assisting your long-term planning it will give you a mass of points which will help you in the immediate few months.

This book is on marketing which, as you all know, includes selling. Once you have defined, or redefined, your markets you have to reach those markets by selling. Selling itself is a huge subject. In this book I have concentrated on marketing and sales action plans with less emphasis on sales techniques. This is not to underplay sales techniques because they are of prime importance. If you take techniques as including:

Paid advertising
Unpaid publicity
Sales letters and mailing shots
Telephone selling
Face-to-face selling

and all the myriad variations of each of these, including the technological improvements in, say, just one aspect – mailing shots – within the next decade, you will see that it would easily double the size of this book.

Each technique deserves a book on its own. There have been a lot of other books written about the individual techniques of selling (letters, advertising, public relations) so I have concentrated on marketing and sales action plans. If you get the marketing wrong, a large proportion of the sales effort will be dissipated or totally wasted. As you will read later, I believe the world, and hotel markets are going to change more rapidly in the 80s and 90s than ever before. So forgive me if I neglect sales techniques a little. But I have included some sections on the different techniques of selling with brief comments and some useful checklists.

Similarly, I deliberately decided to avoid including masses of statistics. They often look very impressive. But there are numerous books, magazines and other publications full of statistics. A lot of bright people take the past statistics and project them into the rest of this century. What does it all mean? We all know that there has been a considerable growth in international tourism, the convention market, business incentive markets overall, with a few 'hick-ups' like the 1973–5 period and lower growth in 1980–3. But does past growth necessarily mean future growth? Some of the most interesting future statistics are produced by the aircraft manufacturers (rather than the airlines) but their top research executives can hardly be described as objective. Can you imagine a researcher in Lockheed or Boeing coming up with a report predicting a decline in aircraft passengers over the next decade? He would not be very popular with his employers. Recently I read in another study paper that 'world traffic will double by 1990 and more than triple by the year 2000'.

Later on I will be commenting on why I feel there will be a growth in some market segments for the hotel industry. But honestly I am guessing and so is everyone else. However, you will still find that whatever the problems are over the next ten years this book is essentially one of optimism, particularly when you read about the Threshold Barrier in the last Chapter.

What I am interested in is 'inspiring' you, the person reading these words at this moment, to make sure that if there is growth you obtain your share of it. That you pick the segments where there will be growth. And if there is no growth that you, my reader, stay profitable by beating the average.

In these days of women's liberation and the feminist movement an author should not talk about businessmen but business executives. I found it very difficult to do this throughout the book. So please bear with me if occasionally I write in the masculine only, where it is obviously intended to include the feminine.

Markets are changing constantly and a book on marketing could well have parts which are out of date by the time it is published. But I had to stop at some point so I set myself a deadline and then stopped writing. And if I digress and wander from a logical pattern, it will be because I want to make a point that may well stick in your mind and suddenly be remembered at an important moment in the future. So I thought it would be useful if I started by elaborating in the next chapters the men and one woman who influenced me over the last twenty years to become a totally committed marketing man. All of these stories in the next section have a moral. Since the first edition, numerous people have raised some of the points behind the four stories. In particular the fourth true story about the prostitute will probably be more relevant over the next few years.

I promise you now that if you invest just a few hours of your time reading this book you will have a greater 'feel' for successful marketing in the next decade or two.

☆ ☆ ☆ ☆ ☆

2

PEOPLE WHO HAVE HAD A LASTING INFLUENCE ON MY MARKETING ATTITUDES

Nobody starts life as a born marketing man, or woman, although I have met some 'born again' marketing men who have suddenly 'seen the light' or got the right message. Marketing is a complex attitude of mind and as elaborated later some people understand marketing in its fullest sense and others are too product-orientated and therefore can miss market opportunities.

But people can change. I have met hoteliers who have attended a course, or had an unusual experience, which has suddenly made them much more marketing conscious than before. One manager, and I do not think he is alone in this, is convinced he became much better at marketing when he stopped living in the hotel. Sometimes people hear a phrase or a statement said in a different way which helps change their tactics and attitude. As a simple example, a number of people have said this about the phrase – 'don't sell a mile wide and an inch deep'. Many times people have said this is where they have gone wrong in the past. Reading, management courses, or your own drive and entrepreneurial flair can make you better at marketing. And very often other people can have a major influence in this direction.

A series of people have influenced my thinking on marketing and readers may well benefit from hearing about them, what they said or did. Now I do not keep a diary and I apologize for a whole series of stories and events which may not be one hundred per cent correct. But they are all based on real events that influenced me in my knowledge of marketing hotels and they are elaborated in later sections. They are all based on true experiences even if time may have made some aspects a little vague. I may have slipped a year here and there or amounts may not be exactly accurate but the message is important.

Thousands of people have influenced me in my career. I am a

mental sponge, a watcher of people, a constant learner. The thousands have influenced me on all aspects of our industry – food, control, forward strategies, standards, hygiene. Hundreds have influenced me on marketing. People who have heard me speak, or been on one of our five day marketing and sales promotion courses ten years ago still write to me to tell me about their bright ideas and I learn from this. But a few people stick in my mind as having had a major influence or just 'opened my eyes'. One is dead. One who is still very much alive, Vic Lownes III, may not remember me. This does not matter.

The people are

Fred R. Bentley, C.P.A.
John Monahan
Victor Lownes III
A prostitute in Jamaica.

I have tried to write about them in approximately chronological sequence following the periods in which I met them and the order is no way an indication of their importance. The last three cover the twenty years I have worked exclusively in the hotel and food service industry.

FRED BENTLEY, C.P.A.

Fred Bentley was the greatest management man I ever knew, a Briton who had worked in America until war broke out in 1939 when he returned to Britain. I worked for him from the age of 21 to 26. He had a small top quality management consultancy firm in the 50s only advising large companies on top organizational problems. He believed any firm of management consultants should never employ more than twenty people and he really preferred only ten staff. His minimum fee under any circumstances was $5,000 (in the 50s!) and I once saw him charge $2,000 in 1958 for *one* day's work sorting out a tricky organizational problem. The client wrote out a cheque without any hesitation as we were still sitting there at the end of the day.

He advertised for experienced consultants *over* 30 years. I applied, aged 21. As I walked in he said 'O.K., sell yourself to me.' I tried and he never said a word the whole time. When I finished he then gave me a lesson on selling myself which I will never forget. He reversed roles and sold himself to me as if he was the cheeky young applicant of 21 and I was the wise man of 70. It was an 'eye opener' on selling yourself for a job. Briefly it was devoted to the fact that although I was only 21 my whole career to date had proven that I had done everything early – passed every exam young – and I *was a quick learner*. Within a few years I would be the best investment he ever made (his words).

He gave me the job and I received three pay rises in the first year – yes, three! Have you ever worked for a boss who gave you three pay rises in one year? He once blitzed me over my expenses. Not for fiddling, but for staying in a lower grade hotel than him. 'Melvyn, when I go to Manchester I always stay at the Midland Hotel. What sort of an image are you creating for the firm by saving me peanuts by staying in a cheaper hotel?' (Hoteliers please note this attitude – there is still a massive market of businessmen who think about image when they are selling and not saving a few dollars a night.)

Bentley was a C.P.A. but he disliked accountants because he said they did not understand marketing. He could never understand when business was bad, as it often was in the 50s, why the accountants' first move was to reduce advertising and marketing. He believed this was the time to spend more money *selectively* and *effectively* on marketing. He taught me a lot about marketing. Unfortunately he died in 1958.

But one story he told me stays in my memory forever. As you know, there are many hotels that operate at consistently high average room occupancies or are always busy in certain months of the year. Or the restaurant is always full. It is very tempting and logical at times to cut marketing, advertising and sales costs and effort, in the periods that seem to fill up naturally year after year and to concentrate time and money on areas of the hotel which are less busy.

I worked with Mr. Bentley for nearly six years before I went to Florida to specialize in the hotel industry. One day we were working in one of the largest fork lift truck manufacturers in Britain who totally dominated the market. They worked on a net profit margin of 11 per cent on total sales. I noticed that they spent 6 per cent on marketing. I suggested to Mr. Bentley that they could easily halve marketing, and net profit would increase overnight to 14 per cent. Perhaps they might even eliminate marketing completely. He looked at me kindly and told me a story.

'When I lived in America prior to 1939 most people travelled long distances by train. You boarded the train and nothing happened. The driver then got on and with a lot of huffing and puffing the train began to move – five miles per hour, ten, thirty, fifty, seventy miles per hour. And the train continued to chug along quite fast, mile after mile after mile, at a steady seventy miles per hour. After this happened for an hour or two you might, if you were clever, like young Greene, decide that you could save a lot of money by throwing out the driver. And it would be *true* that the impetus of that train would continue to keep it going at seventy miles per hour for a time. But you could bet your bottom dollar that eventually the train would slow down.' 'The same point applies to marketing'. Bentley said.

Many times since then a similar suggestion has been put to me:

'The hotel is doing so well, why spend so much on marketing and selling?'
'The food and beverage areas are so busy – let's cut back on promotion there and spend the money elsewhere.'

You will see later that I believe in isolating the 'quiet' and 'soft' periods of every area of the hotel so that the Plan of Action is aimed at improving them. But never neglect the busy areas and times, because very gradually the customers will move to your competition.

JOHN MONAHAN

In 1962 I was working in Miami and getting a lot of experience, but mainly in accounting and control. I worked as a night auditor at The Everglades, on income control at The Eden Roc, on Food and Beverage Control in other hotels. But I was getting no experience of marketing. At that time Miami was a really swinging place – everyone seemed to be in the 20 to 50 age group and it was certainly different from the situation over the last ten years. So I went around asking who was the best man in that whole part of Florida on marketing. Time and time again the answer was John Monahan of The Diplomat Hotel Convention Center, Hollywood by the Sea, Florida. So a friend at Horwath, Maurice Burritt, introduced me to him.

I just said that I wanted to 'sit at his feet' and watch him work. It was an incredible experience. He wore what I thought was a pretty flash suit and as we walked round the hotel and pool he seemed to know every guest by name. 'Hi, Mr. Goldberg, how's your new grandson – don't forget to invite me to the Brith (circumcision).' I thought John Monahan was great but, in my young, patronising, British manner a 'typical salesman'. Near the end of the trip he changed my mind.

John took me through his whole guest history record systems, the filing and mailing systems. The whole highly efficient back-up system – you know, the boring but essential work – which made John Monahan not just a good salesman but the best and highest paid in that area of Florida. His parting words were 'Mel, if I was selling in Europe I would wear a different suit and be a quieter personality.' And he told me to go into selling because he said I had the best attribute of a good salesman. He said 'Mel, you have the gift of being a good listener and you flatter people without realizing it by listening so well.'

VICTOR LOWNES III

Prior to the opening of the London Playboy Club Vic Lownes, their chief executive for Europe up to 1981, was based in a lovely house in Montpelier Square, Kensington. He and his team were planning the opening and marketing of the Club in Park Lane. I used to go to Montpelier Square from time to time and they certainly were an interesting and stimulating crowd of people. Occasionally I was drawn into their creative brainstorming sessions.

I remember once when they were planning the pre-opening selling of the Club and someone asked 'How many mailing shots should we send out?' Now I thought they were going to say around 20,000 to 25,000 when Victor said '150,000', paused and added 'for the first mailing shot'. Now my memory may be wrong and the amounts may be slightly incorrect but I saw the results of that mailing campaign and they were incredible. Victor taught me that if you have done your research carefully on your targets and you are confident in your product, think big – be bold.

Since I wrote this Victor was fired from his job. If you ever wanted an example of how to squeeze the last drop of mileage of free P.R. out of a bad news situation it had to be Vic Lownes leaving London's Playboy Club. For days you would hardly pick up a paper, or watch television, without seeing another interview with Victor.

A PROSTITUTE IN JAMAICA

About twelve years ago I went on an assignment to Jamaica for the Jamaican Government, British Airways and Trust House Forte on the much delayed and at that time unopened Pegasus Hotel in Kingston, Jamaica. I had worked there before and I looked around a lot of the hotels on the Island talking to the management about occupancies, average room rates, and much else. I was staying in an hotel in Montego Bay and was approached by a hooker, or prostitute, in the grounds of the hotel.

She said 'Ten dollars.' I said 'No thank you.' Like a flash she heard my accent and said 'Twelve Canadian dollars.' Again I said 'No' and straightaway she said 'Five English pounds.' That girl was a born foreign exchange dealer.

Some years ago I gave a speech at a time when currency fluctuations were not that volatile and predicted that they would become more volatile. I said that in the future hotel management and marketing men in the foreign tour market would have to study the financial situations of the countries where their guests were coming from, try to avoid countries with weak economies and 'soft' currencies, and seek out hard currency markets, or at least avoid having too much occupancy from any country with a vulnerable currency.

One general manager who was an old friend said 'Come on, Melvyn, we are far too busy running our hotels without becoming financial experts as well – who has the time?' I told him the story about the hooker. She took the time to study exchange rates. The same general manager continued to sell to one major foreign tourism country and experienced severe occupancy problems in the years 1979–82 and 1986.

Many people have influenced me on marketing and I apologize for choosing just a few of those who have stayed in mind over the years. But each of these people helped me to become more marketing conscious. If you had met these people you would have been a better marketeer. I cannot introduce you to them but perhaps these stories have illustrated in a small way the impact they made on me.

* * * * *

3

MAIN ASPECTS OF SUCCESSFUL MARKETING

This chapter may sound a little negative and I know it is easy to criticise. But in Chapter 1, I mentioned that when working in a number of different hotels of varied styles, sizes and services (and in many different countries) I gained the feeling that some companies were not going to get their marketing right in the fiercely competitive inflationary decade ahead, i.e. into the 90s. This is not meant to be a destructive, generalized criticism. But I was finding quite often that a lot of people were continuing marketing and selling as they had done in the 80s, when economic circumstances and a rapidly changing market are going to be totally different in the future.

This comment applies to successful hotels as well as less successful hotels. We have all seen marketing success stories where the executives continue to follow the system because it has been successful in the past, even though circumstances were changing. Usually I came to this conclusion in even successful hotels and hotel groups, wherever the executives were not spending a proportion of their time thinking ahead. All the executives I know think ahead at some time but usually only about one year, i.e. over the annual budgets or targets.

At other times I found that the hoteliers were great product orientated craftsmen but did not really understand marketing in its fullest sense, and that markets have to be redefined continuously. So I am summarizing the major weakness, or potential weaknesses, as follows and then each one is elaborated in a following chapter. Of course there are many people who are very marketing conscious who are worried about the general potential for making sufficient profits in the future where there are a combination of negative factors:

economic recession
fuel shortages

rising operating costs
high interest charges
too many hotels in many areas.

The following are a series of marketing aspects where special thought and attention will have to be directed in the future. This is not to imply that they were neglected in the past but mainly that a fresh look at them with a greater thought and intensity will pay off over the next few difficult years. They are subdivided into:

- Planning Further Ahead than One Year
- Marketing and Redefining Markets
- Pricing Strategies
- The 80s, 90s and Greater Market Segmentation
- Promoting the Hotel
- Marketing and Sales in the Organization
- Marketing and Sales Action Plans
- The Threshold Barrier

Brief comments are made on each of the foregoing in this chapter, then each one is elaborated more fully under its own chapter.

PLANNING FURTHER AHEAD THAN ONE YEAR

As mentioned previously, too many people spend insufficient time quietly thinking about the future, except for the annual budget and, in some rare cases, a five year plan. This chapter elaborates why it is illogical to plan everything in calendar years from a marketing strategy viewpoint, and stresses the importance of taking a longer term stance on marketing particularly where a hotelier wishes to break into new markets.

MARKETING AND REDEFINING MARKETS

There are still too few people who understand and practise marketing in its fullest sense. Talk to some people about their total marketing and sales action plan and they will tell you about their paid advertising plan, or show you superb brochures. Others will proudly show you their new advanced reservations computer. It is great if a potential purchaser can book anywhere in the world from one telephone call in 10 seconds. But advancing technology should never take the place of a total marketing concept which makes the buyer decide to dial that particular number. He will not choose to stay with one hotel group against another solely on the ability to make a booking a few seconds faster than another group. (Although you will lose a potential customer if it takes too long to make a booking.)

A large number of books have been written on marketing generally. This chapter outlines the subject more specifically for hotels and shows how to keep redefining markets regularly.

PRICING STRATEGIES

One of the most difficult aspects of marketing hotels is fixing room tariffs, restaurant prices, banqueting menus and prices generally. Sales executives often complain to me that their hotel's prices are too high and XYZ hotel has just undercut them on a major convention or incentive tour.

Operating management often complain that sales prices are too low bearing in mind ever increasing costs. Who is right? Is there a magic formula to calculate the right price. I do not believe there is. But I do feel that management can be supplied with much more information in order to assist them in what very often turns out to be a decision based on experience, feel for a market, or knowledge of a particular major customer.

THE 80S, 90S AND GREATER MARKET SEGMENTATION

A large proportion of the hotel industry generalizes about markets and does not define market segments in anywhere near the depth that other consumer industries do. In reality competition is not just other hotels, or other countries' hotels, but all the other, highly efficient industries competing in the consumer spending market, e.g. new cars or the latest video equipment. They can often define their target market segment down to age bracket, earning power, place of residence, type of work, reading habits, etc. We in hotels still tend to talk in broad headings about:

businessmen
tourist – local
tourist – by nationality
convention delegates.

I hope to show later that in more successful marketing we must find out more about the segments who:

(a) use our facilities now (present market)
(b) could use our facilities in the future (target markets).

The more we find out what makes our market segments 'tick' the more successful we will be in putting across the right sales message – whether it is written or spoken – and attracting them to the hotel. It is my belief that new market segments will develop over the next decade or two, probably more rapidly than at any previous time. Assuming no major war, we are in for a period of vast technological change and incredible social upheaval. Everyone can see it. No-one seems to fully understand it. But it will create *new* marketing opportunities if we develop the attitude of mind to try to see the opportunities.

This is a vast subject and mainly for ease of reference it has been subdivided into two chapters:

80s and 90s
Market Segmentation.

PROMOTING THE HOTEL

There has often been a tendancy to promote 'The Hotel' as if it is one market, one source of business and one profit centre. You see this very often in hotel sales literature. Chapter 9 illustrates the danger of this and shows what we all know already, this is that hotels are a mixture of different businesses under one roof which may often require quite different marketing and sales techniques.

MARKETING AND SALES IN THE ORGANIZATION

If you examine the role of marketing and sales executives in an hotel's organization you will usually find that it is different in most hotels and many groups. It is also very apparent that some marketing departments and sales executives are far more successful than others, not because they are better at their job but because of their position in the organization. This chapter seeks to draw attention to anomalies in this function and puts forward some suggestions.

MARKETING AND SALES ACTION PLANS

Some hotels have a marketing and sales action plan which is so detailed, often in the form of a huge manual, that nobody really uses it – or dare not up-date and revise it – because of the work involved. Others have an action plan which is so skimpy and generalized that it never really produces results. And other hotels do not have a dynamic action plan, but tend to react to enquiries and present custom, rather than actively seeking to create new additional business. In this chapter I have attempted to set out the main aspects of a successful marketing and sales action plan.

THE THRESHOLD BARRIER

This chapter covers a viewpoint on why I believe there is considerable potential for growth in the hotel industry's future sales, namely the vast number of people who have never been inside an hotel because of what I call the Threshold Barrier. If this chapter provides hoteliers with a little more empathy for 'the silent majority' who do not use hotels now, but could well do so in the future, then this will certainly help improve future sales efforts.

The foregoing are brief comments on each aspect. All the main aspects of successful marketing are elaborated in the following chapters.

TIME

You will see in the following chapters that I am advocating simple but systematic sales plans. I am not going to deny that this may involve you in more time on marketing and selling than in the past.

Most people agree that if you own an hotel or a restaurant it is vital to 'reach out' and sell to past and prospective customers, and not to rely solely on word-of-mouth publicity. Yet many people do not do so. When I am called in to look at an hotel or restaurant which is experiencing financial problems, management often agrees that in the past it has done little selling – if any. Invariably, the reason given is that management was too busy. There are other occasions when a 'sales action plan' is agreed but not completely carried out, because of lack of time.

On the other hand, should you suggest to hoteliers that they join in the annual Beaujolais race, or the race to become the first hotel to have grouse on the menu after the Glorious Twelfth, they will be quite happy and willing to devote time to join in one of these activities.

In the hotel and restaurant industry there are some activities which are so sacrosanct, so traditional, that to criticize them or suggest that the time, money and effort should be spent in other directions, would be looked upon as heresy. Yet I wonder whether the time devoted to these activities is really worthwhile in increased sales and higher profits. One hotel manager, who joined in the Beaujolais race, worked out that it involved his hotel in seventeen man-days. This is ignoring all the costs involved. Similarly, the cost of bringing grouse to the restaurant table must be considerable, when you take into account the money spent (sometimes hiring a helicopter), and the man-days involved.

I am sure the Beaujolais race helps the sales of Beaujolais, but does it help the sales of the restaurant? Agreed these races obtain free publicity, but often this is lost in the welter of the publicity which is far from exclusive to one restaurant. How many people rush to restaurants because grouse appears on the menu? Does this kind of activity sustain an image of the restaurant industry, an image which might be out of date?

One excellent aspect of the grouse race is that it involves the chef in selling. I believe the chef and the restaurant manager can be two key people in the sales role 'outside' the restaurant, yet many people seem surprised at the suggestion.

You can always have time for selling if it is high on your priorities and you make the time.

Excluding selling as an automatic part of every manager's and head of department's (including the chef's) routine, here are a few aspects where an investment in time has proved incredibly worthwhile in higher sales and profits.

First, allocate an hour each week for the management team to sit around and discuss the customer rather than the product. Who is the customer, how did he or she hear of the restaurant, what markets are being missed, and how can you attract more business? Most meetings within hotels and restaurants are about the product, or the customers presently in the hotel. There are far more past customers who are absent, who have to be 'nursed' and attracted back to the hotel.

Second, make time to visit competition regularly and stay the night in competitive bedrooms. This is an extremely valuable investment and essential if you are to sell more effectively through advantage/limitation lists over your competition.

Allocating a member of your staff to read national newspapers and local papers for the catchment area, in order to pinpoint new potential customers who can be contacted with a sales approach, can produce surprising results.

Below is an extract from a newspaper showing the kind of advertisement that can produce a sales lead. It is from British Aerospace showing the hotels they use at present for their interviewing in different parts of the country. Another hotelier I know picked up a very useful event after reading in a newspaper the words 'venue to be announced', by going to see the organizers in order to sell his hotel as the venue.

Bristol, Unicorn Hotel	20 January
Cardiff, Park Hotel	8 February
Carlisle, Cumbrian Hotel	3 February
Chester, Blossoms Hotel	6 February
London, Bonnington Hotel	18 January
Newark, Robin Hood Hotel	27 January
Norwich, Hotel Nelson	25 January
Oxford, Bear Hotel – Woodstock	23 January
Perth, Isle of Skye Hotel	1 February
Southampton, Dolphin Hotel	18 January
Telford, Buckatree Hall Hotel – Wellington	10 February
York, Post House Hotel	30 January

There is a mass of sales clues in newspapers and magazines. But reading them takes time. Following them up and selling takes time. This investment in time is extremely worthwhile. If you can find the time to join in the Beaujolais or grouse races, then you should also find time for other aspects of selling.

☆ ☆ ☆ ☆ ☆

4

PLANNING AHEAD MORE THAN ONE YEAR

The very nature of the hotel industry tends to inhibit operational management from thinking and planning too far ahead. Very often management tends to manage from day to day because the problems arise throughout each day. The smaller the hotel the more the manager (who may be the owner) tends to be involved in day to day management. Even in some larger hotels the general manager may become involved in daily detail for a variety of reasons, e.g. because he cannot delegate, or he likes the detailed day to day aspects of hotel keeping.

The hotel industry tends to operate under a set of circumstances where the work load has peaks and troughs, and very often what I call 'hysterical peaks' particularly on the food and beverage side. Everything is very quiet in a restaurant, then suddenly ten different-sized groups of people walk in without having booked.

And anyone involved in functions or banquets will know what I mean in that all the brigade are poised and suddenly in the space of fifteen minutes 200 people start arriving for a banquet. Many times I have marvelled at the pressure a main central kitchen will work under from, say, 6 p.m. to 11 p.m. on a peak Saturday night when there are often meals being prepared for more than one restaurant, a number of functions – and room service. Yet before 6 p.m. all is calm, and suddenly around 11 p.m. it becomes 'quiet' again, except for the wash up. And everyone seems exhausted. It is the seasons and 'hysterical peaks' that can prevent departmental heads, and sometimes top management, from having the opportunity and energy to think and plan ahead.

And yet we know that the more one can plan ahead, the more a manager can anticipate problems, spot a new market trend and maximize profits. Most companies have an annual budget or target profit forecast with calendar months or periodic comparisons of actual results with budget. As the year progresses past the half-way stage, management sometimes becomes obsessive with the remaining accounting periods in the calendar year, particularly if the results are behind budget. And in the middle of the last few accounting months or periods, management are asked to prepare budgets for the following calendar year. Many managers complain that they are forced into becoming accountants rather than 'getting on with the job of managing'.

Does this situation help us with our forward marketing and in particular with redefining a market role if this becomes necessary?

It is my belief that an obsession with annual accounts is one of the main inhibiting factors in planned, long-term profit growth. If you examine any major industry, you will find there are natural seasons or cycles. And usually they are not exactly twelve calendar months. Sometimes they are shorter, sometimes longer. This applies to the hotel and food service industry as much as any other. But how did it come about?

In the beginning, so the Bible tells us, God decreed that there would be seven days in a week – six days of work and one of rest. It is interesting to note that, at this early point in time, metrication was not adopted – the week had seven days, not ten. As time passed, Man noticed the twenty-eight-day cycle of the moon and that there were thirteen cycles in what was later called a year. Later on, Western civilization came along and changed this to twelve months of varied lengths, with an odd day every four years 'to balance the books'.

And then, along came a series of people who laid down laws as if they were gods – everything had to be measured within a year. Who were these people? Lawyers in the Companies Acts, accountants, tax authorities and the Stock Market, to name just a few.

But is the hotel industry's natural cycle one of twelve months? No. Sometimes it is shorter, generally a season – like the summer, or the entertaining period up to and including Christmas and the New year. And, from a marketing point of view, it could be much longer than one year.

At this point you may well be thinking: 'Come on Melvyn, everyone measures results in a year.' Well, in fact they do not. There are special rules for construction companies involved in contracts running over many years, and in certain continuous-process industries. Moreover, the great insurance institution, Lloyds, measures its members' results every three years. Even the Chancellor of the Exchequer has a series of budgets nowadays rather than one per year.

So there are plenty of precedents.

What are the disadvantages of being 'locked' in a strict one year measurement of business success? The arch villains in this situation are, in my opinion, Wall Street and the Stock Market, and the obsessive fear that many companies have of showing a year of no profit growth, or a decline, with a consequent decrease in share value – and even a possible takeover approach. So as soon as we run into a difficult situation, we often consider a series of actions aimed at achieving last year's profits at all costs. However, these actions could well reduce profits in the long term.

Things a hotelier might be tempted to do to weather a difficult patch include:

- a cut in maintenance and decoration
- reduction in staff numbers – affecting the level of service
- a reduction in the little extras that create the whole experience of staying in a hotel – like the size of guest soap, the quality of the toilet paper
- restricting long-term marketing
- price cutting.

This type of action can rebound. Most companies I know already have a minimal staff level. And cutting back on decoration and maintenance is surely selling one's seedcorn. Recently, I was told by one group that profits would increase by $400,000 in a year if it reduced guest supplies by 5 cents per guest night. Now this might happen through better purchasing. But if it were just a reduction in size, quality, or both, then group costs might be reduced by $400,000 – but profits would not necessarily be increased at all.

And look at marketing. Supposing you want to redefine your marketing goals. Or perhaps you are already in a particular market, but want greater penetration. How long does it take to attract conventions, for example? Usually they are already booked for this or next year. So a marketing investment in one year could sometimes pay off in the second or third year in the convention market. Take the short break market. You would have to advertise and sell quite a lot in one year, as a cost, before the benefit (and repeat potential) paid off in subsequent years.

You all know the old 'rule' about a new hotel. First year it loses money. The second year it breaks even, then the third year shows a reasonable profit. The same applies to a lot of marketing effort and cost. If only a one year viewpoint is taken on marketing results, this seriously inhibits recovery from the present problems, and restricts long-term profit growth.

My case is that basically both operating and marketing management must have a marketing strategy looking ahead two to three years. I am not sure if the five year plans, where companies plan ahead, say, 1985 to 1989, then 1990 to 1995, really produce the level of profit growth that some managers believe because so often they are detailed accounting exercises with 70 per cent figures and 30 per cent (or less) marketing strategy.

The most successful form of long-term profit growth I have been involved with is where a company has fairly detailed annual profit projections and annual sales action plans – and two- to three-year forward marketing goals which are revised annually. So that at the end of 1986 we have a marketing strategy to 1989 and by the end of 1987, a revised marketing strategy to 1990.

To sum up, the forward plan looking ahead two to three years should include:

(a) Strategic aims over next two to three years. Profit objectives. Operational plans. Style, grade of hotel, and standards.

(b) Main sources of business and markets producing these sources.

(c) Detailed 'step by step' sales action plans for each source (e.g. rooms, banqueting, restaurant, etc.) analysed by logical periods compared against targets (e.g. function sales for season up to Christmas) so that the performance of sales executives and/or management can be monitored.

(d) Catering concepts over food and beverage. These are critically important bearing in mind that in many hotels the true net profit on food and beverage is quite often low. Creating the right food service concepts involves not only continuously redefining markets, but also a careful analysis of recipes and menu content bearing in mind payroll costs and skills, as well as food costs.

(e) Control of cost of food and liquor sales (buying, receiving, storage, issuing, preparation, etc.).

(f) Control of payroll (departmental amounts and percentages, staff standards, productivity yardsticks, etc.).

(g) Overheads cost control.

(h) Control of cash flow and capital expenditure including 'timed' expenditure on major renovations, re-equipping, upgrading, or expansion of facilities, where appropriate.

Obviously this book only covers marketing. But as mentioned in the following chapter, if marketing is all embracing as a concept right down to 'marketing for maximum long term profit', then payroll and other costs cannot be ignored and must be included in the TOTAL PLAN.

* * * * *

5

MARKETING AND REDEFINING MARKETS

WHAT IS MARKETING?

In order to maximize sales *and* net profits, there are three major aspects to be considered on a *continuous* basis:

- MARKETING
- PLAN OF ACTION
- SALES TECHNIQUES

Marketing involves choosing the best and most profitable markets to sell to, taking both a short and long term view-point. It involves continuously defining and, in many cases, redefining markets and sources of business. Following this, a plan of action is required to maximize sales from the defined markets. Lastly, you have to develop the right technique to achieve success from the action plan.

The major difference in marketing hotels as against other consumer products is that after a customer has spent money in hotels he has nothing physical to show for his money, as compared with buying, say, a television or a refrigerator. Effective marketing and dynamic selling is more important with hotels because once you have not sold a seat in a restaurant or a room in an hotel, that income is lost forever. In the case of selling consumer products, if you do not sell a product today, you might sell it tomorrow. A hotel bedroom, or a restaurant seat, has no 'shelf life'. Unless marketing is understood fully by the executive at the top of an hotel or hotel group, and there is a total commitment to the continuous need to market, the hotel will always experience the worst of the periodic downward cycles that every country, or area, experiences from time to time, and will not maximize profits from new markets and any upturn in a country or region's economy.

This deep understanding of the continuous nature of marketing by the man at the top must be spread down through the organization, through departmental heads to the actual waiter, chambermaid and telephone operator. If a hotel can train the staff who have actual contact with the guest on the philosophy of marketing, then they will automatically begin to service and sell to guests more effectively. If we add to this basic training in soft sell techniques then the hotel must succeed.

But so often hoteliers explain their marketing by showing you their computer booking service, or the advertising campaign for the coming season. All these are important, but only one part of the continuous circle of marketing. There is a lot of mystique about marketing. Not too long ago every salesman suddenly became a marketing executive. More recently there has been a reaction against the image of the high-powered, business degree type marketing executive, as people have begun to realize that someone, somewhere, actually had to *go out and sell.*

In fact, both are totally inter-related and selling will never be really successful unless markets have been chosen carefully. There are over thirty definitions of marketing. I have chosen five (see below) which I feel are particularly relevant to hotels and food service (and also to travel). In some ways they are views on marketing rather than definitions.

The first definition is by Gerry Draper, and two emanate from my own company. An illustration of the second definition and what we call the 'circle of marketing' is shown in Figure 5.1. By 'research' we mean 'digging out' facts, information, clues, etc. From this circle one can see that 'selling' is just one very essential part of the whole circle of marketing. The fourth definition is by a Swedish firm of advertising agents, Anderson and Lembke. I rather like this view of marketing with its emphasis on beating your competitors. All these definitions have a different emphasis but, read together, they cover our own industry rather than other consumer products. My favourite in many ways is the fifth, by Thomas F. Powers from his book *Introduction to Management in the Hospitality Industry*.

Just think back ten years – which is a relatively short time – to the changes the market demands as a minimum in bedroom facilities and you will see how the market changes. But probably the most rapid changes take place on food and beverage facilities. The capital equipping of a new restaurant may last ten years, but in looking at the feasibility of a new restaurant it is advisable to write the restaurant cost off over, say, only three years, because restaurants become obsolete so fast in marketing terms even if they are still satisfactory from an operation viewpoint.

Talk to many business executives who eat out often or stay in hotels regularly, and you will find a significant proportion who suffer from a severe case of 'menu fatigue'.

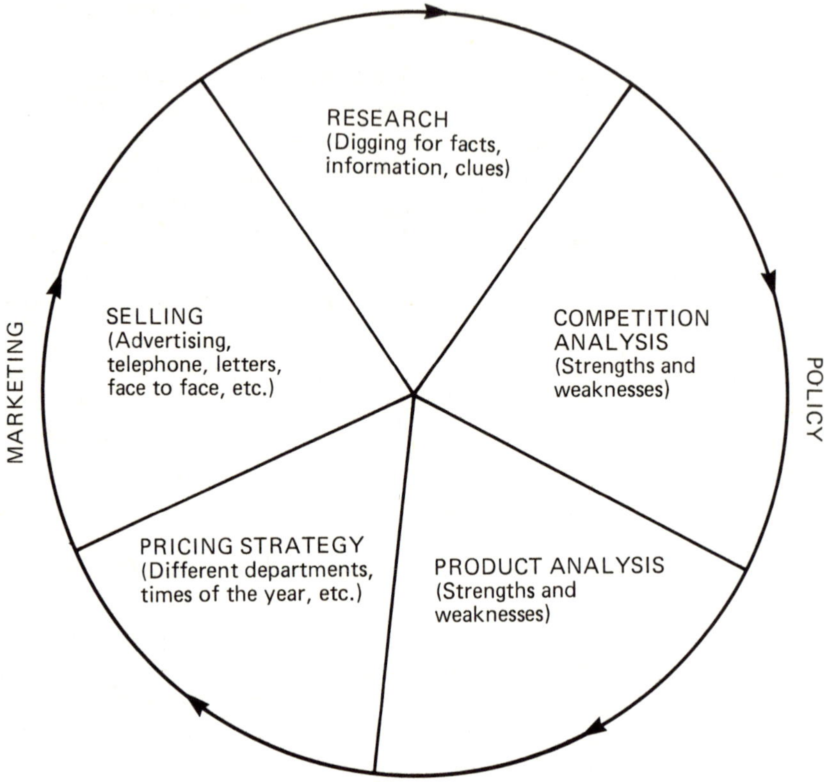

Figure 5.1 The Continuous Circle of Marketing

FIVE DEFINITIONS OF MARKETING

No. 1 by Gerry Draper

> Ascertaining customer needs, tailoring the product as closely as possible to meet those needs, persuading the customer to satisfy his needs and, finally, ensuring that the product is easily accessible when the customer wishes to purchase it.

No. 2 by Melvyn Greene

> Marketing is basically seeking out a demand first and then making the product or supplying the service to satisfy that demand. Selling is rather the other way round – creating a product or service and then trying to find a market for it.

No. 3 by Melvyn Greene

> The ultimate in marketing is to establish brand loyalty so that, eventually, the consumer does not only purchase the goods/services once, but continously. This is achieved only by the producer following the complete process of marketing.

No. 4 by Anderson & Lembke

> We believe that the real meaning of marketing is listening to the demands of the market and satisfying those demands at a profit. From this it follows that *superior marketing* is listening to the market more intently than your competitors and satisfying the demands more effectively.

No. 5 by Thomas F. Powers.

> Marketing is so basic that it cannot be considered a separate function (i.e. a separate skill or work) within the business, on a par with others such as manufacturing or personnel. Marketing requires separate work and a distinct group of activities. But it is first a central dimension of the entire business. It is the whole business seen from its final result, that is from the customer's point of view. Concern and responsibility for marketing must, therefore, permeate all areas of the enterprise.

When they are in their bedrooms thinking of going to eat in your hotel restaurant, or out somewhere in the town, they very often can tell you every item on your menu without looking at it. Good or gimmicky decors pay off sometimes, but if you can regularly try original and fresh menus, dishes and ideas – and promote them in the lobby, elevator and bedroom (see Chapter 11 on Increasing In-House Sales) – the mass market of people who stay in hotels regularly will 'beat a path to your door'.

As you can see from these comments and five definitions, marketing is a total, all-embracing attitude to life and business, continuously watching for changes in existing markets and searching for new markets, adapting the hotel's facilities and services to the new markets, and setting out to attract the new markets.

Marketing involves a lot of thinking time in pinpointing existing and new sources of business. In no way would I like to imply that selling involves no thinking time or less intellectual input – far from it. This is why a lot of people like it, and rush into it without going through the full process of marketing. If this happens a large proportion of selling effort, time and cost can be dissipated. Carrying out the full process of marketing will enable you to be more selective.

As markets are changing continuously, it is important to redefine markets continuously. This is probably the greatest error of the hotel industry, their designers and architects. Hotels and restaurants are built and designed on a fixed basis for a specific market opportunity. Because they are successful to begin with no attempt is made to redefine their role in the market place. When you have a physical building, it is not too easy to change the 'product' to take into account changes in the market. There is, in my experience, a great reluctance to change what *was* a success formula.

But you *can* change the product in various ways, e.g.:

- new decor
- special themes
- new staff uniforms
- different menus
- change in tariffs and menu prices
- new sales literature (hotel and conference brochure)
- grade up more
- grade down slightly

Unless you are continuously reviewing the whole process of marketing there is a danger that present guests and customers may drift away to competitors *and* new customers will not be attracted in their place.

So how do you choose the best markets and sources of business?

REDEFINING MARKETS

Most hotels have many and varied potential markets and sources of business. This creates a situation where the hotel management must avoid the trap of selling 'a kilometre wide and a centimetre deep', or a mile wide and an inch deep.

It is absolutely essential to decide what the strengths and weaknesses of your product (i.e. hotel) are, bearing in mind the demands and requirements of the different sources of business *and* the strength and weaknesses of your main competitors. The last point on competitors is a critical factor. In isolation, your own facilities do not matter – they are only relevant when compared with your competition; for example, if you do not have air conditioning this is not a limitation if all your competitors have no air conditioning. For too long many hoteliers have dissipated time and money by not selecting the source of business which they are best suited for and where they have least competition.

What is required is really two things. Firstly, as much information as possible on the hotel, its facilities, occupancy, catchment area, etc. Then a series of objectively prepared league tables grading your hotel's advantages and limitations. In order to assist you in your future marketing, a series of checklists are shown on information required for marketing, redefining markets and the preparation of a sales action plan. They start with a summary of information under eight broad headings. Quite often this information is available already, sometimes it requires some work and research. It is very similar to detailed background information required for an economic and marketing feasibility study for a new hotel, or a new bedroom extension.

The first aspect of the information is basically on the whole catchment area, moves on to the hotel's facilities, competition and present markets. The first four points on the information are broadly required for marketing and selling purposes, the last four are primarily for selling.

CHECKLIST 5.1: BROAD BACKGROUND INFORMATION

(a) Local Community

1 Trend in population and forecasts of population

INFORMATION REQUIRED

1 Broad background information: (a) local community
(b) local industry, commerce, employment
(c) communications
(d) local events and attractions
(e) catchment area

2 Facilities of the hotel

3 Details of competitive hotels

4 Profile of guests

5 Activity levels

6 Employees – selling ability

7 Specific information on local community, industry, events, communications and catchment area

8 Advantage/limitation list – on own hotel
– on competitive hotel

2 Profile of local residents – age, sex, marital status, etc.
3 Local sports and social clubs, trade and political associations

(b) Local Industry, Commerce and Employment

1 Industrial classification
2 Economic trends
3 Any new factories or offices in last five years
4 Any factories or offices closed in last five years
5 Employment statistics
6 Unemployment statistics
7 Details of main employers:

Industry Type	Profile of Employers
No. of Employees	Independent or Group
If Group, Location of H.O. or Branch	

8 Statistics on visitors to town or specific attractions
9 Statistics on passengers through airport
10 Airlines and travel companies who use airport
11 Traffic count on local motorways
12 Statistics on bus or railway stations

(c) Communications

This should cover existing and planned developments.

1 Location of hotel
2 Road network : local, national
3 Rail : local, national
4 Airports : local, national, international

(d) Local events and attractions

1 Historical, cultural, traditional
2 Scenic
3 Coastline
4 Sports
5 Weather
6 Special events

(e) Catchment area (C.A.)

If selling, promotion and advertising are to be effective it is essential to define the catchment area (C.A.) for potential markets first, because time and money will be dissipated if you market outside the area.

C.A.'s will usually be very different between bedrooms, restaurants, function rooms and bars.

Usually the C.A. for bedrooms is much wider than, say, a restaurant, in that C.A. for bedrooms may be all of a country or, in some cases, all of the world.

Even with a restaurant, the C.A. may be different for lunch and dinner. At lunch time it may be within a limited circle of local industry and commerce, probably up to a maximum of ten to fifteen minutes driving, or five minutes walk. In the evening it may extend to residential areas within, say, a ten mile radius, or a twenty minute drive. These distances depend on traffic conditions.

CHECKLIST 5.2: FACILITIES OF THE HOTEL

Detail facilities sub-divided between:

Areas which produce revenue
Areas which do not produce revenue.

Information on areas which produce revenue:

Number (e.g. 200 bedrooms with private bath, suites, etc.)
Restaurant capacities (number of seats, etc.)
Hours of opening
General appearance and condition
Tariff for each area.

Source: own knowledge, observation and information

CHECKLIST 5.3: COMPETITION

1 Existing competitors – hotels, function rooms, restaurants, bars:
- Size
- Style
- Location
- Type of business
- Prices
- Facilities
- Background
- Any planned expansion
- Independently or group owned

2 Proposed new competition:
- Similar information to above

Note: It is vital to visit all competition from time to time, in order to assess their facilities, service, etc., compared against your own

CHECKLIST 5.4: PROFILE OF GUESTS

Provide a customer profile separately for each income producing area. In some areas, it is difficult to establish a proper profile, because the market is so varied, or mixed, e.g. function rooms, main bars. Profile should provide information on:

Bedrooms	*Restaurant*	*Bar*
Age bracket	Age bracket	Age brackets
Sex	Sex	Sex
Cash, Card, Charge	Cash, Card, Charge	Type or Group
Type or Group	Type or Group	Mode of transport
Place of employment	Mode of transport	Size of party
Place of residence	Size of party	Drink popularity
Mode of transport	Menu popularity	Any complaints?
Single/Double/Family	New customer?	
Room popularity	First choice?	
New guest?	Any complaints?	
First choice?	Chance or guest	
Length of stay	Average spend	
Any complaints?		
Who made booking?		

In the case of firms who spend a lot of money with you, one would require a steady feedback of information on these large sources of income.

Source: observation, conversation, correspondence, records, questionnaire

CHECKLIST 5.5: ACTIVITY LEVELS

This information should be analysed by sales area, season, month, day, meal period.

One would require:
Occupancy statistics – unoccupied rooms
– lost room revenue
Seat turnover percentages by meals and dates
Pattern of empty days for function space, or un-utilized capacity
Pattern of sales in bar

Primarily, the aim is to disclose sales areas which can be improved through a sales effort and where emphasis should be placed.

See further information in Chapter 13 on Management Information – Marketing

Source: records, observations, conversation

CHECKLIST 5.6: EMPLOYEES – SELLING ABILITY

Analyse list of staff employed between:

Those who have a lot of contact with guests
Those who have some contact with guests
Those who have no contact with guests.

Summarize against the first two groups information and opinion on:

Age
Appearance
Personality
Selling Ability
Training Required

Source: observation, conversation, interview, records

CHECKLIST 5.7: SPECIFIC SELLING INFORMATION

1 *Local Community*

(a) Details of local sports and social clubs, trade and political associations:

Name and address
Key contacts
Do they hold functions? If so, what kind, when, how often?
Do they have their own magazine?

(b) Details of 'influential' local residents, councillors (Mayor, taxi drivers, etc.)

2 Local Industry and Employment

Details of all main local employers, including any hospitals, universities, etc.

Name and address
Name of managing director
Name of key persons
Who makes bookings?
Do they have a demand for hotel facilities?
Number of overnight visitors
Number of functions, etc.

3 Communications

Names and addresses of airlines and travel companies, if located near airport, and key decision makers.

4 Local Events and Attractions

List of events, dates, names of organizers and, where applicable, participants.

5 Competition

Details of all competitive hotels.
Advantage/limitations lists.

6 Catchment Area

Defined catchment area for accommodation, restaurant and functions, etc. Names, addresses and 'key' contacts in local papers serving the catchment area.

Readers will notice in these checklists some interesting points. Under Facilities of the Hotel I am recommending that hoteliers should list areas which do *not* produce revenue. You should then ask 'if not, why not?' It is amazing over the last decade how many areas in hotels are now being used to produce revenue, which never produced income in the past, e.g.

lobbies
basement areas (as meeting rooms, speciality bars, etc.)
car parks and hotel grounds
swimming pool
area surrounding swimming pools
bedrooms.

The list is endless. Think like SPACEMEN.

You are basically in the business of selling space. We have all seen lobbies being used for receptions, dance areas (in Miami), display of new cars. I have seen swimming pools with a floor covering which can be lowered from the ceiling so that the swimming pool can be used for fashion shows or boxing exhibitions. One of our clients had a swimming pool which was not used in the winter, and rented it out to local manufacturers of small sailing dinghies. Let us take a function room or ballroom. Everyone complains that they can only be used on busy nights of the week and certain other periods (i.e. before Christmas).

Take a blank sheet of paper and write down all the activities you have seen, or heard, being used in a function room other than functions. I have listed examples in an Appendix. Many of them produce revenue, room hire and rental income and often they can be introduced in the 'quiet' periods. They often attract a new market across the threshold barrier of your hotel who have never used your facilities before. Last year I went to stay at the Hotel Albatross in the beautiful location of Illetas in Mallorca, Spain. It was the quiet season. My wife and I walked in on a Sunday and found the lounge areas absolutely full of people listening to a piano recital. Most of the audience were not staying in the hotel and had paid an entrance fee. A good illustration of an independently owned hotel selling empty space. A copy of the publicity is shown in Figure 5.2.

So please think like SPACEMEN.

Under the heading 'Activity Levels' you will notice a case of lateral or reverse thinking. For accounting and control purposes, room and double occupancy is vital. But for marketing purposes what is vital is the reverse – unoccupied rooms, lost room revenue, empty days on function rooms. Information in Checklist 5.6 spotlights employees who may require further training in social skills and sales ability. Aspects in Checklist 5.7 are really pinpointing key companies, decision makers, advisers to decision makers, etc., so that mailing and sales target lists can be prepared.

After the gathering of this information, what is then required is a series of 'league tables' which show your hotel's (or hotels') position relative to its competition. The objective of the league tables is to put the competition into perspective and to show that for some sources of business there is more competition and for others less. By linking these findings to the respective physical advantages and disadvantages of your hotel and the competition, answers are provided on where to put your sales and marketing effort. We have attended working sessions where just listing the competition for the different sources of business has proved an invaluable exercise.

CONCIERTOS EN MALLORCA

JOAN MOLL
RECITAL DE PIANO

PIANO RECITAL KLAVIERABEND RÉCITAL DE PIANO

I

Obras de compositores mallorquines. Works by Majorcan Composers.
Werke von Komponisten aus Mallorca. Oeuvres de Compositeurs Majorquins

Tema y Variaciones	Miquel Capllonch (1861-1935)
Dos Meteoros	Jaume Mas Porcel (n. en 1909)
— a un bebé alegre	
— a una mujer optimista	
Bolero del Diablo	Joan Maria Thomás (1896-1966)

II

Obras compuestas por Chopin en Mallorca; Works composed by Chopin in Majorca
Werke, die Chopin auf Mallorca geschrieben hat; Oeuvres composées par Chopin à Majorque.

Doce Preludios, del Opus 28	Frédéric Chopin
Scherzo nº. 3	Frédéric Chopin

Domingo 8 Noviembre a las 17 h.	**Sunday** 8 November at 5 p. m.	**Sonntag** 8 November um 17 Uhr.	**Dimanche** 8 Novembre a 17 h.

HOTEL ALBATROS • ILLETAS

PATROCINADO POR:
Consell Insular de Mallorca
Fomento de Turismo de Mallorca
Asociación Empresarial Hotelera de Palma de Mallorca

Figure 5.2 Programme for a Concert in Mallorca

Examples of the information and league tables required are as follows:

1 Make a list of the hotels which are competitive (and the criteria used) – the list will vary depending on the source of business. It is necessary to visit all these hotels to assess their facilities and to stay the night in hotels where you have not stayed previously. This is a vital first step in assessing your real competition and narrowing down the sources of business where you have least competition.

2 Calculate your market share of the total competitive capacity and your main competitors' share. Usually this can be calculated fairly accurately on Rooms, but has to be estimated on Food and Beverage. Sometimes, independent consumer research just asking for first, second and third choice for:

   Bedrooms
   Functions
   Eating out – Lunch
   – Dinner

   can provide invaluable clues to your market share.

3 Not all of the following league tables are relevant to all hotels, but examples of league tables required are:

   Quoted tariffs (single room)
   Single tariffs plus car parking costs
   Quoted tariffs (double/twin room)
   Double tariffs plus car parking costs
   Function charges (food and beverage)
   Room hire charges (excluding food)
   Inclusive conference rates – daily
   – overnight
   'Group' rates (tourists, etc.)

   The parking costs are relevant to many city centre locations where some hotels have free car parking and others do not.

4 Some league tables are required which do not lend themselves too easily to exact gradings but more to broad groupings (e.g. marketing 'muscle'). Examples are:

   Site
   Location
   Car parking facilities
   Noise (bedroom guests – meeting rooms)

Sales and marketing capability and 'muscle'
Group handling facilities (conventions and tours)
Location convenience to air travellers
Location convenience to train travellers
Location convenience to local attractions and entertainment
Conference packages
Restaurant facilities
Other facilities, e.g. health (swimming pool, gym, sauna, etc.)

5 We often use a popularity score basis in order to produce league tables for:

Businessmen – arriving by train, plane or car.
Individual tourists
Group tourists
Conference delegates

by scoring the grading depending on the demands of the different sources of business. Obviously the grading of the score will usually vary between the different sources of business.

6 The various potential markets have to be considered from a number of points of view, including:

Discretionary or essential spending
Company (expense account) or private
Expanding or contracting market
Repeat business potential
Definite or provisional booking
Seasonality
Effect on other markets (e.g. exhibition running over a number of days)
Potential profitability

If you take the foregoing information and also examine:

- your own internal management information (occupancies, covers, etc.)
- Any information you can gather on the trend in the market place (on tourists, businessmen, conferences, etc.)

then by using your own business experience and judgment you should be in a much better position to define more clearly the main sources of business on which your hotel(s) should concentrate marketing efforts. Never neglect established markets and busy parts of the week, month or year. However, many hotels have natural busy periods (e.g. Monday to Thursday nights on rooms, summer season, or function season around Christmas and in the New Year). So try to define markets which will help your quiet, or quieter, periods.

Try this exercise on your own hotel(s), particularly listing the advantages and limitations over your competition for the different sources of business. So often we have found that hoteliers find this fascinating, vital information. It helps to define markets and sometimes just assists a hotelier to get back on the most profitable course. When the markets and sources of business have been defined there is another step which requires careful consideration before you produce a sales action plan. This is to see that the hotel achieves the right *balance* of covers and average spend in the restaurant, and occupancy and average room rate in the bedroom. This aspect of the right balance to achieve maximum profit is elaborated in the next section.

ECONOMIC CRITERIA FOR SUCCESSFUL MARKETING

During the 60s and first half of the 70s considerable worry, effort and attention was concentrated on hotel occupancies. Now, considerable attention is being paid to increasing *average* room rates as well as occupancy. But in a mixed market situation, where there are wide fluctuations in markets and business activity in different periods of the year, how do you ensure that your hotels end up above, or as near as possible to, the right average occupancy and average room *rate* at the end of the year?

The danger is in many ways to oversimplify the objectives. It is too broad an objective to say 'we want to achieve an average occupancy of 75 per cent and an average room rate of $55.' This does not provide operating management, or marketing people, with the right kind of objectives on *sales mix* and *sources of business* required to achieve a target occupancy and average room rate. Too often in the past marketing people have been blamed for selling at reduced rates, when they have not been given the yardsticks advocated as follows.

Therefore it is strongly recommended that the following economic criteria on room tariffs are calculated for each hotel. These are absolutely essential in defining pricing policy, but consideration should also be given to the comments in the section entitled Pricing Strategies. (page 41).

1 The total amount of net operating costs (after contribution from the food and beverage departments) of the hotel. One could calculate the *Total*:

Net operating costs
Net operating costs plus rent (if payable)
Net operating costs plus interest
Net operating cost plus a target return on capital.

2 From this it is possible to calculate the total room revenue requirements (total rooms sales) in order to break even, and to achieve various levels of profit, assuming you know your Rooms Department Cost Ratios, staff numbers and staff standards, etc.

3 On the basis of the foregoing, a schedule should be produced of the average room rates required in order to break even and/or achieve the profit targets at various occupancy levels. At this point, it is very often possible to say that certain levels of profits are achievable, while other levels are impossible. Sometimes in the early years of a new hotel, or where the style and concept demands high operating costs, a calculation will show a target level of occupancy and average room rate which simple business judgment shows can, or cannot, be achieved.

4 Budgets on room sales have to be produced based on sales mix taking into account the different sources of business. Again, quite often based on this calculation it becomes apparent that a target Net Profit Return on Capital cannot be achieved unless the sales mix is varied by a different marketing emphasis.

5 Then based on the current quoted tariff, it is possible to calculate what percentage discounting factors, *subdivided* between the different sources of business, *must not be exceeded* if the average rate required is to be achieved. This is an extremely vital statistic in setting objectives for sales executives – namely the maximum discounting factors.

The two examples, Tables 5.1 and 5.2, are based on a quoted room tariff of $60 single and $80 twin and an average rate requirement per room of $55. It can be seen from the first example that the policy decisions on the discounts shown do not allow the average rate requirement to be achieved as at the mix shown, and discounts allowed, the average room rate required comes out at more than $4.48 less – $50.52. However, by fixing lower maximum discounts in the second example the average is $56.64 – $1.64 above the average rate required of $55.

Table 5.1

	Business Mix %	*Double Occup. %*	*Average Quoted Rate $*	*Discount %*	*Average Room Rate $*
Individuals	40	30	66.00	10	59.40
Conferences	10	10	62.00	20	49.60
Groups	50	80	76.00	40	42.36
			$70.60		$50.52

This second example shows maximum discount levels which do allow the average rate requirement to be achieved.

Table 5.2

	Business Mix %	*Double Occup. %*	*Average Quoted Rate $*	*Maximum Discount %*	*Average Room Rate $*
Individuals	40	30	66.00	5	62.70
Conferences	10	10	62.00	20	49.60
Groups	50	80	76.00	30	53.20
			$70.60		$56.64

6 The information in Tables 5.1 and 5.2 should be compared against your own judgment on business mix and average room rate so that you can see whether they are achievable at various occupancy levels. The point behind this exercise is to achieve *both* a target average occupancy and a target average room rate. This is an actual example and the rates may look low to readers through inflation.

Very often these calculations result in a change in marketing direction and a revision in budgets. Sometimes the change is as drastic as management realizing that a source of business is just not worth having. More often it results in a marketing change of emphasis (e.g. the hotel has to achieve 10 per cent more revenue from businessmen), or it produces a more specific policy, e.g. group discounts are not to exceed 30 per cent or the group rate should not be less than $53.00 per room.

Hotels in certain areas may have only one major business source. Examples are: a hotel in the Mediterranean which has only groups of tourists, and a hotel in a commercial town which has primarily overnight business travellers. But even in these types of location hotels often have three sources of business. The tourist resort hotel has group tourists *and* individual tourists and may be breaking into the conference market. The commercial town hotel has businessmen, conference potential and a weekend market different to that of midweek.

Our experience is that most hotels have at least three sources of business while the larger hotels in major cities can have five or six. Further, these sources may differ totally at various times of the year. The variable factors which make these sources different from an economic and marketing viewpoint include:

- when they come (time of week, year)
- degree of single, double and multiple occupancy
- degree of price sensitivity
- length of stay
- eating habits (do they eat and drink in the hotel?)
- surplus spending power.

All of these factors must be taken into account if maximum sales and maximum long term profit are to be achieved. The market will ultimately fix prices (see next section) but without these calculations of economic criteria it is quite possible not only to overcharge but to *undercharge* in certain circumstances.

PRICING STRATEGY – ROOM TARIFFS

The foregoing section sets the economic criteria in order to establish pricing, maximum discount policies, and goals. These economic calculations are absolutely essential in determining pricing policy. But in themselves they should only be used as essential guidelines to room tariffs. The reasons for this are varied. Supposing a hotel costs a large sum to be built, and therefore its interest charges, or rent, is higher than other competitive hotels. The calculations might show that a certain level of room rate is required to cover rent, or show a target return on capital, but this Average Room Rate Required might be much higher than competitive hotels, or a rate the market will not pay.

Sometimes it is possible that the market would be prepared to pay this higher rate if the hotel is more luxurious, in a better location, or has superior facilities. This may or may *not* be the case. This is where an objective assessment using the league tables as set out in Redefining Markets can be of great assistance. But a higher capital cost is not necessarily a guarantee that one can charge higher prices. Similarly, one hotel may operate with higher costs through inefficiency and this would not justify higher prices. Sometimes the higher costs of, say, payroll could arise through a far older, less cost-effective, design of the hotel. Or the higher payroll may be deliberate policy to provide a higher standard of service which the market might well be prepared to pay for. All these factors should be considered and not just costs. It is the market, ultimately, that fixes prices – not your level of operating costs.

What other factors have to be considered in fixing prices?

For years I have sat at meetings with clients when pricing strategies are agreed for the coming year, or season. It has always appeared to me that there is one significant, unknown factor which we have always lacked at these meetings, even when independent consumer research has been carried out. The usual factors that everyone looks at are either one or more of the following:

- current charges prior to a review
- the estimated inflationary effect on costs for the coming period under review
- the general economic situation affecting markets
- for hotels attracting foreign tourists during the last five years, the currency exchange trends
- the amount of competition and the rate of increase we think competitors are going to charge

In the 'good old days' of fifteen years ago – namely the first three years of the 70s when inflation tended to run at 3 to 5 per cent and currency fluctuations were minimal – most of our clients only looked at the first two of the foregoing factors and, depending on how conservative they were, increased their tariffs by 3 to 5 per cent for the coming year, often from the next financial or calendar year. The situation is much more complex now and our clients tend to consider all of these factors, together with the league tables described previously, and to have different strategies on price increases for the busy and quiet periods, and for the different sources of business.

But the one unknown factor which we will never ever obtain an exact answer to is 'what tariff increase – if there is to be an increase – will the market bear?'

All hoteliers have a major fear or worry.

There are some consumer industries where they can test market a new product, or a price increase in a geographical region and say that a 5 per cent increase in prices will cause a 3 per cent decrease in market share – or increase in market share if the rate of price increase is lower than that of the competition. The hotel industry is not like this. The fear many hoteliers have is that at some level of price increase the whole market, or a significant proportion of the market, could *disappear*. This is a real worry. We all saw this happen in many European tourist capitals like Paris, and in particular London, when the number of American tourists drastically dropped after 1979 as hotel tariffs were increased and the dollar declined in value at the same time. The market did not disappear totally but the total spend of Americans declined much more than the decline in numbers.

Assuming continued inflation over the next few years, even at a lower level than recent years, we are probably in most cases still talking about fixing a rate of increase rather than a decrease. How do we fix this increase and those prices which will show maximum long term repeat business *and* profits?

CONSUMER RESEARCH

Some people believe that consumer research will provide the answer. It is my experience that it might provide some clues, but it may well provide the wrong answers. If you approach existing customers or buyers to carry out research, this tends to cover the market you have now but excludes the far larger market which does not use you for a mass of reasons unrelated to price (e.g. they have never heard of you, or The Threshold Barrier).

And if you complete a verbal or written questionnaire with travel agents, or bulk purchasers like tour operators, on their objective opinion of your tariffs, the research *always* shows that your tariffs are too high. I remember a leading travel agent seriously saying in response to a questionnaire for a new hotel in central Edinburgh that the rate should be $25 per room, and this rate would fill the hotel. He said this knowing that the going rate in Edinburgh in the off season was around double this rate and that even if the hotel was full it could never show a profit high enough to be economically viable.

And I am not even sure if the average hotel guest knows what the room rate is. We once carried out an experiment for a client in a large, 3 Star hotel simply by asking a proportion of guests on a series of days what the room rate was as they were leaving, and in fact had only just settled their bills. Around 24 per cent were with groups and so they had no idea what the room rate was. The remaining 76 per cent were business executives. Only about half had any idea and were prepared to hazard a guess. Out of the total 76 per cent only around one-fifth had any idea of the room rate. The point here is that the vast majority had stayed more than one night and all had incurred extras for meals, telephone calls, etc., which increased the nightly cost. A significant proportion had signed the bill with a credit card, or had a credit account. What guests could give was an impression of 'that seemed expensive' or 'that seemed reasonable'.

EGO FACTOR

What I do know is that the hotel industry reverses many known marketing rules in fixing prices for a consumer product. In most consumer industries you can increase sales by reducing prices. Assuming the particular firm selling the consumer product is operating above break-even point, the principles of marginal costing pay off in higher net profits following the increased sales.

This does not always happen with hotels because although hotels sell a product (in food and drinks) it is one of the few consumer industries which is a combination of product *and* service. In fact, it could be a marketing mistake to reduce prices too far with many hotels, even in cheaper mass hotels, because at a certain level of lower prices the prospective customer gets suspicious, i.e. something must be wrong!

If the Ritz in London, Mark Hopkins in San Francisco and the George V in Paris decided to reduce their quoted tariffs by half, it could well empty the hotels. The normal guest who stays at these hotels would probably switch their allegiances to a more expensive luxury hotel, and the mass of other people would be too overawed to break the threshold barrier and try the hotel. I remember some years ago when the very successful up-market Gosforth Park Hotel north of Newcastle, Britain, opened, that for many years every time they increased their tariffs they expected a slight decline in room occupancy and this did not happen. These are extreme examples of luxury hotels, but to a degree the same point applies to all grades of hotel.

Now bulk purchasers like tour operators will argue the opposite. To a significant extent they are correct in that they must hold down the *total* price of a holiday in order to sell their allocations. But there is a similar point with tour operators in their brochures. For most resorts our 'initial' customer, the tour operator, has a series of hotels usually listed in order of total price. Do they automatically sell all the cheapest holidays first, or do they find that their own customers –

who are the people who sleep in our rooms – will often avoid the cheapest holiday because they are seeking value for money and not necessarily the cheapest holiday? Digressing slightly, I always recommend to clients when they are renegotiating next year's price with a tour operator to obtain the current brochure, have it translated if necessary, and see where their hotel is listed and how it is described compared to the competition. This will often provide valuable negotiating clues. (See page 68.)

In fact the countries who have gone out to promote themselves as a cheap holiday destination have always lived to regret it. This happened to London after the weak £ and Jubilee Year coincided. It happened to Spain. And I suspect it will happen to Florida, which is currently selling itself in Europe with too much emphasis on just being cheap. This kind of marketing gives you no room for flexibility when the market dips a little and currency rates move against you, as they did for Spain at the end of the 70s.

There is a fundamental difference in the consumer product/service we sell, which we ignore at our peril. It is the only situation where we satisfy some of the basic needs of men and women – a warm, comfortable place to shelter and sleep, food for the hungry, and alcohol for enjoyment and relaxation. So our purchaser (guest) has a totally different reaction to prices in hotels, and prices of other consumer products and services. We satisfy fundamental emotional and physical needs of our customers. This is elaborated more under a later section, 'What Motivates People to Buy?'

At the time of writing we are in a business recession and many companies and organizations are being much tougher on their travelling executives' overnight costs. In this situation we may have to provide special price deals, retrospective discounts, etc. for major commercial customers.

The argument is not that hotels should increase tariffs and price themselves out of their different markets, only that we should recognize that low prices lead to lower standards and delays in redecoration and ignores the importance of *the ego factor*. The curtains, carpets and decor, the staff uniforms, the cutlery and glassware we use could be cheap and nasty. But they are usually deliberately the opposite – more luxurious, attractive (and costly) than they need be. Why? Because of the ego factor. By all means reduce prices (or contain price increases) by reducing wastage and increasing productivity. But try wherever possible to avoid reducing the atmosphere, ambiance and service because I *know* people will pay for this.

FACTORS IN FIXING PRICES

What we have to think about and consider carefully in these times of rising costs are a series of factors. Firstly, we should have available economic criteria set out in the previous sections. We also need the information listed at the start of this section. Added to this we need:

1 Customer profiles in order to tell us more about the markets we are obtaining now, and provide clues to markets we are missing.
2 A much greater degree of segmentation with a pricing policy taking into account the circumstances of the different segments.
3 Research to ascertain whether the hotel is a first, second or third choice for the different facilities, e.g. rooms, restaurants, bars. This research should be on a regular basis to see that the hotel is not 'sliding' in popularity.

An amplification of this information is given below.

CUSTOMER PROFILES

An indication of the type of information required is as follows:

Rooms

Age Bracket
Sex
Cash, Card, Charge
Business
Tourist
Convention
Type of Group
Employment
Place of Employment
Place of Residence
Mode of Transport
Singe/Double/Family
Room Popularity
New Guest?
First Choice
Length of Stay
Who made booking

Similar information is required on the Restaurant(s) and Bars, but normally in not quite the same detail. The information can be gathered from observation, conversation, correspondence, questionnaire and reception records. A well designed guest registration card, guest history records, and information from the Billing Machine, Tab or Computer can supply a lot of useful information. Not all of this information is useful on pricing strategies, but could be important in other aspects of marketing. As an example, place of employment and place of residence (which can be totally different) can help to decide where you are drawing custom from and where to direct advertising and sales effort. Similarly, mode of transport and who made the booking can assist in basic selling.

But many of the other factors can help in pricing strategies. In America credit (or charge) cards are very common and few people carry and pay in actual notes. But in Europe and other parts of the world many hotels still have a high proportion of guests, sometimes over 50 per cent, paying by actual cash. We have found that wherever there is a high degree of payment by cash or cheque, rather than credit card or credit account, there is a greater degree of price sensitivity and more resistance to price increases.

We have also found that the lower the average length of stay, the higher the average rate per night. Naturally this is a generalization, but there is some logic in it. When an hotel (say an airport hotel) has an average length of stay of one night, the rate the hotelier can obtain is often higher than where the average length of stay is longer. Obviously people spending a longer time in an area are more likely to notice the total bill, or to be on a daily allowance. And taking the other extreme of a hotel with a holiday market where the guests stay two weeks at a time, the hotel take per guest may be high but the average room rate earned per night is usually much lower than in other hotels. We have often found a degree of price sensitivity which varies for exactly the same product, and room, within a standardized chain, where the only major difference appears to be a different average length of stay.

Research on guest profiles should be carried out to determine the proportion of guests who have stayed with you before, subdivided between guests booked in by a company or where there is a special arrangement with a company, and 'individual' guests. If this research shows a low proportion of repeat business, then the hotel will often have a standards problem related to the price charged. However good the marketing is, it will not become really effective until the reason for the low proportion of repeat business is corrected. One very successful holiday camp company has a 30 per cent repeat potential of people who stay with them *every* year. Presumably there are additional people who return but not necessarily every year. Another exclusive hotel in London has 60 per cent of their guests who have stayed with them before. The timing of repeat visits is also important. Do guests return every year, or monthly, or weekly, and what are the proportions analysed betweeen individuals and companies who send regular visitors?

Many hoteliers will know this information on guest profiles. But in larger hotels with a mix of markets this information would be invaluable background information where pricing strategies are reconsidered.

SEGMENTATION

As outlined in a later chapter, it is felt very strongly that we can no longer talk about broad markets of:

Businessmen/women
Foreign tourists
Local tourists
Conventions.

We will have to research these markets in order to find out much more about them in the future. Let us take an example of the business market staying overnight in hotels. Excluding businessmen, visiting an area for an exhibition, or convention, broadly, business visitors are visiting:

- to buy
- or to sell

If they are buying there is a good probability that the local company selling to them will book them into a hotel, or recommend a place to stay. Are the sellers going to be price sensitive, or worry about another $10 on the room rate? No way. Are they going to risk a sale by accommodating their potential buyer in a poor hotel? They will probably consider his age (for the style of hotel), where he will sleep well so that he is less 'grumpy' and more receptive to their sales approach the next morning. This is not to say they will always put him in the most expensive hotel because he may not feel at ease there. But they are unlikely to cut their costs by deliberately choosing a cheap hotel, if they are paying. And they are unlikely to bruise the buyer's ego by suggesting too down-market an hotel if he is paying.

Generally speaking the hotel industry has one great advantage in this buying situation. The total cost of the hotel is usually very small compared to the amount being paid for the product, contract, or service the buyer is there to examine. Think about this point if a large proportion of your overnight guests are business executives, and buyers as well. Most of the invoices and bills from commerce and industry to *their* customers are much larger in value than $100 to $300 for a two-night stay in an hotel.

And what about the business visitor, staying in an area overnight, who is selling? There are generally two types of salesmen. Those selling a large, or expensive, product or service. And those travelling on the road many weeks of the year who generally are selling a large number of smaller value items. Take the first type of salesman selling a product or service of high value. If he knows anything about selling himself as well as his expensive product, is he going to risk the whole sales approach at the end of the day when most local people ask an out-of-town visitor 'where are you staying tonight?' Is he going to risk mentioning a cheaper hotel?

Now there is no doubt in the case of the second category of salesperson who is 'on the road', that a lot usually have a budget per day to live within and are more price sensitive. But the key point is periodically to analyse and segment your overall business market so you are more aware of who they are, as this information is of paramount importance if you are worrying about whether to increase your tariffs by 3, 10, or 12 per cent, when costs may be climbing at a very unpredictable rate and there is a lot of competition around. Suppose that you find that you get a high proportion of business visitors who are buyers compared with your competitors, or vice versa. Would not this information help you in your pricing strategy?

WHAT CHOICE IS YOUR HOTEL?

It is possible for a hotel to have a high occupancy and yet be vulnerable to a sudden decline in guests if a significant proportion are not staying in the hotel as a first choice. This decrease in occupancy can arise when there is either an overall decrease in an area's occupancy, so that the first choice competitor has rooms available, or there is a disproportionate increase in tariffs. This situation can arise even where average annual occupancies are *not* high, but where there are peak months of the year when most of the hotels are full, or the city or town is what I call a four-sevenths area and full Monday to Thursday with business visitors.

What we have found very useful is the use of a simple questionnaire (Table 5.3) just asking the visitor what is the degree of choice of hotels in the town and catchment area, or within a ten mile radius of the factory/office, for accommodating overnight visitors:

Table 5.3

Hotel	*VIPs and Top Executives*	*Middle Management*	*Other Visitors*
First Choice Second Choice Lower Choice			

Every hotel tends to have a proportion of the overnight visitors who have a preference which is unrelated to price, style or grading. Therefore you will never find 100 per cent of the respondents saying that your hotel is, say, first or second choice. But if you have defined your market segment and pricing strategy correctly, our experience is that around two-thirds (60 to 70 per cent) should rate you as first choice. In fact, it would be very high if as many as 80 per cent rated you first choice although this can happen in a town with only three hotels, say, one motor hotel on the outskirts, one 3 Star, and one 5 Star in the town centre. In an area with a wide connurbation like London or Birmingham in Britain, however successful a hotel is, you will usually find the first choice proportion is not much higher than 60 per cent in a busy period, unless you own a unique hotel like, say, Claridges, or Browns Hotel.

This research should be carried out in busy periods because quite obviously the degree of first choice will tend to be much higher in the quiet part of the week or year. The important factor to watch is really the trend and therefore the research should be carried out regularly every year, or six months. If the proportion stating first choice is steadily declining and the second, or lower choice, increasing, then this is a danger signal on standards, pricing strategy, or value for money. Unless corrective action is taken occupancies are bound to decline. This regular research can often help to highlight a problem well in advance before the decline in occupancy and sales starts.

Ask yourself this question assuming costs have been climbing and you are planning a price increase. Would you feel more confident about a price increase if this regular research showed a high rating which was steadily increasing as a first choice?

Although many of the foregoing comments and principles are applicable equally to food and beverage tariffs, there are comments on these areas in the next section. Pricing strategy is a wide, complex subject with no easy answers. I would never underrate basic management experience of the market and the hotel operation. It could seem that the foregoing information is too much and unnecessary. But if we are in for an inflationary decade during the eighties, and regular constant reviews of tariffs and prices, then the whole decision-making process will be far easier if you have the following back-up information to help you in making the decision:

- economic criteria, estimated sales mix and maximum discounts
- current charges prior to a review
- the estimated inflationary effect on costs for the coming year, or period, under review
- the general economic situation affecting markets
- currency exchange trends – for hotels attracting foreign visitors (tourists and businessmen)
- the degree of competition and rate of increase competitors have made or might make
- guest and customer profiles
- market segments and strategy for each segment
- market degree of choice, degree of repeat business

This information, together with any further consumer research, number of complaints, trends in occupancy, covers served, etc, is vital and may in some cases lead to a price standstill or reduction not necessarily overall but sometimes for a particular source of business. As an example, a hotel may find it has a high choice rating and no problem on increasing room rates for individual tourists, but is too expensive compared against similar competition for the convention market, and is losing business. In view of the large numbers involved, high spend in bars, etc. a reduction (or no increase) in the overnight convention rate might be justified.

PRICING STRATEGY – FOOD AND BEVERAGE AREAS

Pricing menus and drinks in hotel food and beverage areas to obtain maximum sales *and* profits is a very complex subject and in many ways more complicated than preparing a strategy on rooms. Except in older hotels, many hotels have only three or four types of rooms (singles, twins, suites, front view, back view, etc.) and some new hotels built on a standard module for the bedroom block have only one type of room. But menus can have dozens of dishes, all with a different food cost, and the food cost is often unrelated to popularity and the price the market is prepared to pay.

What would be useful is if I put forward certain comments, thoughts and suggestions on the main areas in an hotel selling food and beverages. Four points have often puzzled me about this aspect of hotels.

Firstly, why is it that so often the bedroom guest does not eat in the hotel restaurant or coffee shop where there are competitive restaurant facilities near to the hotel? I am not talking about the long stay visitor but the business executive staying in the hotel for maybe one, or two nights. A proportion do eat in, but a significant proportion go out, and a habit has developed with many regular travellers – 'sleep in but eat out' – which I would like to see changed. If you have a lot of competitive restaurants nearby a proportion of your guests are going to eat out. But this proportion should be as low as possible. Two main reasons for this situation is the aspect of Menu Fatigue mentioned earlier, and poor In-House Selling.

The second point I have seen developing in the last few years is that where a hotel has two (or more) restaurants that appear to be competing with each other and 'splitting the bedroom market down the middle' rather than offering a true price and 'experience' alternative to the overnight visitor and the outside business coming into the hotel. This point seems to have developed lately where, say, the hotel coffee shop has been upgraded and the 'better' a la carte restaurant has gradually limited its menu to a smaller number of dishes. I could name a number of larger hotels with two restaurants which are directly competitive in average spend, evening opening hours and in every way except decor.

A third point is related to function areas. Except in a recession, if you ask the food and beverage manager, or banqueting manager, if the function areas are busy he will often sigh and say, 'Very busy'. Functions are, in my opinion, one of the most exhausting and repetitive aspects of hotel life and I fully understand why they say that they are very busy. But quite often the hotel has only one function per day per function room, and some days (e.g. Sunday) or times (e.g. Monday evening) are rarely booked. And where a function room seating 400 people has a function, it is often well below 400 in size.

Most hoteliers would agree that they must have regular room occupancy statistics if they are to set staff standards, operate and market the hotel. But fewer have restaurant 'occupancy' statistics (total covers, seat turnover ratios, table turnover ratios per meal, compared against a target) and similar information on function rooms. Very often even if you take a function room as capable of taking one function per day (365 per year) the usage percentage is no more than 35 per cent. And if you compare the covers sold against 365 times the seating capacity, quite often the seat usage percentage is less than 25 per cent.

PROFITABILITY BY AREA

The other major point on the food and beverage areas is that some hoteliers do not know whether the areas selling food and beverage are making a net profit or loss – i.e. a contribution to the total bottom line figure of the hotel as a whole. Hoteliers know the departmental profit (or loss) under the Uniform System of Accounts on:

Rooms
Food
Beverage
Tobacco
Telephones
Shops
Sundries

but often they do not have an indication of whether the restaurant, the function rooms, or the bar make a net profit or a loss, and the *total* sales of a restaurant would be hidden as they would be subdivided in the uniform system under the sources of business for control purposes, i.e.:

Food sales
Beverage sales
Tobacco sales.

These comments are not meant to be a 'blanket' criticism of the uniform system of accounts. Most systems in various countries with a developed hotel industry use a uniform accounting system which is based on the American system originally pioneered by the large American hotel accounting firms in the 1930s. No hotel should be without this system, or a variation of it.

But basically it is a control and accounting system and not one designed to assist in policy changes, or marketing. This is why it is recommended that possibly twice a year, or at least annually, the accounts are re-analysed by income producing areas. In order to explain and elaborate this aspect more fully some further information and examples have been included in Appendix A.

In one major London hotel where we first carried out this exercise some years ago, the management was convinced that the function area with sales of around $4 million per year was the biggest area contributor to net profit. In fact it only showed a tiny net profit on a huge sales volume. Our past experience shows that very often many hotel restaurants and many functions rooms operate at a net loss, and this information can be vital in changing policy, creating a greater sense of sales urgency, or in changes in pricing strategy.

ECONOMIC ASPECTS OF FOOD AREAS

Most of the broad principles laid down earlier in this chapter on setting room tariffs apply equally to food and beverage prices. You do need similar economic yardsticks to calculate whether it is possible to make a profit. Even if it is a policy decision that an area cannot make a profit, then you should still be able to measure and control the maximum loss. This policy decision is often made in a hotel where a facility is included to achieve a certain star grading, or it is considered that it is essential to the overall marketing, and achieving a TOTAL hotel profit that certain facilities are included for the guests even if they make a loss.

The economic yardsticks explained in the earlier section on room tariffs should also be prepared on a restaurant. You generally know your staff standards, food costs and can estimate other operating costs. Added to this you can include an estimate of the area's proportion of energy bills and rates (property taxes) so that you could calculate a reasonable estimate of the total sales required to:

Produce a departmental profit
Break even at house profit level
Break even at net profit
Break even at various net profit levels.

Some further points are made later on menu and bar prices, but most hoteliers have an idea of the average spend, or a range of average spends. Dividing the average spend into the foregoing levels of sales will show the number of covers required to achieve the various levels of sales and profit. Very often this exercise alone will show that the target average spend is wrong, or if it is correct, because of the style creating a low seat turnover ratio and the costs of that particular restaurant, it can never do better, than say, break even at house profit level.

Let us take an example of a 100 seat restaurant in a style and price bracket which dictates that you can only obtain one seat turnover at a busy lunch and at dinner. Your maximum covers is, therefore, 365 × 200 or 73,000 per year, assuming the restaurant is open for lunch and dinner every day of the year. Assuming that the estimated total costs of payroll, food costs, departmental charges, and a proportion of your undistributed overheads, rents, property taxes, came to $1.7 million, and the maximum average spend was thought to be $20 per cover, net of sales and valued added taxes, but including food, drinks and cigars.

$$\text{Break even sales } \frac{\$1.7 \text{ million}}{\text{Average Spend } \quad \$20} = 85{,}000 \text{ covers}$$

In order to break even the restaurant would have to achieve an average seat turnover of 1.16 or increase the average spend by around 16 per cent to $23.2. In many restaurants where there are business executives on their own, or three people eating together, a 100 seat restaurant cannot always achieve 100 covers, and there would also be 'quiet' times. In this case if the average spend cannot be improved it might be accepted as a policy that the restaurant will not achieve a net profit. Similar calculation to the above (including room rental estimates) should be prepared on function rooms. However, later on I show that through better sales promotion outside the hotel restaurant, and through in-house promotion, most hotels can drastically improve the restaurant results.

Different style restaurants would show totally different results to the foregoing. Generally the lower the average spend, the higher the seat turnover ratio. Higher seat ratios and lower seat areas per seat usually apply in restaurants *outside* hotels where a restaurateur pays rent, interest charges, etc. And the same situation should apply to eating (and drinking) areas within hotels.

Ultimately the market determines whether your restaurant (and bars) charges are value for money and whether you will achieve the target covers at the target average spend. But it is worth summarizing again a revised list of the factors which should be considered in changing prices or introducing new menus.

I have often sat at meetings where the prices are increased by the average percentage increase in

Food commodity prices
added to payroll increase

The following factors should be considered very carefully in a hotel restaurant's pricing strategy:

- economic criteria, target average spends, target covers per meal period
- current menu and drink prices
- estimated inflationary effects on *all* costs since last review and in coming period
- popularity indices for meal periods, and by period
- average spends (see later comment)
- competition and what it is likely to do
- customer segment profile – outside visitors to hotel
– guests eating in
- total cost of staying in room plus average meal

The hotelier and restaurateur has to find out more about customers and who they are. I have persuaded many operators to take the time and trouble of carrying out research on their overnight guests, and now I am persuading more hotel clients to do this for their restaurants. In every case the results prove invaluable not just in fixing sales prices but in providing marketing and sales action points.

Let us take the 100 seat restaurant mentioned earlier and assume it achieves 60,000 covers per year. This is a useful accounting and economic yardstick, but it really tells us nothing in marketing and sales terms. Are the 60,000 covers, 60,000 different people who only come once a year? Were there 60,000 bills, or checks, for 60,000 people on their own? Or perhaps 20,000 checks with an average of three covers per check. And out of the 20,000 checks would it be invaluable to know that, say:

20 per cent came once in a year
24 per cent came twice in a year
18 per cent came three to five times per year
20 per cent came six to ten times per year
18 per cent were regulars coming more than ten times per year

100 per cent

And how would you react if you carried out this sample research once a year and found that the proportion of regulars was declining? Do you know these proportions in your own restaurants? We must find out more about the people who use our hotels and restaurants, the market segment, their profile, and their spending power. Are they time sensitive but not too price sensitive. What makes them tick? The more we can find out about them the more we can find the right sales and advertising message to attract more of them. And we will be in a better position to choose the most cost effective media to reach the correct market segment.

AVERAGE SPENDS

Most hoteliers and restaurateurs know their average spends on food, and average spends on restaurant-related beverage sales, which provides a total average spend. But by itself this can be misleading because it is only an 'average'. Averages can provide a false impression in locating your market segments. You all know the old story. Sit down and take your shoes and socks off. Put one foot in a bucket full of boiling hot water. Place the other foot at the same time in another bucket full of freezing cold water.

On average you should feel comfortable!!

It is recommended that you analyse your average spends per meal into price blocks, or groupings. If the average spend is $12 you might analyse the average spends as follows:

	%
up to $8	3
$8 to $10	36
$10 to $12	11
$12 to $14	16
$14 to $16	30
above $16	4
	100%

Suppose the pattern for a meal period tended to show the foregoing percentage proportions. You will see that there are two clear average market spends, 36 per cent between $8 and $10, and another large group at 30 per cent spending between $14 and $16. In fact, only a minority are spending around the average of $12. More analysis and information would be required to draw conclusions and make decisions on this kind of information but if this was a regular pattern, it would tend to indicate that there were two distinct markets in this restaurant. In some countries 'mixing markets' makes little difference. But in many countries 'mixing markets' can sometimes be disastrous because it can often drive both markets away.

Past experience shows that this type of spend pattern arises for various reasons. Sometimes the menu prices are structured so that the customer cannot spend at the average level, but is forced into the two brackets because the main entrées are clustered in those price brackets. Usually this arises because management have not really thought out the market segment thoroughly enough. Very often this pattern occurs where there is another higher priced restaurant and the two are competing. Where two restaurants are competing then some of the bracket spending above $14 may have been 'taken' from the higher priced restaurant.

Coffee shops, open for long hours, will often show spend brackets which are well apart from the average, and depending on the location, markets may mix amicably, e.g. business executives and people out shopping. It is recommended that periodically this type of average spend is analysed into price bands, together with regular popularity indices on dishes for the various eating areas in an hotel.

TIME SENSITIVITY

Quite often business executives with a high spending power may choose to eat in a coffee shop because they are in a hurry and do not wish to spend more time in a leisurely up-market restaurant. It is customary to assume that the fast food scene is a high volume, low price market but the two do not necessarily go together.

Many businessmen are primarily time sensitive at lunch and may not be price sensitive at all. In fact they might pay more for a good meal served fast. This is not to say that we should turn hotel restaurants into a typical McDonalds fast food restaurant, far from it. But we should find out, through our customer profiles, whether we have a significant proportion of our customers who are time sensitive. We should then systemize and gear the operation to satisfy this market.

We once carried out a popularity study on a restaurant in a famous London hotel. More than half the lunchtime covers were chosen from the trolley even though there was an excellent à la carte menu. The joint on the trolley was not much cheaper than the other entrées so why did customers choose it? The visual display and presentation of the trolley might have been a factor but this restaurant was not famous for its roast joints like, say, Simpsons-in-the-Strand. Besides, the restaurant was so large that most people ordered what was on the trolley without being able to see it clearly. Our research showed that the principal reason was that customers were relatively time sensitive. About 60 per cent ordered from the trolley at lunchtime; this decreased to 15 per cent ordering from the trolley in the evening, when people have more time and when roast dishes may not be so popular anyway.

FIXING A MAXIMUM SPEND

Excluding the five star hotel with a superb restaurant and an extensive wine list, let us examine the subject of average spend. Most experienced hoteliers and restaurateurs have a target average spend which they try to improve without affecting sales volume and driving away trade. On the other hand they do not want to have customers coming in during the busy meal periods eating just one course or ordering a cup of coffee. So virtually all restaurateurs introduce a minimum charge in the peak periods; alternatively, they price the menu so that no one spends below a certain amount. This is sound economic sense unless you are very quiet in the usual peak periods.

Many restaurateurs feel that if the customer wants to spend a lot of money, why not give him the opportunity? So they offer various high priced dishes as starters, as a main course, and special desserts (and special coffees and cocktails) in case he is in the mood to spend. I am sympathetic with this as a general policy, but in the mass market of middle-spend customers, isn't there a case for fixing a maximum or ceiling price rather than a minimum? Many people say if you avoid smoked salmon, lobster and the most expensive items, and choose the house wine (which I normally do), two people will leave my restaurant with change from $60 to tip the cloakroom attendant – or words to this effect. The amount of $60 is not as important as the principle.

With one client we decided to take this policy a stage further. The restaurant had a fairly extensive menu but only six wines on the wine list. We specifically planned the pricing strategy so that if a couple had one cocktail, the most expensive dish out of three courses, the most expensive bottle of wine, and coffee, adding taxes and 15 per cent tip they could not possibly spend more than a certain maximum amount. The spend bracket for two people was carefully researched in the catchment area, and the market segment range of spend fixed as a target with a maximum possible spend per couple and naturally half this per cover. The marketing philosophy was that the owners were very happy with the price segment *and* the maximum, and the customer would not experience a shock because he had spent much more than he expected when he walked in. The restaurant was, and still is, very successful.

Inflation meant that after a year the maximum was increased. Then we encountered inflation together with a recession. The decision was made not to exceed the maximum price spend and to hold it at that level whatever the rate of inflation for at least one year. This was done by rethinking and changing dishes, menu specifications, and by better buying, particularly of wines. In a period of inflation *and* recession this policy pays off in repeat business, higher sales volume, and as a bottom line profit.

FOOD COST PERCENTAGES

Traditionally in hotel food operations we have controlled costs on a percentage basis. We talk about a target food cost of, say, 35 per cent, or in the United Kingdom a target food gross profit of 65 per cent (100 per cent minus 35 per cent). This method of controlling food costs is a useful economic yardstick, but it is totally wrong from the point of view of marketing, pricing strategy *and* net profits. Firstly, once again, it is an average percentage. Secondly, it ignores payroll cost. And, most important of all, it does not take into account what the market is prepared to pay. Let us take an extreme example. The food cost percentage, and therefore gross profit, is usually much better *as a percentage* on a bowl of soup compared with a starter of, say, smoked salmon ('lox'). But what would you really rather sell in terms of actual *amount* of profit?

Traditionally many restaurateurs and chefs took the food cost of a dish and multiplied approximately by three. Then it became recognized that this priced out of the market certain dishes, where the commodity purchase price was expensive (e.g. lobster, smoked salmon, etc.) Generally throughout the 80s it was recognized that you could not expect to achieve a target food cost percentage of, say, 35 per cent and still find a buyer for these higher priced items. During the next decade the trend will be much more towards establishing a fixed amount of profit per dish which is more related to increasing sales volume, seat turnover ratios and actual amount of profit. Nobody has ever banked a percentage. It is the actual amount of money that counts.

Similarly, as good wines increased in purchase price we persuaded some clients to drop the idea of selling wines on a percentage mark-up basis and to change over more to a standard amount of add-on per bottle. This certainly helped to increase total sales, particularly of the slower moving higher priced wines, and increased overall net profits.

FUNCTION PRICING

The right kind of imagination can do a lot to make a routine function something absolutely special whether it be a central feature like an ice carving, attractively produced menus, or something personalized to the name of the company or the people organizing the function. Derek Taylor's excellent book *How to Sell Banquets* is well worth reading on this aspect. Many restaurants can quite honestly obtain higher prices because the food, service, or atmosphere is unique, or just a little better than the competition. This is more difficult with functions. Most functions are fairly routine, and it is difficult to produce a gastronomic experience when you are feeding large numbers. Further, this aspect of a hotel's sales quite often has more competition, particularly on price.

Many of the points raised previously on restaurant pricing strategy are equally applicable to functions and will help to maximize both the number of functions and, where attendance is not compulsory, the numbers who attend. Points like seeking an amount of profit on food and wines rather than a percentage can help to increase sales. I believe that by the 90s food and beverage management will automatically talk about pounds and pence, or dollars and cents, per dish, rather than food percentages. They are going to ask a colleague from another hotel 'How many dollars do you make on an eight ounce fillet steak?' rather than 'What percentage do you make?'

The other major cost on functions is payroll. Unless the trend moves over totally to self-service buffet style functions, payroll costs are always going to be high. In many countries most of the waiters and waitresses are 'casual' employees taken on just for that function or a series of functions. So they are not usually a fixed cost.

Very often a prospective function organizer is offered a series of sample menus covering a range of prices. The prices usually vary depending on the *commodity* cost of the dishes making up the suggested sample menus. Payroll does not enter into the calculations. Most hotels fix a staff standard for functions based on their style of hotel of one waiter to a table of ten people, or one waiter to two tables. And yet payroll is getting more expensive all the time. Where competition is tough, or we in the hotel industry want to stimulate overall growth in the function market, we should consider waiters (as well as food cost) as another 'variable' in the pricing strategy.

Suppose we said to a prospective function buyer, once the broad menus are agreed:

> 'Mr. Jones, we have three alternative types of functions where your guests are sitting down to a superb meal, and three different price levels.
>
> 'One is our standard function, the other is a function where you are not in too much of a hurry and have more time. And the third is our VIP function.'

The first might have one waiter for every ten customers, the one where they have more time might have one waiter for every twenty people, and the VIP might have two waiters per table of ten. This would be gently explained to the prospective buyer, with the different prices.

In one 'slump' year I know one hotelier who decided to take action well before the pre-Christmas office party period, because he feared massive cancellations of functions. He offered local companies who were cutting down on numbers, or thinking of cancelling, the chance to reduce costs by *sharing* a dance or disco with a completely strange company. His argument was that everyone eats in a room with strangers (except at their own table) when they eat in a restaurant, so why not in a large function room? It worked and in fact a number of the companies expressed their thanks to him for trying to save them money. That was pretty radical thinking.

What I am saying is that over the next decade we are going to have to rethink a lot of the ways we fix our pricing strategies because they are based on tradition. Yet the world is changing.

Periodically we should sit down with our team of executives and assume the hotel was *brand new*. We should go through the exercise of fixing room tariffs, restaurant, bar and function prices, and try to forget completely what we are charging now. Assume no prior experience. Look at the competition, find out about the market needs, think fresh. When the exercise is finished we should compare the results with the prices we are charging now and we must consider carefully, if they vary, why and what we should charge.

PACKAGING UP IN PRICING STRATEGY

The foregoing sections deal with pricing strategy for room tariffs, restaurant and function prices. At times of recession, or in some circumstances even in busy times, the question of whether to discount on normal quoted tariffs is often raised. Could I make it quite clear that I am not against discounts. There are many circumstances when there is an opportunity to obtain business in a quiet period (e.g. a function on a Monday night). Or there is a possibility of obtaining a booking for a definite large number of people like a group tour with high double occupancy, or an over-night convention, when a discount might be good marketing tactics. In these cases discounting up to an agreed maximum percentage, as shown in the earlier section on Economic Criteria for Successful Marketing, is logical.

But too often I have found on actual consultancy assignments that there is an automatic reaction to put forward a price reduction at once, as the first tactic for obtaining more business. In particular I notice that sales executives in giving a sales presentation sometimes suggest a discount at an early stage where in fact the prospective buyer has not heard the whole presentation, and may not want a discount. And it is not just sales executives who fall into the trap. In obtaining business in a quiet period, or developing new markets (e.g. weekend and short break holidays) the tendency can sometimes be 'how competitive (cheap) can we make it?'

The first question about a quiet period should really be why is it quiet? What are the reasons, the problems that prevent business from coming in those periods? Unless there is no business at all, what motivates the present market and custom to use you in the 'quiet' times? Very often the different sources of business require a pricing package in order to promote it as this provides the buyer (whether it is a weekend break or a convention) with a chance to fix a maximum budget. It is my contention that this pricing package does not necessarily have to be priced as low as possible, but could be packaged up – or both.

Some years ago I remember the manager of an hotel in the Scottish ski resort of Aviemore telling me he set out to attract more of the honeymoon market than he was obtaining to date. He produced a special brochure and part of the package price was a bottle of Moet & Chandon on ice in the bedroom on arrival. In fixing the price he first thought of including each bottle at cost price only. Then he thought he would see what would happen if he charged the full price for the champagne in the total holiday price and offered both – the basic price with no extras and an alternative with the champagne and other extras. Every couple bought the honeymoon with the extras. There are many other people who are willing to 'trade up' who are not necessarily on honeymoon if it is presented to them in the right way.

Another client was going to enter the weekend break market for the first time and were prepared to invest time and money promoting and developing this market over a three year period. I persuaded them to offer two weekend packages. One was the standard package including accommodation, breakfasts, two dinners, service charges and taxes. The other was a VIP package 'for that special occasion' which was the standard package and a half bottle of champagne on ice on arrival – a box of Elizabeth Shaw mints – fruit and flowers in the bedroom – free cocktail before every meal, breakfast in bed, etc. The results were monitored and on average just over a quarter, 27 per cent, purchased the higher priced weekend break.

Another example of a situation which was not creating a new market but was a chance to obtain a bigger slice of business. Our client had a large hotel near a major airport with a number of competitive hotels. Most of them were new and few had significant advantages over the others. All were experiencing low average room occupancies, around 60 per cent. A major international company was launching a new product and wanted to hold the series of launches for their agents world-wide by flying them all to that airport. So the location at the airport was fixed. They wanted 300 rooms for each series, four days per series, spread over nearly twenty weeks.

The company had asked five or six hotels to quote. Together with the client we worked long hours preparing advantage/limitation lists compared with the competition. And everyone racked their brains to finds ways of quoting the minimum price to obtain this large amount of sales income. I persuaded the client to put forward two quotes and we were told afterwards that we were the only hotel who did.

The first was the Executive Package which was the usual conference rate for an overnight conference reduced 'to the bone' and no hidden extras. The second was the VIP conference package including:

Accommodation
All Meals
Use of exhibition and conference rooms
Fruit and flowers in every bedroom
One bottle of gin, sherry and whisky in every bedroom
Opening cocktail party first evening

One evening at the theatre
Last dinner special Elizabethan evening
Complete programme for wives

The total price per delegate of the VIP conference package was nearly twice the price of the lower Executive Package, but the company bought it with hardly any hesitation or alteration.

We often consider packaging up for VIP dinners, conferences, or for a special weekend. But quite often we ignore the opportunity at breakfast. In fact the trend is to move away from including a full breakfast in the room tariff and only include continental breakfast, or nothing in America. Have a look at the breakfast menu shown in Figure 5.3 from the Ritz Hotel in Lisbon, an Inter-Continental Hotel. This kind of menu could really work successfully where there is room service and the principles would still apply where breakfast is served in a restaurant. I know it works. My wife and I stayed there and we both thought the Sparkling Breakfast was great but did not choose it until Saturday when I did not have to work. We both felt you had to try it. (See following page.)

Many people discount because travel agents and, in particular, tour operators often say the market is very price sensitive. Most tour operators are very shrewd and clever negotiators – if you take a short-term viewpoint.

I always recommend clients to obtain the current brochure when they are renegotiating their price with a foreign tour operator, have it translated if necessary, and see where their hotel is listed and how it is described compared with the competition. That will often provide valuable negotiating clues. For years I have watched 'bulk buyers' negotiating prices which are unrealistic considering the long-term future of the product they are buying (i.e., the hotels) and are, therefore, not in their interests.

I would like to put a scenario before you of a hotelier, Sam Salt, negotiating his rates with a tour operator for next winter. The characters are fictitious and so are the rates. John Smith is the tour operator, Ms Sheraton Hilton is the sales executive, William Black is a competitive hotelier. Sam Salt is speaking.

> 'I have listened to your remarks, John, about next winter's market, and I agree with most of them: that there is no sign of an end to the recession and that we hoteliers are going to have a tough time next winter. And I appreciate you showing me the market research predicting a bad winter for holidays between your country and London. It doesn't surprise me that my competitors are worried and

PEQUENO ALMOÇO		**BREAKFAST**
Servido entre as 07h00 e as 12h00.		Served from 07h00 – 12h00
O PEQUENO ALMOÇO REAL	950$00	**THE SPARKLING BREAKFAST**
1/2 Garrafa de espumante bruto Salmão fumado da Escócia e espadarte fumado e Bife do lombo grelhado com ovo estrelado e A sua escolha de pequeno almoço Inter-Continental		1/2 Bottle of brut portuguese sparkling wine Scotch smoked salmon and smoked swordfish and Fillet of Beef with fried egg and Your choice of Inter-Continental breakfast
Com morangos ou melão (na época)	150$00 (extra)	With fresh strawberries or melon (in season)
O PEQUENO ALMOÇO ARISTOCRATA	500$00	**THE DUKE'S BREAKFAST**
A sua escolha de pequeno almoço Inter-Continental com Bife do lombo grelhado com ovo estrelado e bacon O cereal à sua escolha		Your choice of Inter-Continental breakfast with Grilled minute fillet steak with fried egg and bacon The cereal of your choice
Com morangos ou melão (na época)	150$00 (extra)	With fresh strawberries or melon (in season)
O PEQUENO ALMOÇO TRADICIONAL	350$00	**THE TRADITIONAL BREAKFAST**
A sua escolha de pequeno almoço Inter-Continental Escolha de cereais Ovos, à sua escolha, acompanhados com presunto, bacon, salsichas ou cogumelos		Inter-Continental breakfast at your choice Selection of cereals Eggs, any style, served with ham, bacon, sausages or mushrooms
O PEQUENO ALMOÇO INTER-CONTINENTAL		**THE INTER-CONTINENTAL BREAKFAST**
(Incluído no preço do seu quarto)		(Included in the price of your room)
Inclui sumo de laranja natural ou qualquer outro sumo, Croissants, pãezinhos ou bolos secos, torradas, Manteiga, compotas diversas ou mel chá, café, chocolate ou ovomaltine		Includes fresh orange juice or other fruit juice, Croissants, rolls and buns, or toast, butter, marmelade, Jam or honey Tea, coffee, chocolate or ovomaltine
Todas as taxas incluídas		All taxes included

Pequeno almoço
Breakfast

Figure 5.3 A Breakfast Menu

prepared to give you a rate of $18 per pax (person) double occupancy, including continental breakfast, service charge and VAT. I also agree that there is a mood of panic among some hoteliers because prospects are bad and interest rates high. So your offer of $20 per pax sounds generous. But I have worked out some basic calculations.

'My heat, light and power bill has gone up 38 per cent in three years.

My property rates have increased by 72 per cent during the same period. The pattern is the same with most costs, except for repairs and redecorations which I reduced to a minimum last year. It is fortunate that my property is in a good state of repair and décor. I have calculated that I may break even at $20 per pax if I allow a reasonable sum for repairs, renovations and depreciation. In the same very tough years your rate paid to me only increased by 18 per cent.

'I agree that you must hold down the total price of your holidays in order to sell as many as possible and you are correct in pointing out that my competitors would be very happy with $20 . . . you have already shown me the signed agreement with William Black at the Excelsior nearby even though this is confidential.

'I could kick myself for not doing it before, but I got *your* German brochure for this present winter and had it translated into English. You list a choice of eight hotels in London, starting with the highest priced. I find that I am the second most expensive and the Excelsior is seventh, very nearly the cheapest. If your customers' sole criteria was price – as you stress – how is it so many choose *my* hotel?

'What I like best of all is the glowing way you describe my hotel, the friendly staff, the good state of décor and my quiet location. Together with my sales executive, Sheraton Hilton, I have produced a new advantage/limitation list of my hotel *and* my competitors, so we know these glowing comments in your brochure are correct. We have also checked that my breakfast is superior to my competitors.

'I put it to you, John, that you have been in business for many years, and in your kind of trade a key economic factor is the degree of repeat business and recommendation. I would bet that your CSQs (customer satisfaction questionnaires) rate me as high, if not higher, than many of my competitors.

'After some calculations I have set my new rate at $30 per pax double occupancy. I really want your business, John, but I want it at a profit. I feel that my rate of $30 is good value for money.

'John, we'll have to end our meeting soon because I have an appointment with another tour operator. Sorry to rush you but I don't want to keep him waiting, and you will need a day or so to think this over.

'Give me a call next week.'

This little scenario is put before readers to stress some points. Firstly, the hotelier has done some homework. Secondly, he has obviously been on a course on negotiation! Primarily he has planned his tactics and the timing of his next meeting very carefully. He may reduce his price from $30 to do a deal but he will probably achieve more than the tour operator's offer of $20. Obtaining a translation of the tour operator's brochure could be invaluable in negotiations like this. The hotelier is also selling on higher satisfaction for the tour operator's clients and more repeat business rather than selling on price alone.

Although much more extensive, this is very similar to an actual meeting I attended where the tour operator finally agreed $28 per person.

> Concentrate on price and you have only one way to go – down. Switch from price to value and you have many paths all of them up.

One of the finest statements I have ever read on the whole subject of price and value was written over one hundred years ago and I have no hesitation in repeating it below.

> Value . . .
> It's unwise to pay too much, but it's unwise to pay too little. When you pay too much you lose a little money, that is all. When you pay too little, you sometimes lose everything, because the thing you bought was incapable of doing the thing you bought it to do.
>
> The common law of business balance prohibits paying a little and getting a lot. It can't be done. If you deal with the lowest bidder, it's well to add something for the risk you run. And if you do that, you will have enough to pay for something better.
>
> John Ruskin (1819–1900)

Very often in negotiating on price I have read this out and it has helped to win an argument.

Some hoteliers and sales executives automatically assume that the only way to clinch a major deal is to offer discounts. This could be the easy way out – in many situations the buyer would sooner have the proposition 'packaged' with a series of extras included, rather than having a reduction in the price. Many people say that the market is price sensitive today. What they mean is that the tour operators say the price is sensitive. Often research shows that the ultimate purchaser (the guest) may show an opposite reaction.

A leading sales executive said to me recently that the only right policy is 'pile 'em high – sell 'em cheap', quoting the famous policy statement by the founder of Tesco, a chain of supermarkets. But we are not selling cans of beans, and this attitude may well drive us out of business.

Send sales executives, receptionists and reservation staff out to look at competitors' rooms and list league tables of comparable tariffs. It might dawn on them that your quoted tariffs are not as high as they may seem. I have seen many sales staff and receptionists 'breathe in' as they quote the tariff for the room at $40, $60, or more, because they feel it is high. Once they have seen the competition's charges they will have much more confidence in selling their room rates.

Curiously enough, however sophisticated people become, everyone likes something for nothing. And if you include something in a package which appears to be free, people love it. In the Daula Hotel, Kano, Northern Nigeria, we introduced a rose for ladies leaving the dining room. The response was staggering. There are a mass of 'small' items which make people think you care and make them return.Too often we have a number of irritating add-ons. The small charge for a morning newspaper or – probably the worst – the cover charge in the restaurant. I know all the reasons for it, but it annoys the majority of customers. I rather like the idea of giving a departing guest a take-away gift which is associated with the area, like a selection of local cheeses, or a paperweight from a local stone, with your own name or emblem on the item or on the wrapping. I have a key ring, a leather coaster for my office desk, and a long shoe-horn which I use virtually every day – all reminding me of the hotels who gave them to me. Naturally the quality of the gift would depend on the style of hotel. Why give a departing guest just a receipted bill and a credit card slip when he leaves after spending possibly $2000 or more on a holiday?

It is a very good rule in obtaining repeat business to give guests something when they arrive and something when they leave.

In good or bad times there are always some people who will spend more money if you give them the chance. And there are always some companies or organizations who are selling a very expensive product, or trying to make a good impression on a product launch, where a hotelier can do the same. Usually the hotel costs are small compared to the overall costs of marketing, in relation to the development costs of a new product, and compared to the sales price of the product.

There is a place for discounts on quiet nights and periods of the year where the market is more price sensitive. Retrospective discounts to major buyers where they have given you more than a certain amount of business in the past years are also useful. But before hoteliers use discounts as a marketing weapon, first:

1 Find out much more about the market, its motivations, price sensitivity, etc.
2 Isolate quiet periods clearly and try some creative selling first, before discounting.
3 Try packaging up rather than pricing down.

What we must avoid is the degree of discounting which lowers the average rate earned per room to a level which is so low that however high occupancy is, the hotel will never show a reasonable profit level. We must not fall into the trap the airlines have fallen into of selling 'bottoms on seats' regardless of profits. Belatedly airlines are packaging up with a lot of advertising promoting larger seats, 'free' drinks, slippers, etc. The problem is that once the market has got used to low prices, it is very difficult to increase them to an economic level.

Talking about pricing strategy is easier than writing about it, because when you are talking someone can always interrupt, ask a question, and you can cross-fertilize ideas. When I told a friend I was going to write a Section on Pricing Strategy he described it as a 'time bomb' where you can never be right. But if this section makes you argue, puts it into perspective, or just provides you with a few clues to your own strategy in the future, I will be very satisfied.

* * * * *

6

THE 80s AND 90s

Anyone who tries to predict ahead in these uncertain times is asking for trouble. Yet businessmen, industrialists, economists, must plan ahead and this involves a degree of prediction. It takes about a year to write this kind of book, and then another year to have it printed, re-written, corrected and published. A politician once said 'a day is a long time in politics'. A period of two years is a long time to put pen to paper on predictions, and then find that perhaps they are totally wrong the day the book is published. But looking ahead should make us plan ahead and this must have advantages. I am reminded of a quotation by Epitectus: 'What is it to be a philosopher? Is it not to be prepared against events?'

As an example of the difficulty in predicting too far ahead, just look at the spot price of oil. When I wrote the first edition the price of oil was climbing steadily to $30. One could predict that the major oil producing countries within or outside OPEC (Britain) would gradually increase prices and cause inflation in the oil importing countries.

At the time of writing, the price of spot crude oil had fallen in a six-month period through the $20 barrier for the first time in seven years, and then down through the $15 price barrier. There is a surplus of 2 million barrels of crude oil a day flooding on to world markets! Should the current war between Iran and Iraq end there would be an even larger glut.

Saudi Arabia, Kuwait, the United Arab Emirates and Britain could cut output to remove this surplus but seem unlikely to do so. The delicate economies of Venezuela, Mexico and similar countries could collapse. However, this situation should benefit many countries who import oil (i.e. India) and some who send large numbers of tourists round the world to Britain and other countries. It should benefit countries like America, Germany and Japan. Some smaller countries I have worked in recently (Ireland and Cyprus) see the collapse of oil prices as really good news.

There has been growing world terrorism. Should the war between Iraq and Iran spill over to adjacent countries, e.g. Kuwait, the price of oil could increase rapidly again. Who can predict ahead one month, let alone ten years? In fact, the only known predictable fact is that we are all going to die one day. Do you ever think about that – your own death? Have you ever sat around with your friends and discussed when it does happen – the end of your life – what you will have achieved in your life? For many of us in the Western world someone will have the difficult task of carving a few lines on a headstone to try to sum up our whole life's achievements.

When I look back at the last twenty five years, and look forward hopefully to another twenty five years, I can see quite clearly, so clearly, that the sum achievement of my life, the main thing people will say about me, is shown on the illustration below.

If we obtain a major assignment anywhere which necessitates a series of flights, I can guarantee you the air traffic controllers will work to rule. Strikes, go slows, work to rules, and industrial disputes appear to follow me around. But this does have a major advantage. It gives me a lot of time to read, and time to think. I am a compulsive reader and I like to think about future trends and their relevance to the hotel industry.

FUTURE ASSUMPTIONS

There are numerous books which look ahead from either an economic, technological or sociological viewpoint, and usually a mixture of all three. What I would like to do is tell you about the thinkers and writers who have influenced my speeches on looking ahead to the 90s and in particular the ones who have something relevant to say about the future of the hotel industry's markets, although they did not mention hotels and I had to interpret their views to the hotel industry.

In looking ahead you have to make certain assumptions because if you do not, you cannot even start. For instance, you have to assume certain future developments will, or will not, happen:

1 There will be no outbreak of war between the major powers, and obviously no nuclear war.
2 If wars break out between the 'smaller' nations they will not be in areas of strategic or economic significance, or if they do they stay contained in that area, i.e. the war between Iraq and Iran.
3 Major oil producers (like Saudi Arabia) and other producers of key raw materials will not have their production interrupted and the countries will continue to be run by leaders sympathetic to the West.
4 There will be no major shift of territorial influence by the West or the Russian and Eastern Bloc.
5 China will stay pre-occupied with its own internal economic and modernization problems and will not be expansionist.
6 We will not see a series of bad harvests in the main food producing countries (e.g. America, Canada, Russia, Australia), particularly of wheat.
7 The present so called world economic recession will not worsen.
8 Inflation will still be with us but this will not turn into the level of hyper-inflation experienced in Germany in the 30s, i.e. the kind of inflation that certain smaller 'special situation countries' are experiencing of over 100 per cent per year will not spread to more countries.
9 There will be no major ecological disaster or nuclear accident.

If we believe that any, or some, of these are likely to happen then we might as well 'shut up shop', or just live from day to day. If we assume that these major factors, or any I may have omitted are *not* going to occur then we have a basis to look ahead with a more positive outlook.

SOCIAL AND TECHNOLOGICAL TURMOIL

There are higher levels of unemployment at present in the industrialized nations than for some time, other than the difficult year of 1974 when the OPEC countries increased world oil prices rapidly from what they claim was a low starting level prior to 1974. And yet most people in the Western world are better off than the previous decades of the 50s and 60s, and many older people would have to agree that materially we are far better off than when they were young. There is no doubt that if we consider being better off in terms of material assets then far more people own their own homes, possess cars, televisions, video-tape recorders, cameras, etc. than one or two decades back.

And yet a lot of people seem very unhappy. There is considerable social dissention and stress. Crime has increased in most countries. There is not just a generation gap between parents and children but you can see a gap in 'younger' people which is as short as five or ten years where they cannot seem to communicate. Racial tension seems to be increasing and there is a polarization of views between people who are active politically.

Employer and employee relations appear to have worsened in most countries. Even in the so-called Communist and Socialist blocks where the owner of factories, plants, and stores are the employees, the situation seems far from happy (e.g. Poland).

And haunting the whole scene is the spectre of mass unemployment.

Many sociologists, economists and writers paint a depressing picture. However, there are a lot of positive aspects to the development of society which are obscured by the enormously fast rate of technological change which I believe was triggered off by the American and Russian space programmes. This rapid change only really began about fifteen to twenty years ago. These space programmes lead a drive toward miniaturization and the use of machines to assist men in their work (i.e. robots) which has been there since the dawn of the industrial revolution but has been speeded up suddenly in the last twenty years.

Many great thinkers and writers have written about this. Two have influenced my thinking. I am not sure if they have got it right, but they did help to clarify many things for me and I would urge readers to read their books. It would be useful to set the scene for the next decade if I summarized some of their ideas on the future for readers, although their views look further ahead than the 90s in many respects.

The first is *Le Défi Mondial* (The World Challenge) by Jean-Jacques Servan-Schreiber who also wrote 'The American Challenge', a book which glorified American management methods and seemed to infuriate management of most other countries, particularly the French. Servan-Schreiber sees the industrialised economies of the West as 'exhausted' and hopelessly dependent on imported raw materials. He frets over the mountains of petrodollars accumulating in Arab hands and paints a terrible portrait of Third World nations, crushed under the weight of famine and illiteracy, seething with resentment and considered entirely unfit for development by the West. Only a dramatically new approach, built on the concept of developing human potential can, in Servan-Schreiber's view, bring hope to this hopeless situation.

Servan-Schreiber says he has the key to unlock the trilemma of Western decadence, Middle East greed and Third World misery. It lies, he argues, in the cybernetic revolution, the microchip, the industrial robot and advances in telecommunications that soon will permit the world to be woven into a single 'informatized' unit. Thanks to microchip technology, the poor of Asia and Africa will be able to leap from primitive societies to developed nations. Even better, the cybernetic age will create a demand for so many new programmers, teachers and doctors that unemployment may soon become a spectre of the past.

The author calls for a new Marshall plan, based on Western and Japanese expertise and Arab oil money and aimed at a massive transfer of information technology to the Third World. 'There is no need for negotiation' he argues, 'because the benefits of such a transfer must be "obvious to all". The OPEC countries need opportunities for investment, the West needs markets, the Third World needs all the help it can get.' The model that inspires him is modern Japan. He portrays the postwar tycoons who built Toyota, Honda and Mitsubishi as geniuses who faced conditions even worse than those in the Third World. Without raw materials, they had to rely on human resources and they were incredibly successful.

Servan-Schreiber unfolds a fascinating future which at least is optimistic and positive, rather than all doom and gloom. Having worked in underdeveloped and developing countries (Jamaica, India, Northern Nigeria) I wonder whether he underestimates the human element. I am not sure that American, European and Japanese technology can be superimposed on many underdeveloped countries as he believes . But his vision of the microchip future is worth reading as in a sense it is with us now and will alter our lives more significantly by the 90s than most of us can ever imagine.

A much more fascinating book, from a human relations point of view, is Alvin Toffler's *The Third Wave*. He also wrote the book

Future Shock. I can remember quite clearly being given the book in 1973 and could not stop reading it. The Third Wave is very heavy going but put me straight on the sociological stresses we face over the coming years.

Toffler argues that we had 3,000 years of an agricultural revolution (the first wave), followed by 300 years of the industrial revolution (the second wave) which is turning sour. In many respects he is quite right. I first started work practically worshipping, or at least admiring, huge organizations because I was brainwashed to do so. I remember standing outside a large factory AEI-BIRLEC in Birmingham, England, twenty-five years ago and watching thousands of employees pouring out at the end of the shift. I dreamed that one day I would run such a huge factory. Nowadays the thought horrifies me. Alvin Toffler argues that the industrial revolution is doomed because it is built on a series of false premises.

Firstly, large is good, leading to lower unit costs etc. whereas the employees of the 80s hate working in large organizations. Secondly, standardization is good, although we can see clearly that an increasing number of people will pay more for something a little special or different, like the special limited number versions of cars and special weekend packages. Thirdly, the industrial revolution divorced the producer from the consumer. Very often the producer never saw the consumer who might even be in a different country. (Readers will notice that there are points here relevant to hotels, particularly the standardized chains.) Fourthly, the industrial revolution is based on expendable energy which will be used up, or in very short supply within fifty years. He argues that the cult of centralization, popular throughout the last one hundred years, creates inefficiency and divorces top management from markets. Toffler then described a Third Wave Civilization where large numbers of people will work at home in Electronic Cottages, the traditional family unit will change, small (possibly within big) will be good, and technological developments and the microprocessor will revolutionize our work and leisure time.

How do I see the future and what is the relevance to the hotel industry?

I have stressed the need for us to think much more deeply about our markets, their motivations, problems, spending power, etc. – and the need for a greater degree of market segmentation. As this is important I have separated my views on the future and some of the new or expanding market segments I see developing within the next decade, taking us into the 90s. We are going to have a period of rapid change which will create social turmoil for large sections of the population. This is not necessarily a prediction, as you can see it happening now except that the pace of change and turmoil will quicken.

TECHNOLOGICAL CHANGE

This change will be in technology through microchips and the miniaturization of machines as well as computers, and this will have a major impact on our working lives. Whole job sections of the community will disappear overnight and it will have a bigger impact on some industries than others. Repetitive, assembly line jobs will be taken over by robots and other industries, like printing, will change beyond recognition. (There will be no need for print compositors.)

Any employment and industries which require retrieval, filing and reference systems will change. We will no longer need a whole bookcase or shelf for encyclopaedias as our children will be able to type or press out a question on a very small memory computer when they are studying, and read the answer on a small screen and/or have a print out result. Possibly by the 90s your child will be able to ask the question and the computer storage facility will understand simple word sounds or code words (HAL in '2001'). These computers will be much smaller and cheaper than the present series of encyclopaedias and much simpler to keep up to date. Reference libraries, filing systems, etc. will be revolutionized and this will affect most offices and industries.

This technological change has always been with us. I had an elderly aunt who started life with the job of making hand-made cigarettes. Along came a man called Bernard Barron who invented a cigarette-making machine and my aunt had to train for another job in an entirely different industry, together with thousands of other people who worked producing hand-made cigarettes. And for the first time Bernard Barron mass produced cigarettes which were cheap enough for the masses and ended up employing far more people than ever worked on hand-made cigarettes.

Bernard Barron was a generous philanthropist, although modern doctors might curse the day he ever invented the first cigarette machine.

Technological change has always been with us. It is just that over the last decade and probably over the next thirty years (Alvin Toffler's Third Wave), it is going to be far more rapid than ever before. There will have to be massive retraining and a total change on aspects of our life like retirement dates, holidays, leisure, etc. Unfortunately the stress and tensions in society arise because the majority of people do not want change, and who likes 'going back to school' or being retrained? Although both technological and sociological changes are going to affect the hotel industry, most hoteliers see the social changes of more relevance in marketing trends.

GEOGRAPHICAL GROUPINGS OF WEALTH

Firstly let us see how the wealth of the world may be distributed in order to aim our future long-term marketing strategy. For a long time after the Second World War this was easy to predict as America was by far the wealthiest country, sending tourists and businessmen around their own country and abroad to the hotel industry. It is interesting to note that without the growth and technological development of the aircraft manufacturing industry and the airlines who took enormous financial risks, the rapid growth in international tourism, which averaged 12 per cent growth per annum throughout long stretches of the years up to 1972, would not have taken place. And this growth to many countries was led by the American tourists and businessmen.

We have seen the growth in the economy of America falter, but I believe this is not long-term. There is no doubt that a country like America, which can put men on the moon, will solve their energy and balance of payments crises. Only 7 per cent of Americans have a passport, and the vast proportion have never been outside their own country. This will change and Americans will again become significant travellers and users of hotels by the 90s, both as tourists and as businessmen.

When we study industrial groupings of countries for mutual self interest, if not for political reasons, in the past they have often arisen solely out of geographical closeness. Communications, transportation costs and many other economic factors must be lower when you trade with a neighbouring country rather than one a long ship, plane or train journey away. How else can we explain the reason behind the grouping of the EEC countries? It isn't as if we speak the same language, have a common history of peace, or even like each other. But we are close geographically.

As in the past, I see one major geographical grouping dominating the 90s with energy, numerous other raw materials, population and technology, which could be unsurpassable by that time, this is:

America
Canada

In my opinion these countries will continue to have a major influence on the 90s. Their inhabitants will have considerable disposable income to spend on hotels (and restaurants) in their home countries, *and* as foreign tourists.

Churchill wanted an economic union of Europe *and* America. The biggest mistake the Europeans made was not to offer a union with America. We will regret this lost opportunity because an economic union between the EEC and America would have been very successful.

Looking ahead to the end of the 90s, there is another geographical area grouping which could be formidable as an economic growth area and cultural influence. But this is an area which most people really believe is a 'pipe dream' as a combined united economic area.

As a generalization, oil revenues only really make a substantial impact on the residents of a country where that country has a small population. Norwegians will become more wealthy from North Sea oil than Britons. Saudis will become more wealthy than, say, Nigerians. Very few people really appreciate the significance of the wealth oil has created for the countries with small populations. The surpluses of oil for export and foreign currency are beyond imagination.

In the Middle East we have a situation of extreme wealth and influence. But the area has problems. There are problems of food production, water for drinking and irrigation. And, of course, the area has been the scene of friction and warfare, not only between the Arab countries and Israel, but between Arab countries and different religions (Lebanon). On food problems there is no doubt that the country most skilled in growing food in the virtually impossible geographical and climatic conditions in that region is Israel. Probably the most advanced small nation in desalination is, once again, Israel. I have had the experience of working in both Israel and some Arab countries. I really do believe that there is a deep yearning for peace in all the countries I have visited.

If, and it is a big IF, there was peace in this area, then the potential of this geographical region is phenomenal. There was a period of 1,000 years when Arab was at peace with Jew. The combination of Arab oil and Israeli technology on food production, solar energy and desalination, could turn that area into one of the most influential geographical groupings of the 90s. As a *combined* area for tourism the Middle East's potential is 'explosive' once there is peace in that region: can you imagine a situation where tourists would travel freely to Lebanan, Jordan, Egypt and Israel?

I do not see the European Economic Community growing in anywhere near the significance of, say, an American, Canadian economic grouping. Some of the countries in the EEC may thrive, but the economic growth and political union of Europe cannot be forced, and in its true dynamic force may be fifty or a hundred years off, rather than in the 90s. After all, it took the different States in America about a hundred years to become truly the United States of America, and many people argue that they still have a long way to go.

The building of a fixed link (a channel tunnel) between Britain and France could stimulate a much faster growth in tourism between Britain and the Continent (and vice versa) than most people realise.

Overall I see the EEC showing steady economic progress and a development of trade with their close neighbours, the Russian Bloc. This should be beneficial economically, providing the EEC countries put up a united front to sell their much-needed products to the Communist countries on the same credit terms as they would export to, say, Australia or America, and not on the basis of some past credit terms where we are financing the development of the Communist Bloc, when our own industries require finance.

There could be little growth in the Russian Bloc which seems to have all major faults of too much centralization, lack of incentives, being product-orientated more than market orientated. There will be trade and some growth in the number of people from these countries who travel abroad on business, to specialist conferences and as tourists in escorted tours.

South America has increased its external tourism steadily and I expect that there will be considerable growth in the number of South Americans staying in overseas hotels throughout the next decade.

China will take a long time to industrialize and use the new technological developments. But I do see a significant number of people from China travelling abroad in groups to learn, study, and attend seminars. They will stay in hotels at the cheaper end of the price bracket. I know of one hotelier who has received a steady flow of business from this source. In 1980 I was asked by the Commercial Attaché's Department of the Chinese Embassy in London to find them a hotel they could purchase! The population of China is, as everyone knows, so huge that you only need a very small percentage travelling abroad to create a lot of income for hoteliers. Conversely I believe that one of the huge growth situations the tour and travel industry could face in the next two decades is tourism *to* China.

The sheer initiative and drive of the Japanese will keep them expanding, and they will open new export markets in Russia and China. There will be growth and a trend towards more economic unity in the geographical sphere of South Korea, Japan, Australia, Phillipines.

SUMMING UP

Although we read a lot about unusual destinations, research shows that tourism to America and to the established tourist points in Europe will grow during the next decade. The European Travel Commission predict that in 1990 Europe will constitute the destination choice of 75 per cent of the world's tourists. The study envisages 242 million international tourist arrivals in 1990 compared with 135 million currently. It is predicted that the number of American visitors to Europe will increase again. The growth in the Japanese market is likely to show sustained growth well above the world average.

Other studies predict new generating markets from Brazil, Mexico, Argentina, Venezuala and from a number of Middle East countries. There will also be expansion of a two-way flow of visitors between Europe and Singapore, Hong Kong and Korea.

In hotels the public demand for minimum standards and minimum facilities will increase steadily. I do not see a worldwide growth developing in capsule hotels, although many people would disagree. There is a Capsule Inn in Osaka which calls itself a business hotel for the year 2100. This unique facility has 418 'capsules' spread over three floors of a nondescript downtown building. Each plastic capsule is five feet high, five feet wide and six feet, seven inches deep. Almost every night, nearly every capsule is full. And people pay to stay there! A comparison of room sizes for budget hotels with a Capsule Inn is shown in Table 6.1.

The interior of the establishment that introduced the idea in Japan's second largest city looks more like a laundromat than a place to spend the night. But what appears at first to be washer or dryers, stacked two-high in long rows along the dimly lit corridors, turn out to be sleeping 'capsules'. There are other attractions. Each capsule has its own television set, radio, alarm clock, mirror and air conditioning. Television, vending machine refreshments and comfortable sofas are also available in the lobby on each floor, where guests lounge in orange terry-cloth robes supplied by the management. The capsule hotel may be a uniquely Japanese development.

Table 6.1
Budget Hotel Room Sizes

Chain	*Room Size in Square Meters*
Capsule Inn (single)	3
Washington (single)	10
(double)	13
Arcade	13
Minimote	15
Campanile	17.5
Super 8	24.5
Days Inns	26.8

I feel that the opposite trend will take place. People will pay more for space, and that future hotels will have larger rooms, probably with private small saunas, and certainly small jacuzzis in the bathroom area. Unless they have been neglecting capital expenditure, there is considerable evidence that older top quality hotels, with character, will develop a new following – if they ever really lost it. With high ceilings, sense of space and style, a growing market will pay more to stay in them, particularly if they have no more than around 200 to 300 room and suites.

In fact, smaller more personalised hotels could experience growth in demand. Apart from large conventions and certain unique areas (like Las Vegas) it is felt that the very large hotels will experience difficulties in achieving high average occupancies and high average room rates over the next decade. It is also my belief that large, American-style, standardized chains with their philosophy of high minimum standards but 'no surprises' for the guest will change their marketing stance to retain minimum standards but to give every hotel a different decor or theme which the owners can promote. Some co-operative marketing systems with high minimum standards but with widely different styled hotels, like Best Western, may gain on other franchise groups unless the other groups reduce the level of standardization.

In the next chapter we shall explore how the social and technological changes, and the new markets, will affect the hotel industry.

* * * * *

7

MARKET SEGMENTATION OVER THE NEXT DECADE

Earlier sections have commented on the possibility (some say a probability) that we will have radical changes to our social structure and in the way business and industry is organized. I have spoken about the need for geographical economic groupings, and yet at the same time forecast a break-up in centralized authority and power on the political and industrial front.

Although there is a current trend to huge mergers/take-over bids above $2 billion, my belief is that they will only be successful if authority and decision-making is delegated down the line to smaller autonomous sections and to companies where management is 'nearer' to employees and ultimate customers.

We are seeing the beginning of executive and employee buy-outs of separate sections of a larger company by the executives who appear to have the ability to make the company far more profitable than when they are part of a large group. These executives appear to have little trouble raising finance, even though the sums involved are large.

One recent management buy-out of Mecca in Britain was for $150 million. The same trend will develop with large hotel groups which run hotels which are not all profitable, particularly after charging head office overheads.

There could be advantages in conglomerates in the hotel industry 'floating off' separate companies on the Stock Market with their own quotation. About three months before the start of a new financial year the directors of separate divisions and subsidiaries start presenting the case to Head Office for capital expenditure. The management of these separate companies are absolutely convinced that they could expand profits substantially if they had the capital to re-vamp and update present premises and expand by acquisition.

Many major hotel companies have three or more divisions or subsidiaries - hotels, restaurants, pubs, contract catering, tour operators, etc. By the time the total requests for capital are added up, the amount involved is usually far more than is available. I have sat in on many of these meetings where the main board of directors and head office executives require the 'judgement of Solomon' to decide who gets what, and how much. Many subsidiaries end up with half the amount they have asked for and sometimes receive nothing. So profit growth is often inhibited through lack of capital.

And yet quite often some subsidiaries are within Stock Exchange groupings where the Price Earnings (PE) ratio is higher than the holding company's PE ratio. At the time of writing, in Britain restaurants as a stock market grouping have experienced a PE ratio nearly twice the level of many holding companies. If the holding company was to float off the subsidiary in order to take advantage of these higher PE ratios, it could show a 'capital profit', retain a major stake in the subsidiary, and at the same time raise large sums of capital to plough back into future expansion. Many non-hotel holding companies could float off their hotel subsidiary, take advantage of the higher current PE ratios and, at the same time, retain management control.

In the early 70s I worked on the possible merger between the hotel division of The Rank Organisation and the hotel subsidiary of Scottish and Newcastle Breweries (Thistle Hotels) into a completely separate company. Rothchilds were the merchant bank involved and the code name was 'The Third Force' because it would have produced the third largest hotel company in the United Kingdom after Trusthouse Forte and Grand Metropolitan hotels. At the time Thistle Hotels were primarily in the North of England and Scotland, and Rank Hotels were mainly in London with only three provincial hotels. Two of these provincial hotels were in the only two major cities where Thistle was not represented (Bristol and Leeds).

A merger would have created a major national group 'overnight'. For various reasons it did not go ahead. But the basic principles behind the merger were sound and certainly applicable to many hotel companies who do not have national coverage or, taking a broader view, companies who do not have international coverage, although they may have strong representation in certain Continents.

As societies change whole industries will alter in nature. Companies dealing directly with the consumer – like hotels and restaurants – will have to show particular flexibility to change as the consumer does. Working hours will change with more shift work to operate and supervise expensive capital intensive equipment. The trend towards flexi-hours will increase. A considerable number of people will work at home if not all the time at least part of the time, communicating with a central or head office by audio-visual telephones. Many more executives will have less need to visit their offices and could connect small briefcase size computers from most countries in the world direct to their major computer at head office by telephone to receive latest prices, output figures, stock delivery dates, latest management accounts, technical data, etc.

The typical family unit will change in many ways. Marriage will not 'die as an institution'. Although many people use the increasing divorce rate as evidence that the state of marriage is declining, in fact what is surprising is the number of divorced people who re-marry so that the total number of married people is not declining anywhere near the rate that divorce is increasing.

There has been a major development in sexually related illnesses like Herpes and AIDS that could lead to a revival in 'the couple' as a longer term market within marriage or just living together. There is certainly going to be considerable technological and social change over the next decade.

I believe that eventually after change and turmoil things will settle down. It might take a whole generation to train people in the new skills and industries, but in most of the developed and developing world there is a Brave New World ahead. Whenever there is change more marketing opportunities arise than when there is a long period of stability with little change. Even in a depression some people are still capable of making a lot of money, not necessarily because of exploitation, but because they see marketing opportunities when the mass of people do not.

Here are some examples of market changes and new segments. They cannot be all embracing because there are changes happening now which cannot be seen clearly. But here are some examples of how social and technological changes create 'danger' situations or marketing opportunities. Firstly a broad 'social' point, relative to people's homes, which in a sense acts as a warning note.

THE HOME VERSUS THE HOTEL

Traditionally, the hotel had something better to offer than the home, it was more luxurious, more exciting, or even just different. During the last decade in many countries people have modernized their homes, or moved into new houses with all the modern facilities. Where many people did not have them in the 60s or 70s, they have now installed central heating, double glazing, showers, extra bathrooms, extensions, playrooms, wet bars, wall to wall 'close' carpeting, tiled bathrooms and kitchens. Some older hotels, particularly on the bedroom side, have not kept pace with this trend.

The trend of people improving their own homes will continue. Some forms of consumer spending create pollution (cars), noise (music centres) and an anti-social backlash and even legislation (smoking). Expenditure on the home creates none of these problems, and is often viewed as an investment rather than just an expense. There will be steady growth in people up-grading their own houses or apartments.

Hotel owners and people planning new hotels must be aware of this trend, and ensure that hotel facilities are still slightly better than those in private houses – more comfortable, or different. There are still some hotels without modern personal facilities who will survive and thrive because they are unusual, nostalgic or historic. I have a friend, with a seventeenth century hotel which does not have private bathrooms to each bedroom. But the hotel is so unique that there will always be a demand for this kind of hotel. It could well be a premium demand because it is just like staying in an English aristocrat's private house. In fact his sales message is 'welcome to my home'.

Similarly, one of the most successful formulae in Europe is the old attractive smaller hotel with a new bedroom block discreetly built with modern personal facilities at the back. I am not arguing that only new and modern hotels will be successful in the 90s, because 'nostalgia' will be one of the easiest and most marketable products. Hotels like the Plaza, New York and the Savoy, London will always be popular. Very often they have larger rooms and bathrooms than newer modern city centre hotels. But the 'older' hotels must have regular 'facelifts' and in the long term must have all the modern personal comfort facilities, like air conditioning.

Many people, particularly businessmen, stay in a hotel not because they want to but because they have to. This means they tend to be more critical. One of the clear trends over the past two decades is that the public's demands in hotel facilities have steadily moved more up market. Even the major tour operators sending a mass market from the colder climates of Europe to the sand, sea and sun of Italy, Greece or Spain, at one time included hotels without private bathrooms in their brochures. Nowadays all the hotels in their brochures have private bathrooms. Once a businessman stays in a large bedroom of, say, Holiday Inn size, he tends to feel very restricted if he stays in a smaller bedroom.

The message I am trying to put across in this section is that unless a hotel is old with unique attractive features, it is essential that the hotel industry recaptures, or retains, the edge over the customers' private homes.

SUITE-ONLY HOTELS

The social trends are not necessarily just to luxury but to better facilities. Many people avoid staying in luxury hotels for a variety of different reasons. Often they feel inhibited by the words 'de luxe', 'luxury', or by 5 stars. There are many hotel companies who deliberately choose a 4 star category, even if they could obtain a further star.

The key to success in the hotel (and restaurant) industry is to advertise, promote and promise potential customers 90 per cent of what you know you can achieve. If you promise 100 per cent the slightest shortfall will disappoint them. If you promise 90 per cent and give them 95 per cent they will be agreeably surprised. Promising luxury could be dangerous unless you are completely sure you can deliver.

For some time now the emphasis has been on the bedroom with larger more comfortable beds, in-house movies etc. Within the next few years every hotel will have upgraded the actual bedroom. I see the next concentration of effort, thought and marketing on the bathroom.

I have stayed in hotels with two king-size beds and yet a small bathroom, or a very small bath. Total restyling of bathrooms will be with us over the next decade. Even where bathrooms are not large enough for 'his' and 'hers' washbasins and jacuzzi baths, some aspects, like tiling, become unfashionable every five years where once tiling would last twenty years. After years of throwing away old fashioned Victorian bathroom fittings they are now coming back in fashion!

It is becoming more apparent that business executives want to work in their bedrooms. They want to write, use their portable computers, hold business meetings and entertain business prospects in the privacy of their own room. In my opinion there will be a growing trend to suite-only hotels and executives will be happy to pay more for this. Many existing hotels could easily convert into two-roomed, suite-only hotels. In the year prior to being privatized by the Government, I advised British Transport Hotels on their marketing. Many of their bedrooms were huge. One plan we were going to introduce was to convert the larger bedrooms into mini-suites with an attractive partition between the bed area and the working area. I am convinced that there is going to be a growing demand – not necessarily for more luxurious hotels – but for facilities like suite-only hotels.

By suite-only hotels I do not necessarily mean the trend in some American suite-only hotels where there is no or very limited food and beverage facilities. These are more like apartment blocks. In America some of the first developments for some companies (like Guest Quarters) were conversions of apartment buildings. I see future development as more up-market with a full range of services, i.e. a normal hotel which has all bedroom suites and no individual bedrooms.

SOCIO-ECONOMIC GROUPS

No doubt market and consumer researchers are going to disagree, but I do believe that the normal method of grouping consumers into socio-economic groups is fairly meaningless for future marketing. You will remember that the traditional groups are as follows:

Grade A Households – Upper Middle Class
Grade B Households – Middle Class
Grade C1 Households – Lower Middle Class
Grade C2 Households – Skilled Working Class
Grade D Households – Semi-skilled and Unskilled Working Class
Grade E Households – People at Lowest Levels of Subsistence

We should not abandon the use of social grading in consumer and market research. Far from it, there is no better alternative in most aspects of consumer spending. A slightly more elaborate explanation of the six grades is shown in Appendix B. But it is felt that this kind of grading has limitations for the different sources of business in most hotels, except possibly a strictly holiday hotel. Let me give you some illustrations.

Some years ago we were working for Thomson Holidays, one of the most efficient tour operators, sending more than one million Britons abroad each year on holiday. I learned a lot from Thomson's brilliant marketing. They owned and operated around thirteen hotels at the time with nine in Mallorca. They commissioned some consumer research by Gallup in their own hotels and the results were fascinating. The vast majority of the visitors were very satisfied with the hotels and thought they were good value for money.

But I became very conscious of the limitations of using socio-economic groups in locating high spend markets. Some lower groups (possibly without mortgages) had much more discretionary spend than other groups. A family would be placed in a group depending on the father's occupation and earnings, and yet the mother's occupation might place them in a different group. Some fathers earned very little, but the wife and two children were all working and all living in one home.

Once I advised the owners of a hotel and casino, which was on an island, on their marketing. When we first analysed the occupation of the guests most of them were 'company directors' which really did not tell us anything. So we dug a little deeper and found that the occupations included butchers, hairdressers, jewellers, caterers, publicans, owners of car showrooms, owners of dress shops, etc. At first I could not quite see the link and then it dawned on me that they were all in cash takings businesses, staying in this hotel and spending money in the casino.

So rather than look at socio-economic groupings in the future we have to try and locate markets with the most surplus spending power, e.g.:

husband and wife both working
one or both in cash takings businesses
where the whole family work and live at home

The foregoing are illustrations of a thought process in marketing. What we will talk about much more is market segmentation as illustrated in the following sections.

THE INSTANT MARKET

People are tending to want things instantly. They want instant coffee and tea. Often they are not prepared to wait for each course, but want fast food. They buy things now, and pay for them later. And we often follow America. An example has been the rapid development of credit cards in Europe in the 80s, following their dominance of the American scene for decades. It is not just the security of not requiring to carry cash but the facility to buy now and not wait till one has saved the money.

A social development is that far more people buy products, order services, book holidays on impulse, and at a shorter time beforehand, than in the past. Not too long ago a large segment of the community booked their summer holiday just after Christmas. Executives planned a business trip weeks ahead. And people would plan a night out with a meal well in advance. This has changed with a much larger proportion buying at short notice. Because of this hotels must have systems so that they can take full advantage of this trend. And marketing and sales messages must persuade people to book at short notice with many of the techniques of Direct Response Sales Techniques adapted to hotels.

Ask this question. Assume you were a businessman or a couple thinking of taking a short break holiday, how easy is it to book at short notice? Make yourself go through the steps assuming you live outside your area, so that by having empathy you can spot the problems and improve your present booking facility and procedures. Assume you are not a hotelier and your wife says to you on Thursday (or Friday) 'Darling, you look tired, why don't we take one of those weekend breaks?' And you agree. What would you do? How would you find the telephone number at short notice of a certain hotel, or a central reservations office. Would this prospective buyer find *your* telephone number, or a competitor's? Do people keep sales literature? It is interesting, but I use a very expensive shoe horn every day I am at home with the name and telephone number of the Inter-Continental Hotel in Geneva. And I have a pen holder fixed to the side of my telephone from the Konover Hotel in Miami, again with their address and telephone number on it. If I had to book at short notice in a hotel in Geneva, or Miami, isn't there much more chance that I would use one of these hotels? But who keeps expensive sales literature, or cuts out the adverts you see from time to time in the media for major hotel companies' central reservations?

Hotel groups with computerized central reservations and independent hoteliers in a marketing co-operative with a similar computerized facility, will have a major advantage providing, of course, the impatient customer can locate the telephone number without too much trouble.

Every day my secretary brings in my tea and places it on an attractive leather place mat given to me by Thistle Hotels with their central reservations telephone number on it. If I suddenly wanted to go to Birmingham for a few days which hotel group am I likely to telephone first? The calendar on my office wall is from De Vere Hotels. The central reservations telephone number is there quite clearly for a whole year. The pocket diary I use is from Anchor Hotels and my key ring, which includes a miniature clock, is from The Forest Park Hotel, Platres in Cyprus.

WOMEN

In the last ten years I have been stressing on every occasion that the biggest growth market, staring everyone in the face, is women staying in hotels, or eating in hotel restaurants. There are women executives and women going on holiday (without accompanying men) in all age groups. We have always had a significant number of

American women, often middle-aged, travelling alone, or with female friends. But the growth in other nationalities going on holiday is rapid. Some are divorced or single and many more married women are nowadays taking an extra holiday on their own.

Probably the fastest growth segment for hotels over the next decade will be women executives. Everyone notices how some minority groups are more motivated to succeed and try harder. I see women nowadays as a majority group with all the drive of some minority groups. Many parents I know claim that their daughters study harder and work harder than their sons. One of my clients with a 'businessman's' hotel in a British industrial town had less than one per cent occupancy for women guests in 1971. This increased every year and was 19 per cent last year. In 1985, 52 per cent of all the females in the United States aged 16 and older were in the work force. Only 37 per cent are full-time housewives; the rest are at school, retired, or disabled.

When this social change is mentioned to hoteliers a significant number think 'So what?' They do not actually say this but they imply it, or you can read it on their faces. I invented the management technique, 'The So What Technique'. This arises whenever anyone makes a statement, very often in selling, which creates the reaction 'So what?' – there must be something wrong with it. I have seen this reaction when people say 'all our rooms have a private bathroom'. Or 'We are the largest hotel group in the world'. Or 'We open a new hotel every week on average'. So you are entitled to say 'so what?' when I get excited about the growth market in women executives staying in hotels. People say 'they eat, and want to sleep the same as businessmen. What is so important about this trend?'

Firstly, women often read different media to men, and therefore this media should be included for more future advertising in attracting your share of this growth market. Then you find that most bedrooms are designed by men for men. Mirrors are often wrongly located, and too often women have to make up in a steamy bathroom. Only recently I saw a mock-up bedroom for a new hotel with a full length mirror *inside* the bathroom door. Traditionally there is only one thing in a bathroom specifically designed for women, and this was introduced for operational reasons not for marketing, namely the sanitary towel disposal bags. Similarly, last week we stayed in a superb London hotel and my wife found there was not one hanger in the wardrobe where she could hang up a skirt.

And God help the lone woman executive when she goes to eat in the restaurant. Maitre d's and restaurant managers tell me this is what often happens in practice. They are showing someone else to a table or taking an order. A good restaurant manager always takes an order, if this is his responsibility, with an eye on the entrance. A women executive arrives. What happens? Restaurant managers have told me they often assume she is going to be joined by a man, in a moment. So they keep her waiting, maybe only ten or twenty seconds, but to her this seems like an hour. Many women executives I have spoken to claim they hate hotel restaurants and often eat in the bedroom. And you can imagine what happens if they go into a bar in a 'business' hotel.

What I am trying to emphasize is that if you redesign the bedroom with both sexes in mind, and train your restaurant and bar staff to pay particular attention to lone women executives, this growth market will 'beat a path to your door'. In the restaurant of one hotel group we tried a series of a kind of Captain's Table, circular in shape, for people on their own who just wanted to chat. Of course, lone executives were given the choice, but these 'singles' tables were very successful. But women do not want 'women only' lounges or bars.

Most of the available research on women travellers has been conducted in America. There, the findings are that the average woman executive is six years younger than her male counterpart. She tends to be in sales, marketing, public and press relations, or personnel work. She makes ten to twelve trips a year, but tends to stay longer than a man. Nearly 40 per cent of her trips are to conventions. She is more likely to be single than the typical travelling male. Many women are concerned about personal safety and hotel security. If persuaded, they would prefer to eat in the hotel than go out to eat. They are not comfortable in hotel bars, and prefer lobby bars and lounges that are open, airy and relatively quiet. They want a room which is very clean, attractive and spacious with good lighting. Women ask for closets high enough to accommodate floorlength dresses and a good supply of hangers – including skirt hangers. They like good lights for make-up and a large vanity area for all their jars and bottles, and they prefer individually operated temperature controls and a clothesline in the bathroom. Many of them use room service a good deal when it is available.

Staff must be trained to realize that the restaurant bill for a couple should no longer automatically be presented to the man – in fact the woman may be the boss. If the staff are not sure, let them place the bill in the centre of the table. Travel agents and travel managers can also help women executives travelling to certain areas for the first time by giving them advice on local religions, customs, etc. so that they do not make any serious business or social blunders.

SHORT BREAK MARKET

Another example of a social trend and market segmentation is the short break holiday. Many hotels which were traditionally four-sevenths (busy Monday through to Thursday nights) have very successfully promoted weekend breaks although experience shows that it takes two to three years to become sufficiently known in this market to attract a 'following' and repeat potential.

We studied the profile of this market in order to obtain clues to improve future marketing and sales promotion. In the major tourist cities like London or Edinburgh we found no definite profile, or market segment, except that visitors on short breaks to Edinburgh tended to be over 40 years old. Very often these particular packages included a rail fare and the buyers were a wide cross-section of the whole market and from different parts of the country.

But where hotels were in a smaller town or city the profile was much more specific. In one case of a 90-room hotel with a weekend average occupancy of 55 per cent, mainly from weekend breaks, the profile provided some invaluable clues.

Firstly, most visitors travelled by car. And a significant proportion had not exceeded two hours driving time. This helped to define the catchment area much more specifically for future promotion, although a maximum of two hours driving means the catchment area for different hotels in a group varied considerably, for different locations depending on the road network and driving conditions to the hotel. Some three quarters of the market were over 45 years old, at the age where they no longer had to worry about baby sitters, or leaving their children. This was the group who had reached a stage in business life or career where they could leave off work earlier on a Friday, or arrive in later on Monday morning. And a significant proportion were self-employed in cash takings business. With the employed person a high proportion of the wives worked as well, so they were two-income families.

The occupancy was virtually all double. But one of the key points about the profile was that something like 80 per cent of the 'couples' were not alone but spending the weekend with another couple, and a high proportion were three couples away together. Sometimes out of six people there was one decision maker who suggested going away and in nearly every case the decision maker was a woman.

From this we altered the whole of the advertising geared to this profile, selling more specifically within the catchment area, and changing the wording to the theme of 'get away with your friends to a house party'. A considerable part of the sales effort was a series of letters and mailing shots throughout the year to past weekend break visitors. This aspect was very successful although it was not always the same parties who returned each time. Within six months of starting the mailing and promotional campaign, the weekend average room occupancy was up to 80 per cent which was around the average for the midweek room occupancy but, of course, the weekend had a much higher double and bed occupancy percentage.

KRAMER V. KRAMER

Are there other social changes and new market segments beginning to develop which may be significant in a few years' time? I believe there is one which is going to create sales and profit opportunities and that is the single-parent market. It is true that single parents may be unmarried mothers with very little money, but it is equally true that a lot of them were married and are now separated or divorced. A growing number are single-parent fathers.

Do you remember the film *Kramer v. Kramer* with Dustin Hoffman and Meryl Streep in the battle for the custody of their son? Not necessarily the courtroom battle but the single-parent father is a new and growing situation.

A considerable proportion of single parents may be short of money, but not all. A significant number will sometimes spend more than they can afford. Most when taking holidays, short-break trips or eating or drinking out, if asked, will say money is tight; but at particular times of the year are prepared to spend more than usual. So, in this respect, the single parent is no different from anyone else. On holiday recently, where I was staying, there was the usual mixture of couples on their own of various age groups, and six two-parent families with children. There were also three single-parent mothers with their offspring – an indication of a growing trend. I notice that in holiday resorts or hotels with sports activities there tend to be more single-parent fathers with their children. I have observed many with their children in hotels abroad, and on short-break holidays in Britain, and I have seen them eating in restaurants. Some spend money like water!

One hotelier I spoke to described the spending of the single-parent father on holiday with his children as 'guilt money'.

However, more women than men are in the position of having to bring up children on their own. Some grandparents say to their daughters: 'We'll pay for a holiday this year.' Many single parents hold down executive jobs with paid holidays. And, of course, many single parents have remarried and have limited access to their children. Often this access is alternate weekends, or two weeks a year during the holiday period. Once in a steak restaurant, I heard a father talking to his two sons at the next table. He was obviously divorced because of the questions he asked the boys about their mother's activities! Apart from buying them an expensive meal he also asked them what sort of presents they would like. The answers were unbelievably expensive.

Please believe me when I say I am in no way trying to discredit single parents. But I am stating a marketing fact which creates an opportunity for us which we should grasp. As with women executives who are only just beginning to use hotels and restaurants, single parents often feel awkward when they walk into a restaurant with their children.

Hoteliers or restaurateurs who think through this market's 'problems' carefully with empathy will find they will obtain a lot of repeat business and recommendations. Many hoteliers in the holiday market go after the family business as a deliberate policy. Why not the single-parent family business?

We should change attitudes in order to attract this new market. Holiday brochures and many short-break brochures give a major concession for children, in some cases up to 18 years old, who spend the night in their parents' room. Yet often the concession for a child sharing a room with one parent is very small, or nothing at all.

My belief is that those restaurateurs and hoteliers who set out carefully and systematically to change their literature, their own attitude, the attitude of their staff and the whole sales approach to this market will find it a lucrative growth market in the next few years.

ACTIVE LEISURE

People are becoming much more health conscious, or perhaps they are more conscious of ill-health. But there is one aspect of leisure which has shown considerable growth and this is *active leisure*. Large sections of the population of both sexes appear to have become physical fitness fanatics, playing tennis or squash, jogging, etc. Many of them do not feel right if they cannot have a regular work out, or jog, when they are away from home.

Many hotels are beginning to recognize this trend and many more will have to provide the facility as part of their essential future marketing. Commonwealth Holiday Inns of Canada provide a Gym and Tonic area near their swimming pools with a circuit of exercise machines suitably supervised. They have a colour code so that you can start with the 'easy' circuit and build up.

Other hotels recognize that the jogging craze is long term and include a series of maps in the bedroom – one, two or three miles with directions to nearby parks. It is felt that more hotels should notify guests that they have a supply of track suits and shoes in case they have forgotten. And the route maps should make the jogging more interesting by showing out-of-town joggers points of special interest on the run. An example of a jogging map from the Hotel Ritz in Lisbon (an Inter-Continental Hotel) is shown in Figure 7.1. Incidentally the instructions were in different languages. In Trusthouse Forte's new hotels in America they have jogging tracks on the roofs of some of their larger hotels.

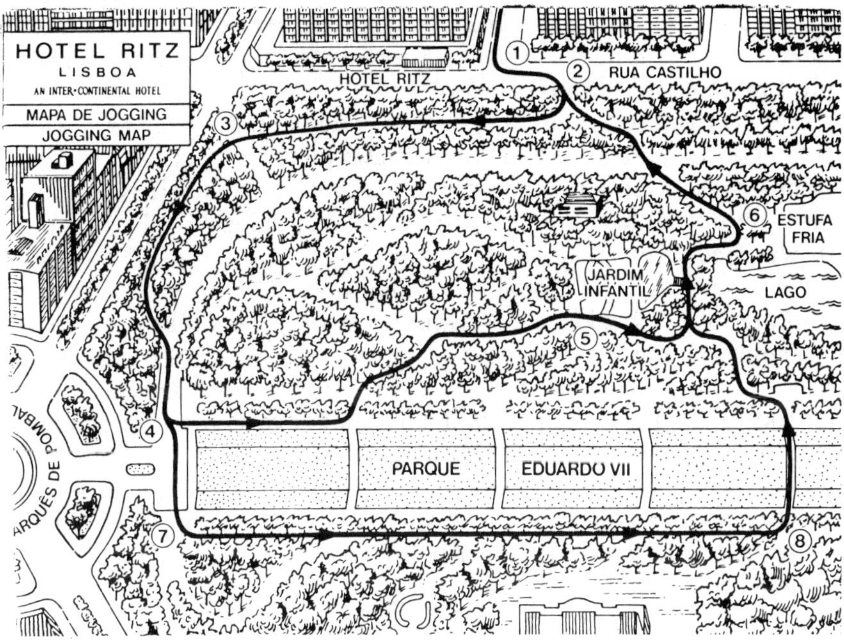

Figure 7.1 Joggers' Map

There are fairly small combined exercise machines, which would easily fit into a small unutilized function room, designed to do a circuit exercise so that four people can use them at the same time. Where you haven't sufficient land or space for tennis courts, or a swimming pool, you might be able to fit in Paddle Tennis, which is only one-third the floor area of normal tennis, or a jacuzzi to relax in. Even if your hotel is not adjacent to a golf course, with tennis courts as well, you can still do a lot to provide exercise opportunities for the guests who want them and it does not have to be too expensive. If you do not, your competition will.

A SECONDHAND PRODUCT

Let me put you through a thought process to illustrate a social change which creates marketing opportunities. Most of your hotel guests are fairly well-dressed and generally do not wear second-hand clothes. Similarly, at home they may have some antique furniture but generally their furniture is not second-hand and they do not sleep on a second-hand mattress. However we are selling them a second-hand product. We are selling them a bedroom which has been used by hundreds or thousands of strangers. Previously the bed has been slept in by a complete stranger. That stranger has used the same bath and toilet as your guest. No other consumer products are used so many times by so many different people.

This is why good housekeeping is so vital so that when a guest has checked in there is no evidence that a complete stranger has used that room before. Unfortunately if you are a non-smoker it is virtually impossible to hide the smell of tobacco as it 'clings' to the curtains, carpets, bedcover etc.

Ten years ago few people would have dreamt that the anti-smoking lobby would have become so strong. This lobby has made non-smokers more conscious of stale cigarette smoke and made many smokers self-conscious, even guilty about their 'habit'. And yet not too long ago it was masculine to smoke, certainly in the movies and on television.

This social change creates marketing opportunities. After a speech I gave in Scotland in 1978 to Thistle Hotels, a subsidiary of Scottish & Newcastle Breweries, with fifty hotels, they introduced a series of non-smoking rooms, usually a complete floor in each hotel. They were not the first in the world to do so, but certainly were the first in Britain. The idea is that all curtains, carpets, etc. are thoroughly cleaned to remove any trace of tobacco smell. That room is never knowingly let to a smoker, even if it is unsold. Chambermaids are also non-smokers. Wherever this has been tried the occupancy of the non-smoker rooms is much higher on average than the other rooms and previous occupancies.

I remember standing in the reception of Thistle Hotels' Royal Scot Hotel in London when they first introduced the idea. The response from their guests was overwhelmingly favourable. Of course, it takes time and energy to set up non-smoking areas and they have to be promoted. But the investment is well worthwhile, particularly if your competitors do not bother at all, as is often the case.

The same social change applies in other areas. I first saw a non-smoking seating area at a convention in the Doral Hotel in Miami Beach. Recently a convention organizer told me that he chose one hotel for his convention out of three similar hotels on his final shortlist because this one hotel had set aside one third of the room as a non-smoking area, and sold this as one of their advantages.

It was some years ago when I first experienced the same point in a restaurant which was, I believe, in the Victoria Station restaurant in Union Street, San Francisco. A simple partition down the centre subdivided the smoking from the non-smoking area and in no way were you pressured into either area. I have recommended this to many clients in the last five years, but many do not try the idea because they claim that most tables have a mixture of smokers and non-smokers. However, one client with a group of restaurants did set up a small non smoking area, found it was far too small, and monitored results carefully before and after introducing the areas. They found an immediate overall increase in sales of around 20 per cent which carried on consistently for a year, until they completely changed their menus so that it was impossible to measure the actual increase of introducing non-smoking areas anymore. There is still a minority of restaurants outside America with such areas, but I have seen them introduced as far afield as Kano in Northern Nigeria, and Crete.

One key factor in introducing non-smoking areas in bedrooms and/or public areas is that in no way must your sales literature or staff imply that you are anti-smoking, or make smokers feel more guilty than they do already.

In 1984 I ran a top management course for the Dan Hotel Group in Israel. One of the developments following this course was that in 1985 they became the first hotel group in Israel to set aside a proportion of their bedrooms as non-smoker bedrooms.

Last year I carried out some research on sixty hotels which had introduced non-smoker bedrooms. Thirty hotels had found the concept very successful, and fourteen had found it unsuccessful and had dropped the idea. I carried out some further research on the fourteen 'failures'. Six should never have introduced them because either the hotel was too small, or the mix of rooms prevented them from 'isolating' a fixed number of rooms on a regular basis. Out of the remaining eight, six of the managers smoked!

There were only two other managers who smoked out of the other fifty-two in the survey. In all of the eight hotels the non-smoker bedrooms had been introduced with no staff training whatsoever, particularly in reception. Instead of offering the idea in an inoffensive way, some receptionists were asking 'are you a smoker?', automatically putting the guest on the defensive. With all new ideas, training is essential.

Figure 7.2

MENU FATIGUE

Perhaps out of any hotel's varied sources of income, the aspect which is likely to change most radically in the next decade is in 'the eating areas'.

If it has not done so already the typical hotel dining room will disappear. Certainly the normal lunch and dinner menus will be meaningless and the hours of opening for these meals will change. Various social, sociological and technological changes seem set on destroying the usual meal periods of lunch broadly between 1 p.m. and 2 p.m. or dinner between 6 p.m. and 7 p.m. (in America), 7 p.m. and 8 p.m. in Britain, or 9 p.m. to 10 p.m. in, say, Spain.

Many more people are going to work flexi-hours. Many more people are going to work shift hours where there is expensive equipment which has to be used 'round the clock', or in the growth leisure industries. There are estimates that by the 90s as many as 25 per cent of the population could be working from home, if not all the time, at least part of the time. These 'home workers' will enjoy not having the hassle (and costs) of travelling to work every day. But they are going to be bored. They comprise a natural market who will 'buy' a weekend break, or a meal out in a restaurant, on impulse at short notice. Probably by the end of the 90s, if not earlier, only a minority will still work in a traditional 9 to 5 job.

This means that these people who work 'odd' hours will want to eat at 'odd' hours and hotel restaurants who do not cater for this will suffer.

Business executives will be arriving at very awkward hours and may be hungry when they check in. Or the time clock in their stomachs is still in New York, 6 hours different to Britain, and they must have some nourishment. I am not recommending that you introduce a series of different restaurants to cater for the different markets. But the restaurants of the future must be more flexible in design and there may have to be a varied menu situation. Restaurants must be designed with flexibility to change the lighting for the different moods of the day, or to convert to a self-help buffet for, say, Sunday brunch.

Joe Allens in London has the breakfast menu on until well in the afternoon. A lot of people really enjoy a cooked breakfast. So why just give it to them at breakfast times? I remember another classical example of using a varied menu by the late John Dean, manager of The Royal Turks Head Hotel in Grey Street, Newcastle upon Tyne, England. The hotel had a mixed market, business executives and visitors to the fine shops and theatre in Grey Street. John Dean had a limited menu on at first in the evening up to around 8 p.m., for the people who were going to the theatre and who were time-sensitive. After 8 p.m. the full à la carte menu was brought out, and later in the evening a more limited menu with specials took the place of the à la carte.

Lord Forte's superb Café Royal, in the heart of theatreland in London, introduced a pre-theatre meal which again recognized the theatre goers' problem – would they ruin a good meal and obtain indigestion by rushing the meal before the theatre? At the Café Royal they had a 'split' meal if they wanted it. They had the starter and main course before the theatre, and then returned to the restaurant afterwards for dessert, coffee and brandies. A great way to increase your average spend with special desserts, and brandies and liqueurs.

More and more people are eating out and staying in hotels. Business executives who stay in hotels a lot are likely to pick up what I jokingly call an illness, or disease. Many regular travellers claim they suffer from it. It is called 'Menu Fatigue'. When you are in your hotel bedroom you generally know, without seeing the restaurant's menu, exactly what is going to be on it. Most hotels produce a menu which is 'safe'. I believe that any restaurant owners who tries new ideas, or just something a little different, will find that people will beat a path to their door. When you have something special on in your restaurant, or just a special, unusual dish, go *out* and sell it. A later section in this book covers In-House Selling. But in twenty-five years of staying regularly in hotels I have *never* been asked, when checking in, whether I would like to reserve a table in the restaurant, 'as we are often fully booked'. There is usually sales literature in the room but in the long run people sell, people want to make bookings, and other people take bookings. I can only recall two hotels in 25 years where I have received a polite call around 6 p.m. asking whether I would like to eat in their restaurant. My attitude must be 'Why not?' rather than go out.

In general eating out and commercial food service outside hotels have seen massive changes in eating habits. We have health foods and healthy foods – two entirely different things. There have been enormous swings to fast food, system catering and self-help. Ethnic foods are extremely popular. Yet I have the suspicion that hoteliers are too cautious to try these same successful trends in their hotels.

We can all see that more and more people are eating Chinese and Indian food. And yet we stick to many standard dishes cooked in a bland fashion, or become over obsessive with French cuisine. Let me turn to America for some published statistics.

In America consumption of hot and spicy food is increasing rapidly. In the last five years US consumption of hot spices (including the red pepper family, black and white pepper and ginger) showed an increase of 45 per cent. And the trend is even greater than these figures indicate, since they exclude many popular hot flavoured items such as mustard seed, canned green chillies, bottled hot sauces and fresh ginger. To me this shows a significant swing in a national taste pattern. My own feeling without these back-up statistics is that the same trend is happening in the United Kingdom.

Some hoteliers are forgetting that we all fall into *different* market segments, depending on the time and place. The well-dressed top executive with an open-ended expense account for business use, eating in the finest hotel restaurants, may well take his family out for a Kentucky Fried Chicken meal. Running a marketing course for one hotel group's top management, we decided to eat out one evening rather than eat in the hotel. The eighteen hoteliers on the course agreed unanimously that we should eat out at a top Manchester Chinese restaurant. The same hoteliers agreed that they would be hesitant to have a 'Chinese evening' in their hotel, or even some special Chinese dishes.

We in the hotel industry must become more adventurous in order to reduce the chances of menu fatigue and ensure that a lower proportion of our overnight guests eat out in competitive restaurants *and* we attract more outside visitors into the hotel's restaurant(s). In fact there is one term widely used in Britain, and in many independent countries which were once British, which I would like to see banned from the hoteliers' language and this is 'Chance Trade'. This is trade which comes in off the street supposedly by chance. Not many things really happen by chance. You have to make them happen. Either they have been recommended, or heard of you. Maybe your exterior, entrance, menu display and signposting attracted them in. Or more than likely your paid *and* unpaid publicity, mailing shots etc., have reached a target. In a hotel's restaurants there are people who book in advance and those who appear to come in by chance. Let us make sure that the latter grows in volume but through your steady systematic marketing and sales effort – not by chance.

DRINKING HABITS

Eating habits have changed radically in the last decade and will probably change just as fast in the next ten years. But in many ways drinking habits have in a sense changed 'quietly' but just as radically round the world. Who would have thought that the Japanese would become such heavy consumers of whisky? In traditional beer-drinking countries, like Britain, there has been an enormous swing from traditional beers to lager and real ale. In the late 60s I visited Scotland regularly to advise Scottish & Newcastle Breweries on the development of their hotel subsidiary, Thistle Hotels. I remember most Scots said they would never change from McEwans Export, or Tartan Keg, and drink that southern drink, lager. But they did – en masse. In Britain during the decade up to 1981 the proportion of lager sold, out of the total sale of beer, increased from 9.9 per cent to 30.8 per cent! I recall talking to one of their top managers, Jimmy Pratt, who at the time ran the public houses in Glasgow. He suddenly said 'One day we will all drink green beer'. At the time I could not understand what he was getting at, but I do now. You do see young Britons who would normally be standing drinking beer in the pub but who are now sitting drinking green cocktails in new style restaurants, rather than pubs. Similar changes are happening in other countries. In America wine sales per capita almost doubled in the last decade. There was also a marked change in the type of wine being drunk. In 1960 white wines controlled only 17 per cent compared to red wines 74 per cent share. Today white wines dominate with 54 per cent of the total wine market.

But what really amazes me about drinking habits in restaurants generally is the way we are drinking – *water*!! Imagine this commercial I heard a few years ago:

> 'The unmistakable growl of Orson Welles sets the scene as Dracula kneels beside his victim and plunges his long teeth into the milky whiteness of her throat. But the vampire is a hard-to-please consumer. "It is good", he concedes. "But it is not Perrier".'

The advertisement, part of a radio campaign run in the United States, is a dramatic reminder of the strides a new product can make in a surprisingly short time. Who would have thought, ten years ago, that you could make an honest living selling bottles of water to a mass market? Yet now mineral water companies are talking of the UK market alone being worth $200 million at current prices by 1990. With Perrier again making the running, imports now hold nearly three-quarters of the British market. The comparatively high quality of tap water in the British Isles makes it all the harder to persuade people to pay out good money for a bottle of H_2O. But, by adopting an intelligent lifestyle approach to selling, brands such as Malvern and Ashbourne are proving that a healthy new market can be carved out.

The size of bottles can influence liquor sales. Many business executives eating on their own like to have wine, particularly with their dinner. They do not necessarily want a whole bottle and yet many hotel restaurants consider it slightly down-market to promote half bottles on their wine list.

And what about larger bottles?

My son, Anthony, was telling me about The Evergreen restaurant in Covent Garden, London, where they sell champagne by the bottle, magnum, and then the sizes increase to a two magnum, four, eight, 12, 18 to 24 magnum size. When he was last there a customer bought the large size priced at $300. Anthony was told they very often sell the largest sized bottle of champagne. And what a great idea to let the customer take the empty bottle home as a keepsake with the name of the restaurant clearly shown on it.

If these considerable changes in drinking habits occurred in the last ten years, there are bound to be other changes in the future. Hotel bars, restaurant wine lists, and function wine lists must acknowledge these changes, and spot new trends as they emerge.

FORMAL BUT FUN

Up to the 50s eating out was very formal and many people dressed for dinner in holiday hotels. Many restaurants would not let men in if they didn't wear a tie, or women if they wore trousers – a cardinal sin. Life changed rapidly in the 60s to become much more casual. I know of one very successful hotel restaurant, The Last Drop Hotel, near Bolton in England where their Saturday night dinner-dance jumped in popularity in the 60s when they announced that customers would *not* be allowed in if they were wearing a tie. Formal dinner-dances 'died' to be replaced by discos, or a mixture of the two. By the 70s there were many offices where no men wore suits and women wore jeans, a situation unheard of in the 50s.

Successful hoteliers and restaurateurs made money in the last decade by *practised deliberate studied casualness* – through staff, menus, design and decor. It took a highly developed marketing and professional sense to do so.

I feel that we will have a trend back to a more formal situation by the 90s.

Today, many women executives dress well (sometimes in suits) and often dress better than men. I know of a pub/restaurant where the owner packs out the 'quiet' Monday night with a 'suit only rule' for men. I hear a growing number of people in their 20s/30s saying that it is nice to dress up for a dinner party occasionally.

I could be wrong but my feeling is that the successful entrepreneurial hotelier and restaurateur will make more money in the future from 'formal but fun'. The dress and style will be more formal but within an informal atmosphere.

SECURITY

On a management course for about twenty top hotel general managers in the same company I asked them to list from 1 to 10, in order of priority, what they would devote their energies to each day. Would they rate highly inspecting the bedrooms or perhaps the kitchens? Did they place their emphasis on income control, on food control, on staff rotas or perhaps, marketing or selling? They all wrote them down in order of priority.

The results caused a laugh but should not have surprised me. The top rating was something I had not really thought about. It was 'dealing with memos or calls from head office'. Marketing and selling rated very low in their order of priorities. What rated highest following 'memos from head office', particularly for the hotels in London and large cities was 'security'. In one large London hotel the manager said there was an average of one bomb scare per week. Most of the scares were obviously not serious but he had evacuated the complete hotel nine times in the previous twelve months although, fortunately, no bombs were found. One other manager with an hotel near a famous rugby ground regularly received a 'crank' call every Saturday after the match. I had an experience of staying in this very hotel on a weekend conference when the alarm was sounded when I was in my shower.

In the three years since the first edition it has become a very real problem internationally. There has been a major increase in terrorism and highjackings. We have had highjacks of planes, cruise liners and even the delegates at one OPEC conference. We must plan to prevent someone trying to highjack a hotel!

But it is not just terrorism. Although nowhere near the level of some American cities, we have seen an increase in robberies of bedrooms in British hotels and even some rapes. In discussing this with my clients they often tend to look upon the subject as an operating problem and not part of marketing. There was a view a few years ago that if security was 'tight' it was unwise to advertise this as an advantage because potential guests might feel 'why do they need to have tight security?'. This is not the case now.

A major advantage of electronic key cards for guests is that each card can be 'destroyed' when the guest leaves so that each guest has his/her personal code. Similarly, personal guest safes are bound to grow in popularity because too often it is quite a public announcement to anyone else near reception when one wishes to obtain valuables. Again each guest can set his/her own code number to open the safe.

There are some hotels where very wealthy or well-known people only stay because there is a completely separate entrance and lift/elevator to the suite(s), or because they know security is good. I persuaded one hotelier who had close circuit television on each bedroom floor to promote this as a major marketing advantage. He found that women executives, in particular, felt this a major contributing factor in choosing this hotel rather than his competitors in the same price bracket. I see a situation in the future where many people will only stay in hotels, particularly large hotels, where there is close circuit television on each floor, but also a security official constantly observing the monitors.

Similarly, many hotels will re-introduce the lift (elevator) 'boy' because it will make guests feel more secure. They could pay for themselves by doing some in-house selling. Spyholes in doors and adequate locks will be a must in many city-centre hotels.

Obviously the promotion of a secure and safe hotel would have to be discreet so as not to worry guests. But if you have security features which your competitors do not have, it is well worth stressing this in your marketing and selling.

CONCLUSION

One constant thing in our lives is change. And yet most people dislike change. In the foregoing sections I have tried to illustrate a few examples of different circumstances for the hotel industry and social changes which create marketing opportunities. These points covered:

The home versus the hotel
Suite-only hotels
Socio-economic hotels
The instant market
Women
Short break market
Kramer *v.* Kramer
Active leisure
Menu fatigue
Drinking habits
Formal but fun
Security

This list is not meant to be all embracing but is an illustration to show you a thought process in spotting marketing changes.

It is important not to go 'overboard' on some of these new social trends and end up 'shooting yourself in the foot'. For some time yet the majority of executive overnight guests are likely to be men and it is important not to give them the impression you do not want their business or that you might neglect them. Similarly, there will be a large proportion of smokers for decades to come.

Healthy eating is a growing aspect of our society. But the majority of people are not on a diet and are not vegetarians. In fact, many people like to 'let themselves go' when they stay in an hotel. Many people I know who rarely eat a cooked breakfast at home like to have one when they are away. Many want to neglect their eating régime and diet when they are your guests and it would be wrong if you made them feel guilty when they stay with you.

Most conference delegates do not rush to your gym at the end of a working day, but like to relax and socialize in the bar. The majority of people on holiday, or taking a short break, enjoy relaxing by doing nothing or walking. When you consider the large capital investment many hoteliers are making in gyms and leisure centres, it is surprising how little is done for people who wish to walk locally, shop or tour the area by car.

There are more hoteliers providing a route map for joggers but where the hotel is in an attractive walking area I rarely see a walker's map.

There is no doubt that health clubs can show a very quick payback period (i.e. a high cash flow return on capital) – sometimes less than a year if there is a membership demand from local residents and business executives in the catchment area. But they are unlikely to do so just from hotel guests.

My own research shows that only a small proportion of guests staying one night use health and leisure centres – around 15 per cent. For guests staying two or more nights around 50 per cent use some aspect of the facility. But this declines to around 25 per cent on the second visit. However, having the facility tempts a significant proportion to stay over an extra night. A very low percentage actually use the gym – a much larger proportion use a swimming pool, if available.

There is no doubt that having a leisure centre is a major decision factor in choosing a hotel particularly for conference organizers. And there is considerable evidence from my own research that it makes a high room rate acceptable even where a guest does not necessarily use the facility.

Research in 1985 by Marriott's in New York showed that only 18 per cent of the under-45 business traveller wanted their health clubs (called Nautilus). In the age bracket 45 and older only 7 per cent wanted these facilities. Digressing slightly, it is also interesting to note in the same survey that a majority of the business traveller respondents said they usually pay between $71 and $110 per night for a room, but when it comes to New York City 71 per cent said that $150 a night in 'the big apple' is not prohibitive.

These health club facilities can be very profitable at least in the first year or two from the local catchment area, and they are perceived as a major advantage by conference organizers, holidaymakers and many business guests even if they do not use them.

Other trends are appearing. The public is going to become much more hygiene-conscious in the future, as a result of being more health conscious, and because of the publicity from prosecutions by the health authorities. Unfortunately, many fine hotels in Europe are old, and kitchens with older floor surfaces and wall coverings might not be as easy to keep hygienic as some newer kitchens. Where you do have a superbly clean kitchen, use this as a sales tool. Most people are fascinated by hotel kitchens. Offer to show people round (at an appropriate time) and include 'a trip round the kitchens' in your brochures and sales literature. Not too many people will accept the offer, but making the offer will illustrate your confidence in the state of the kitchen, like a restaurant I saw on the Continent where the entrance went through the kitchen. I expect the whole role of some employees like kitchen porters and dishwashers to be rethought, regraded and retitled, possibly as hygiene supervisors.

The typical family unit is changing. More people who are married are deliberately choosing never to have children. And these couples have incredible spending powers. As well as homosexual couples there is a growing number of men and women, who are not homosexual, who choose never to get married (for a variety of different reasons) but live together sharing a house or a flat. I know two heterosexual men in their early forties who share a superb house in Chelsea, London. One is an engineer, the other an accountant, and both have no intention of ever marrying. They eat out regularly in restaurants and are always going on holiday because they can afford it.

In a resort hotel in America, I noticed a significant number of men on holiday with their children, spending money as if it had gone out of fashion – and there were apparently few women around. The owner said the men were divorced fathers who had custody of the children for a certain period each year and he noticed that they spent a lot of money and, in his words, never said 'no'. He called it 'guilt' money. Another 'new' marketing opportunity.

The real message is that all our conceptions about how people live and work are probably wrong. What real plans, menus and pricing strategies are you using to serve the single household? Most places still seat the single person in Outer Mongolia, making them feel unwelcome, and they do the same when two women come in at dinner. Additionally, the menus and the table arrangements are most suited for the Old-Style Couple and not for people sharing a meal, sharing the check. Two men or two women probably don't want to sit as close together as the OSC. The restaurant manager has to sell to each person since they are not a couple but two very distinct individuals with separate finances and different tastes. Around 40 per cent of American adults are not married. Restaurants will have to be designed for a mix of Old-Style Couples, two women or two men, singles, or three women and one man.

The normal twin-bedded hotel bedroom may have to be redesigned to recognize that more double occupancy will not be OSCs – with a washbasin outside the bathroom, and a lavatory separate from the actual bath area (as in many Novotel bedrooms).

There are also indications that the average age of eating out in better restaurants (not junk food) is decreasing as young people are taken out to better restaurants more frequently by their parents. They are over 'the threshold barrier' and therefore more inclined to eat out regularly as a habit rather than necessity. This is good news for restaurateurs who look after and keep an eye on the young couple when they try a better restaurant for the first time.

The world is changing. New markets are developing. I hope that these illustrations will show hoteliers some of the opportunities which lie ahead. It takes takes quiet thought, planning and energy to try new ideas. And it takes time – generally a rare commodity. Some ideas will misfire. But any hotelier who does not replan for the rapid and major changes which lie ahead, will be overtaken by competitors who do.

* * * * *

8

WHAT MOTIVATES PEOPLE TO BUY?

LORD EMPATHY

Large numbers of books have been written on marketing and selling but very few specifically for the hotel and food services industry. Those written for our industry often stop at marketing, or concentrate more specifically on the sales side. This is not written as a criticism of my fellow authors. Probably this arises because the experience of many authors is either in marketing, or in the actual selling, although marketing also embraces selling.

In the previous sections I have tried to take readers through the whole continuous marketing process including what it is, how to redefine markets, economic criteria for successful marketing and the difficult subject of pricing strategy on rooms, food and beverage. I have also included the two previous chapters designed to help you, the reader, think ahead about trends and relate them to your own hotels and restaurants.

In what is more or less the second part of this book I want to cover marketing and sales action plans and some of the sales techniques in reaching the markets. But first it would be useful to consider what motivates people to buy, or spend money. In this book you must have noticed my frustration in that we often do not really know what motivates people to use hotels and restaurants. If we knew the answer to this we would have the key to success. After working with clients we are now improving the success ratio, but there is still a long way to go.

Recently a telegram was sent to my office addressed to 'LORD EMPATHY'. The client was jokingly referring to my obsession with the use of the word 'empathy' as a key thought process, or ability, in successful marketing and all kinds of selling. My definition of 'empathy' is the ability to sit in the other person's seat, or wear his shoes, and imagine what really makes him tick. What motivates him, what are his worries, his problems?

An experienced receptionist knows that a lot of business guests returning around 6.30 p.m. from a hard day's work tend to be over-critical and impatient in waiting just a moment for their key. The receptionist knows they have had a rough, tough, day, cannot take it out on their wives, and therefore may blast off at the hotel. I knew of one receptionist in the Angus Hotel, Dundee, who was incredibly popular because she very kindly asked some of the tired-looking business executives 'Have you had a tough day?'. Some of them would pour out their hearts to her. Later she was promoted to management.

Empathy tells us that when that little man walks in and says that he would like to talk about booking his daughter's wedding in your hotel, he doesn't mean this at all. It is his *wife* who would like to book the wedding and she may be the decision-maker to sell to, not he. Empathy tells us that the young executive given the job of organizing the company Christmas party is shaking in his boots. The big boss usually calls in an up-and-coming junior executive and says, 'I have a simple job for you, John, I would just like you to organize the office party this year. You choose the venue, you know, John, somewhere nice as my wife did not like the ABC hotel last year'.

Young John thanks him, walks outside the door and bangs his head against the wall. 'What bad luck. All my bosses will be there, and their wives, and it's bound to go wrong.' Any hotelier who, with empathy, realizes that this young man's future career is at stake, and acts with confidence and integrity, is going to obtain the booking – again and again. That young man could be his friend for life, and could become the chief executive one day.

Empathy tells us that most people don't know a thing about wine. Most people do not know the etiquette and order of speeches at weddings. Most convention or management course organizers are more worried about whether you have a spare bulb, or fuse, in case the overhead projector fails, and empathy should tell us he worries about 'We hire any kind of equipment for you from a firm just down the road'.

Empathy gives us clues to successful selling. Empathy turns us into problem or worry solvers, rather than product sellers. Empathy makes us much more successful.

MOTIVATION

Therefore, before starting on the sales side of this book, let us pause and consider what really motivates people to buy, or to spend money on anything – any form of spending money, not just hotels, restaurants, or a holiday, but all expenditure. Get together with your deputy, colleague, or boss and list on a sheet of paper all the motivated reasons for spending money.

I did this with a group of top sales executives recently, and their replies are shown in Table 8.1. No group of people will arrive at the same list but it is usually similar. When we have agreed this we will then relate what you consider are the key motivational factors for some major sources of business. This list is not in order of significance but the order as called out by a group of twenty-four people, working in smaller groups of three people.

This is not a complete list and as mentioned before these are motivational factors that make people spend money on *anything*, not just hotels. We avoid points like 'they spent money because they received a mailing shot, or saw an advert'. This was not what we wanted as a reply. What we are seeking is the point, or message, in the advert which motivates them to buy. After all, hotels do not just sell a room, food and a drink. The public can get that anywhere and cheaper generally. Selling a room, food and a drink is too product-orientated. If you analyse what really motivates people to buy we must be more consumer- than product-orientated by selling 'a good night's sleep' rather than a room, 'a meal experience' rather than food, and 'relax and unwind' rather than just a drink.

After completing the list we asked the executives to tick the motivational factors which could influence people to spend money in hotels. Nearly every one was ticked. There was some argument about

1 FEAR
7 POSSESSION/ENVY
8 BASIC NEED
9 RELIGION
10 GUILT.

Most people felt that number 8, basic needs, was covered by other factors. Sentiment was included – 'where we spent our honeymoon', etc. But everyone felt the other thirteen points were strong motivational factors for hotels, except number 16 on shortages in some countries only. Delegates linked physical and mental health and well-being together as important factors.

Table 8.1

Motivational factors that make people buy or spend money

1 FEAR	– insurance
2 SECURITY	– burglar alarms, spy holes, new door
3 LONELINESS	– televisions
4 CURIOSITY	– televisions, historical buildings
5 STATUS – 'KEEPING UP WITH THE JONES'	– there were many examples – quoted from video tape recorders to a Rolls Royce
6 EGO	– this seemed to relate to STATUS
7 POSSESSION/ENVY	– this seemed to be related to items under STATUS
8 BASIC NEED	– it was agreed that this was water, salt, bread and a blanket for warmth
9 RELIGION	– money spent on Christenings, etc.
10 MENTAL RELAXATION	– hobbies
PHYSICAL HEALTH	– sports – relaxation
11 PRICE	– buying something reduced in price
12 VALUE FOR MONEY	– not necessarily related completely to price
13 INVESTMENT	– shares, stocks, cost of a product launch
14 PERSONAL COMFORT	– central heating, air conditioning
15 GUILT	– present for wife!!
16 SHORTAGES	– in some countries with import controls
17 EDUCATIONAL/ RESEARCH	– correspondence courses, evening classes
18 SENTIMENT	– photographs

We then took five sources of business and listed the motivational factors in degree of importance which influenced the different sources. (see Table 8.2). The sources were:

1 A wedding
2 An annual holiday for a family of four
3 A product launch
4 A local firm booking a room for an overnight visitor.
5 An executive out selling and staying in hotels regularly.

What was interesting from this exercise is that price ended up being 'value for money'. This was only listed as the first point with number 2 – the family of four going on a holiday. Even with the

Table 8.2
Main Motivational Factors

1 *WEDDING*	2 *HOLIDAYS*	3 *PRODUCT LAUNCH*	4 *ROOM FOR BUYER*	5 *ROOM FOR SALESMAN*
STATUS	PRICE	INVESTMENT	COMFORT	COMFORT
EGO	VALUE FOR MONEY	STATUS	STATUS	VALUE FOR MONEY
SENTIMENT		VALUE FOR MONEY	EGO	
PRICE	COMFORT		INVESTMENT	LONELINESS
SECURITY	HEALTH			STATUS

salesman travelling a lot and probably on a budget, everyone felt that his first motivation had to be comfort, otherwise he might as well stay in a local 'doss' house if his first motivation was price. With the product launch, investment was rated first. Everyone felt with the wedding in a hotel function room that status, ego and sentiment ('I want to give my daughter the finest day . . .') ranked before price although they all felt price was important. Most people find this exercise fascinating and naturally the answers will vary depending on a hotel's style, location and competition.

What I am hoping to achieve with hoteliers and hotel sales executives who have read this book is a change in emphasis and presentation of words as you sell which strikes a chord with prospective customers and in the market place generally, so that more buyers think 'this hotelier really understands me, my worries and my problems'.

PACKAGING THE WORDS CORRECTLY

In most consumer industries a buyer spends money and has something to show for it. If he buys a television, washing machine, new car, etc. he pays for it and can actually use, touch and feel it long after he has bought it. When a consumer spends a large amount of money in a hotel for a convention, wedding or holiday, he often has nothing very tangible to show for it. He may have good memories, photographs, and his sales should increase, but he has no physical asset after paying his cheque.

'Well, we know this' you must be saying, 'what is the point?' Well, the point is precisely that you do know this. And because of this it may creep into your sales approach without your realizing it. I have heard many inexperienced hoteliers talking as if expenditure by guests in their own hotel is just a cost, only a payment out. I have heard hotel staff, when asked what it costs to stay the night there, say 'Well, sir,' (pause) 'it will cost you $80' (another pause to watch the reaction). This is particularly the case when hotel staff and receptionists have never stayed, and paid for a night in that style of hotel. They should say 'The charge is $80 for the room which has air-conditioning (or a special view) as well as the usual facilities you would find in a first class hotel,' and place a registration card in front of him.

In preparing league tables for the hotel compared against competition it is a useful thing to use receptionists to collect the data on competitive hotel room rates. This way they will begin to see that $80 for your hotel is not necessarily a very high price.

Every so often we should totally reverse thinking on the questions we ask our guests. Very often the questions we ask are of a negative nature 'Tell me what went wrong'. We go up to a guest in the restaurant and ask 'Was everything all right, Sir (or Madam)?'. Or we use questionnaires in the bedroom which very often ask guests to tell us where we went wrong. There is nothing wrong in this. What I am suggesting is that periodically we ask guests the opposite – 'Tell us where we went right or what it is that you like about the hotel that brings you back?'.

Subdivide the guests between first time visitors and regulars. Ask the first time visitor why it is that they chose your hotel and not the competition. Who made the decision? Who made the booking?

Then ask regulars who come back time and time again what it is that draws them back to the hotel, subdivided between the various areas in the hotel (bedroom, reception, restaurant, etc.) If you did this on a regular basis (two or three times a year) there is absolutely no doubt that you would gather some very vital clues in order to help improve sales in the future.

What we have to do is to train all staff, not just management and sales staff, firstly to try to find out as much as possible about that potential buyer and what motivates him. They then have to talk not just about his costs but about what he (or she) will receive in return (the comfortable quiet room, or the meal in our redecorated restaurant). We have to use the word investment in the appropriate situation where the prospective buyer is selling something. Health, feel better, investment, impress your relatives or business colleagues – these are the words we must use in sales literature, advertisements, and in face to face selling. Any hotelier who does this, analyses motivational factors and uses the right words, together with his advantage/limitation lists will have a very successful future.

*   *   *   *   *

9

SELLING — GENERAL COMMENTS

For the marketing and selling hotels to be more successful, there are four major aspects which have to be considered and reviewed regularly:

1 Marketing and re-defining markets
2 Sales organization, training, motivation
3 Plan of action – marketing and sales
4 Sales techniques.

The first aspect, marketing and redefining markets has been dealt with in previous chapters of this book. The other three aspects are covered in the following chapters. But even if you define the right markets, choose the most dynamic organization, prepare a great action plan, and train everyone to improve their sales techniques, it is still possible to achieve little progress for a variety of different reasons.

Quite often I have been asked to analyse why a particular sales effort, or a continuous sales effort, has not paid off as well as the hotel and/or head office management planned. When I have been asked to analyse where something has gone wrong I only accept that kind of assignment if I can also recommend solutions to solve the problem. Criticism can be destructive unless it is presented with constructive solutions. However, some of the main reasons why sales decline, or do not increase to target, are summarized as follows:

1 Selling a mile wide and an inch deep.
2 Lack of research and insufficient time spent on preparation.
3 People try one thing and give up.
4 Management and staff are too product orientated, rather than consumer orientated.
5 Sitting back waiting for business/enquiries to come in.

6 Employees and management do not really believe in selling.
7 Head office versus hotel organization problems, or sales versus operating management problem.
8 Some hotel groups and hotels work in isolation of what their competitors are doing.
9 There is no real systematic marketing and sales action plan.
10 Sales techniques could be improved.
11 There is no systematic follow up.

SELLING A MILE WIDE AND AN INCH DEEP

Many of these 'faults' are inter-related but let us firstly consider 'selling a mile wide and an inch deep'. Usually this stems from a very enthusiastic, dedicated management and sales team. Too often management saturate a market with telephone calls, personal visits and mailing shots in the belief that a massive effort is bound to achieve results. Sometimes it does. But generally only when there is a steady, carefully planned, well-researched systematic follow-up to the initial blitz campaign. Very often all you find is a very exhausted sales and management team getting more and more concerned over the mass of enquiries but lack of sufficient real bookings.

There are broadly two kinds of bookings, or sales situations. Firstly, the one where a customer telephones, writes, or calls in, and says that they wish to talk about reserving a room, booking a function, or organizing a conference. This is the incoming enquiry. At this stage the prospective customer must have considered your competition, has probably seen your prices, and maybe your facilities. Careful further selling is still required to obtain the actual booking. But this is an *incoming* enquiry and therefore a much easier sales situation than going 'out' to sell with an outgoing sales approach (by telephone, letter, mailing shot or face to face call). The second *outgoing* sales approach is absolutely essential if the hotel is to receive more incoming approaches.

It is possible to obtain a booking from incoming calls at the first, or second, sales situation. But the 'colder' sales call takes a series of essential steps if the maximum return is going to be obtained from the sales expenditure and sales time. Sometimes sales people believe a mass of bookings will just arise as the hotel becomes better known, and so they cut out some of the steps. This automatically leads to less effective selling. What are the various steps?

1 Firstly an organization or a company who uses hotels, or could use hotels, has to be located.

2 Then the demand for the hotel's facilities has to be determined from this organization. It may be just bedrooms, the restaurant at lunchtime, or one annual dinner dance. Or it might well be all three plus, say, a regular training course in an hotel.
3 The names of the decision-makers and advisors (or influencers) of the decision-maker have to be found out.
4 Who do they use now? Who is your competition? Do they use your hotel already for some aspects, but could use your other facilities?
5 Numbers involved, potential spends, time of the year – all these points have to be found out.
6 Then the initial sales approach has to be made.
7 You have to get them to see the product if they have not been there before. A customer may have attended a function but never been inside the restaurant, or seen how good your bedrooms are.
8 You may have to see them more than once to agree prices, dates, special equipment, etc. and they still may not have made a definite booking.
9 And then you have to close, i.e. obtain the booking.
10 There is then the follow-up for the next booking, next year or the next time, or to obtain their other business.

This list of ten steps is not all-embracing but they are absolutely essential and take time and patience. The earlier research will tell you whether the sale is worthwhile and enable you to be selective. Assuming the sale is worthwhile, all these additional steps are also worthwhile, and essential, particularly if your competition is selling to them at the same time.

When a new hotel is opened, or a function room is revamped, and sometimes when management want an all out sales effort, it is essential to avoid the scatter shot approach. The first five steps are all research, digging for key names and contacts and these steps are *vital.* But it takes time, energy and patience. Many people have an abundance of energy, but everyone I know lacks time, and many people lack the patience required for a systematic successful sales approach. Let us take a typical example of a hotel deciding to enter the conference market, or obtain a greater share of this market.

What I have seen happened many times is that they buy a mailing list of conference organizers, which is often quite extensive, running into well over a thousand names. Then they produce a good mailing shot, and covering letter, and sometimes an expensive conference brochure as well. And they send them off to the one or two thousand conference organizers, perhaps with a reply paid card for more information, or if they require a visit. They might try two or more sales promotional 'shots' to this list.

The first point on this is that *any* hotel can buy the mailing list. Secondly the conference organizer has received a series of these promotional efforts from a whole range of hotels. Most hotels do not have a variety of conference facilities which will take any type and size of conference. And these mailing lists rarely tell you the size of the conference, how many per year, etc. that the conference organizer will hold. So a good proportion of the lists may hold conferences which are not suitable for the hotel. This type of promotion may produce results, but it is my contention that it is too much like selling a mile wide and an inch deep.

Other than the large convention hotels, most hotels only need a hard core, or 'regular' conference clients, of maximum, say, a hundred companies and organizations who are going to use the hotel regularly. Bearing in mind that there are day conferences and functions, if an hotel had a hundred companies using the hotel for only one conference of two nights per year, this would be a significant amount of business for many hotels on a regular basis – plus the other overnight conferences which can be attracted as well.

I know one hotel (with 150 rooms) which has a main client list of only twelve, where eight of the clients hold regular management conferences and training seminars, for five days, gathering on Sunday night to start Monday morning.

This puts the 'problem' into perspective. Naturally it depends on the size of the hotel, but many hotels only have to find, say, fifty regular conference clients, and some less regular conferences. Therefore it pays to take time researching names very carefully before building up a mailing list, and in fact the list may be small enough to visit each one personally. Firstly, start with past conference users of the hotel. Then contact users of the hotel's other facilities, as they may hold conferences. Then research the local catchment area. Seek out local companies who are part of an international, or national group. Locate organizations who hold management and training courses, like insurance companies, computer firms, management consultancies. Steadily build up a list of organizations who could use your hotel's conference facilities and where they are the right size and style. Naturally find out the name of the decision-maker or his advisors. This takes time and patience but is well worthwhile. You will gradually build your own index of more likely prospects. As you start to sell you will be able to grade them. Eventually you will end up like the hotel mentioned previously with a hard core of clients to service and follow up, plus a more selective list of possible users of the hotel's conference facilities. And to keep these clients you 'nurse them like a baby'. This is much more like selling 'an inch wide and a mile deep'.

Some organizations go in for blitz campaigns whenever an hotel in the group is not doing too well. They bring in a concentration of sales and other executives from other hotels in the group and saturate an area with telephone sales calls – and personal visits if they have time to make a proper appointment. Then they all go away. I know of one hotel which used four salesgirls to call on every office, factory and company within a three-mile radius of the hotel. I have studied a large number of these campaigns over the past decade and there is little evidence that they are successful relative to the enormous time and effort put into them.

The only one which was effective was a concentrated telephone sales campaign, with a carefully produced list of questions, which had one primary objective and this was to obtain a list of companies who used local hotels, what facilities they used, the name of the decision-maker and the person who actually made the booking. This campaign produced a very worthwhile and beneficial end product of sales opportunities which the actual hotel staff could steadily follow up during the following weeks or months.

Many people expect to get a booking from a first sales call. This could happen with an 'incoming' enquiry but rarely happens with an 'outgoing' first sales call. It is imperative that the objective of the first call, and quite often the second call as well, is to carry out research, i.e. obtain as much information about the prospective customer as possible, his needs and problems. Only then can you really begin to sell effectively. It could well be that no attempt is made to sell at all on the first visit. But the sales person goes away, has time to think about the present hotel the buyer is using, the advantages over that hotel, and has time to prepare a more effective sales presentation and approach. The approach that produces the best results is one where the sales executive, or hotel manager, spends more time initially in discounting the broad approach and saves time in the long run by producing a smaller, more manageable list of prospective buyers.

AVOID SELLING THE WHOLE HOTEL

Similarly, it is necessary to concentrate available resources and energy on the sources of business most likely to produce results in increased sales and profits, and avoid trying to sell and promote every aspect of the area. I was called into one hotel where the management team were extremely good. They were working very hard trying to increase the sales of the hotel. Results were improving steadily, but not fast enough, and the management team were working extremely hard on selling without obtaining satisfactory results. The hotel had excellent small meeting rooms, an extremely good situation, and was near a major communications point.

I asked management to list the areas and aspects of the hotel that they were trying to sell in their brochures, advertising, and sales approach generally. They were in fact trying to sell virtually everything. We listed them as follows:

Overnight business visitors to local factories
Business users of major communication point
Tourist users of major communication point
Weekend breaks
Overnight smaller conferences
Smaller and larger day conferences
The restaurant
Weddings
Functions.

There were a number of competitive hotels near the major communication point. We then drew up an Advantage/Limitation list (which is amplified later in this book), not on the hotel as a whole but on these various sources of business, and drew up similar lists on the competitive hotels for the different sources of business. It became very apparent from this listing that my client's hotel had far more competition for some of these sources than others. In fact, it became very clear which sources to concentrate on over the next year. They were (1) overnight visitors to local factories (2) weekend breaks (3) overnight smaller conferences and (4) weddings.

Prior to this they had been spreading their time and energies over nine major sources of business. The intention was not to ignore the other five, only to concentrate sales resources on four for the coming year, and then review the situation. After making the decision the whole management team took on a new lease of life and were far more effective than when they were trying to promote every aspect of the hotel.

In the minds of some hoteliers there is one hotel and one market. Brochures and sales literature usually promote the hotel as if it was one business, with one market segment. In fact, it is a series of different businesses with different markets which just happen to be under one roof. The market segments may vary considerably. Very often the market attending functions is totally different from the overnight convention market, weddings, or the market segment in the bedrooms. And yet often the brochure and even the face-to-face sales approach promotes one thing – the hotel. Surely we require different advantages for the different sources of business compared with main competitors, and we need more specific sales literature rather than an overall brochure. As an example, promotional literature for weddings will stress different advantages of the hotel from, say, promotion to the organizer of a series of management courses who is more interested in where the electric points are, and the shape of the room, even if both sources are using the same room.

A further point where sales results do not arise is where people try one method of promotion and then give up. In the later chapter on Action Plans it is emphasized that a steady systematic series of contacts and sales efforts is required before results are achieved. Too often people send out one mailing shot, or try one advert and then give up if the response is not immediate. Naturally the lack of response could be because the mailing shot just does not sell, or the advert is badly located. But there is a kind of inertia which has to be overcome where the prospective customer decides that he will respond and telephone you, or accept your invitation to have a look at your meeting room, or bedrooms. If the sales message is right, at some point the buyer will think 'why not', but this may not arise from the first approach.

SALES VERSUS OPERATIONS

In the last twenty years my partners, consultants and I have worked for nearly every major British hotel group, approximately a dozen Continental and North American hotel groups and numerous individual hotels. I have studied the organization structure of many of these groups in detail, and, of course, looked at the sales organization. I have never seen two which are alike, although some are similar, primarily because the management may have come from a similar background (e.g. a significant number of British sales executives worked for Grand Metropolitan Hotels at some stage in their career during the 60s and 70s). When people ask me what the most effective type of sales organization is, I have to answer that I do not know.

Most companies' sales organizations are all different and they all seem to work. Some sales organizations are more centralized than others particularly in selling rooms. Many American hotel groups do not have sales organizations in the same way as other countries. They rely more heavily on paid advertising and advanced technology for very efficient central reservations. Advertising in the media in America, particularly on television, is far cheaper and more cost effective than advertising in Europe, and this probably explains the different emphasis.

Historical development also plays a part in the type of organization. In Britain, larger groups who started with hotels in London and then expanded into the provinces tend to be more centralized with less selling, if any, carried out by the hotel manager. Provincial hotel groups who expanded into London tend to leave more of the selling to the manager.

What I am conscious of is that at times sales and operating management will 'trip over each other's feet' in going after the same business, and presumably there are times when they miss opportunities because they both assume the other is dealing with it. In some hotels there is a chasm between the two 'sides' of operations and sales which should not exist, but does. You may think this is an exaggeration but there is enormous aggravation between the two which is unnecessary. I have spent hours listening to hotel operating management pouring out their hearts over their company's sales team, and similarly have heard the other side pouring out their frustrations. It is worth considering the main 'complaints' so that any reader involved in this situation can be more aware of them and hopefully will be in a better position to find a solution. These points are not always applicable, but are more common than they should be.

- Sales executives claim that management are too product-orientated, turn down or discourage business, resent the presence of a sales force and never say a word of thanks when they bring in a sizeable amount of business.
- Operating management claim that sales people have often never worked in a hotel, interfere with the operation and raise complaints on the hotel. They claim that sales people often only obtain business by discounting and do this at times when they could fill the hotel anyway. Above all, they claim sales people are not responsible for the budget or target Net Profit and couldn't care less about the bottom line figure.

What I would like to do is to put forward suggestions – do's and don'ts – to try to improve the team spirit. Firstly, operating management must accept that sales people are absolutely essential for virtually all situations where the initial part of selling is outside the hotel's immediate catchment area, e.g. to conference organizers a long distance from the hotel, foreign tour operators and travel agents. Operations and sales must agree beforehand the quiet periods which require particular emphasis and the maximum discount they can provide. Whenever feasible on a 'large' deal, operating management should accompany sales to key negotiating meetings so that they work as a team.

Where sales executives have not worked in hotels before they should spend some time working in the hotel's various departments. This should include the kitchen, particularly if they have to sell functions so that they do not sell a dish which is impossible to produce for large numbers. This would be an invaluable investment. Conversely, heads of departments (including the chief accountant) and most certainly the general manager, should periodically go out selling, even if this is just on follow-up sales calls to past customers. If this was done for just two separate weeks in the year it would provide them with an invaluable feel of the market's pulse. And my experience is that it does produce a lot of business. These two suggestions on working on each others 'areas' could help enormously to break down barriers, where they exist.

Sales executives are sometimes appointed by an hotel group to sell for more than one hotel in an area where the hotel is too small to justify a full time sales executive. I have never known this work effectively. Even where a company has two small hotels in an area of different grades, the salesperson tends to spend more time selling the better hotel.

Management must agree with the salesperson where his or her work starts and ends. Some sales executives stimulate enquiries, get the prospective customer to the lobby and then hand over to operating management. Some take the situation through to the booking. Others stay with the customer until the conference or function has been completed. In some hotels, where the sales person's work starts and ends is totally blurred. Whatever decision is made on the point where the salesperson 'hands over' this should be clearly defined, and if practical put down on paper, so that everyone knows where they stand. This must also apply to sales people from head office. Often sales people show tour operators, or conference organizers, around an hotel without introducing them to the hotel management.

I once booked one of our management courses in a London hotel with the conference head office sales manager who at no time introduced us to anyone from the actual hotel management. Days later I met the general manager of the hotel, at another hotel, and casually mentioned I had made a booking. Instead of being pleased, he was furious with the man from head office. All staff should be warned when a buyer is being shown round the hotel. I know one major conference hotel where they have a series of red lights only the staff can see, which are switched on when a conference buyer is due in the hotel. The lights are behind reception, behind the porter's desk, in the restaurant, etc. I am not sure if I like this idea and an experienced buyer should visit a hotel anonymously. In fact in this hotel I was told they switched the lights on whenever the chairman and managing director visits the hotel. But staff should be told that the buyer is due, the time, his company or organization name, and his or her name.

Sales executives employed by the hotel to sell locally should be part of that hotel's management team, at deputy management status and responsible to the general manager, with possibly a dotted line to the head office marketing or sales manager, not the other way round.

The situation of sales versus operations does not arise in all hotels, or hotel groups, but it does in a significant number. It is hoped that by highlighting the problem, and putting forward the foregoing suggestions, that readers may be able to correct this situation if it applies to them.

WORKING IN ISOLATION FROM COMPETITION – ADVANTAGE/LIMITATION LISTS

In producing an effective sales action plan one of the first steps is to write down the different sources of business for the hotel, e.g.

bedrooms – business use
bedrooms – tourists
restaurant
functions
weddings
conventions
exhibitions
seminars
etc., etc.

It is then necessary to list your most immediate competition for the different sources of business. If the hotel is in a major international tourist town or city like San Francisco or Edinburgh, then it could be argued that every other international tourist city is a competitor. But in this case I am assuming that a tourist has decided on your town as a staying point and therefore the competition would be within your immediate catchment area. When you ask some sales executives and hoteliers to list this real competition there is sometimes a tendency to generalize and name certain other local hotels. Some people will name the so-called better hotels at a higher star grading and say they are the most competitive. Other people will mention cheaper, or low priced hotels as their main competition.

But if the advantages and limitations of your own hotel are listed compared with the advantages and limitations (A/L Lists) of the competition, not overall, but by the different sources of business, then a completely different picture can emerge.

What is often the case is that hotel management work in isolation from their competition, what they are doing, how much they are charging, what are their advantages and limitations. Some hoteliers, in drawing up an A/L List on their own hotel, produce a long list of limitations, sometimes longer than the advantages. Empathy tells us that the reason why they are 'negative' about the limitations of their own hotel is because they have to live with these disadvantages in the selling and operation of the hotel. These 'problems' are constantly being brought to the hotelier's attention and therefore it is understandable if he (or she) over-reacts to them.

On the other hand other competitive hotels also have limitations and there is no hotel in the world with only advantages for every different source of business. In order to find out the limitations of your competition and your advantages over them it is essential to visit them, stay the night there in different rooms and study them carefully. Not enough people do this and very few executives are given a specific budget to spend studying the competition. Some hotel managers visit competitive hotels to eat with the competitor's manager, and return the invitation at a later date. This is not what I mean. I gave a speech to a team of sales executives who worked for a major international group. I asked them where they stayed when they visited other towns. They looked surprised and said in their own local hotel in that town, if there was one.

It may be necessary to carry out a little 'industrial espionage' but it is vital to

Stay the night in competition
drive, walk, get a taxi to them

eat there
examine all their facilities
find out their rates for a typical function, day conference, overnight conference, etc.
assess their standards

Some hoteliers view this 'spying' with horror. I do not regard it as spying. When a car manufacturer brings out a new model, other manufacturers will buy the new model and literally take it apart in order to learn from it, and assess how they can compete with it. We in the hotel world must recognize that the next decade is going to be highly competitive. A few examples of the type of advantages hoteliers, sales executives and we as consultants have found over competition are listed below. They exclude the obvious ones which most people could list from the hotel's brochure.

1. A hotel had the only car park in town where all the people attending a function could actually park when the function rooms were full.
2. Two competitors had underground car parks where it was extremely difficult to park a wide car because the ramp was so windy and narrow, and even more difficult to drive out (particularly after a few drinks).
3. Competition had good size bedrooms, but very small bathrooms.
4. Most competitive hotels had air-conditioning, but main competitor's was very noisy.
5. Competition had only one mix of beds. All rooms were twin-bedded whereas our client had a proportion with double beds.
6. Outside noise problem was much worse in the competition than one client imagined.
7. Inside noise problem between bedrooms and corridor was much worse, although the competitor was a new hotel.
8. One client found theirs was the only hotel out of six competitive 4 star hotels who had an inner door which reduced a lot of the noise from the corridor.
9. One major new competitor in the smaller meeting market (up to 100 people) had a new suite of meeting/conference rooms. But the ceilings were so low that most screens for visual aids could not be extended fully.
10. Two beautiful chandeliers at either end of a conference room meant that the room had major disadvantages in projecting anything on to a screen particularly as the speakers sat on a stage at one end.

11 One competitor's meeting room was long and narrow with disadvantages for some types of conferences.
12 A major competitor in top grade hotels had all rooms with private bathrooms but no showers.
13 A client had the only hotel in a city who could sleep all the delegates in the hotel when the convention room was full. Other hotels had to sleep a proportion in other nearby hotels when the convention room was full.
14 A client had the only hotel in town with a champagne bar – which was a big attraction and a unique selling point.
15 One client had the best variety and selection of meeting and conference rooms in a major city. No one else could offer the conference organizer such choice.
16 In one major tourist and conference town we found our client was the only hotel with an air-conditioned large conference/function room.
17 Another client found they had the only large ground floor room which could take a heavy floor load for extremely heavy equipment at exhibitions.
18 A client had by far the best back-up facilities for copying, interpretation, secretarial, telex and 'outside' telephone lines than the competition although the main conference room was in an old building and not purpose built.
19 A client was the only one locally who offered the service of picking up and transporting guest speakers, if required.
20 One large city hotel was one of the few in the city with a really good separate check-in area and lounge for large group tours, conventions and business incentive groups.
21 One client thought their function prices were higher than all the competition, but found this only applied to food. They used a low mark-up on wines and spirits which meant that for a typical function menu, and one third of a bottle of wine per head, they were in fact sixth on a price listing of eight competitive function rooms, although they had much better facilities (the most expensive were listed first).

There are many other examples which could be quoted other than the more obvious ones, but the foregoing is an example of some which can only be determined by study and careful analysis. This kind of analysis is essential if you are to draw up the league tables mentioned in Chapter 5 and produce dynamic A/L Lists. You can only prepare them by going into your competition regularly, taking a cold, hard, objective look at his facilities, standards and pricing strategy, *and* doing the same to your own hotel, analysed by source of business. If you do it, and your competition does not, then you will be at a major advantage in marketing and selling the hotel. If every hotelier prepared A/L lists the concentration of thought on stressing the advantages, and reducing the impact of the limitations would ensure that the whole hotel industry surged forward.

A CERTAIN ATMOSPHERE

There are still many hotels who sit back waiting for business to come in. I am usually told that they 'want to sort out some problems in the hotel first. When we get the product really right, then we will start selling.' In the hotel industry the product is never really right, and this is the way it should be. The day we think we have a good product is the day we stop striving to improve things. In a total 'people' situation like the hotel industry you can never achieve 100 per cent perfection whatever some hotel advertisements may say. But this striving to improve the product should never be an excuse for not selling.

The other assumption we should not make is that all the management and staff really want to sell. Do they really want to chase more business? After all, it only gives them more work, more headaches. It is wrong to assume that all management and staff have the same motivation to sell. Providing the hotel is doing reasonably well, why should they 'kill' themselves? I have sometimes seen a banqueting manager's face fall when the food and beverage manager, or the sales executive, excitedly rushes in and announces they have just landed another new function. All it means is more work.

The other assumption which could be wrong is that employees will sell more in bad times. Most staff have no idea of the economics of running an hotel. My experience of talking to hundreds of employees is that the vast majority believe the hotel they work in is far more profitable than it is. Many of them equate sales with profit, or they forget all about overheads. So an early move in many hotels would be a series of short seminars explaining to the staff the basic Profit and Loss Account of the hotel, and stressing why increased sales are absolutely vital to the hotel and to *them*. This is an essential 'investment' to make them more sales conscious.

We must recognize that some staff need more motivation, or a different kind of motivation, so that overall the whole team sells with enthusiasm.

Many employees do have a financial incentive to sell and deal with more business through the addition of a percentage service charge, or the tipping system. But a significant proportion of the employees (e.g. kitchen staff) and most management do not share in these financial rewards. And even where they do receive extra income for more business there are many employees who reach a level of income where above this level they really believe it isn't worth 'the sweat'.

There are many types of profit sharing schemes, specific financial incentives, employee of the month awards, etc. Sometimes they work, in other situations they do not. The types of incentives aimed at boosting sales which I have found most effective are as follows:

1 A bonus to all the reception team for every night room occupancy reaches 100 per cent, or a certain target level. Or a bonus where room sales pass a certain level of money on any night. Both overcome the problem of the very common situation in many hotels where the guests have a different length of stay, of turning away business because the hotel is full, but not achieving 100 per cent occupancy. The second really applies where reception staff have control over the room rates, or the majority of them. I have sat with reservations and reception staff after around 6 p.m. in the evening as they literally chase every available avenue to obtain one more booking.
2 Employee of the month (and year) awards. If these are well organized, with an objective form of assessment in a logical points fashion, they can really motivate staff. Often I have found them more successful when there is no incentive in the form of actual money, but the award, or prize, is a present or holiday. I once asked a series of award winners what was the best aspect of the award. Nearly all of them mentioned the press relations aspect of their photographs appearing in the company's newsletter, the local press and the hotel trade press. One waitress who had won an award told me she had posted copies of the company in-house newsletter to twenty different relatives in other parts of the country.
3 Incentives linked to increases in covers served, average spend, etc. As mentioned later in this book incentives can be useful in motivating staff to increase sales to existing guests. But they only tend to work if they are based on a specific target which can be measured rather than a generalized overall increase. And employees must be able to influence the increase in sales themselves. Examples of where we have found these incentives work most

effectively are an increase in the number of desserts sold as against the same period last year. Or an increase in the number of liqueurs and brandies sold, rather than an increase in the overall average spend. Of course, the objectives of the incentive to increase the number of desserts, or brandies, sold *is* to increase average spends. But they seem to work more effectively when the target is a number in quantity rather than amount.

The foregoing are examples of incentives which do work in some hotels. But many do not appear to work over a long term period, and they require concerted regular motivation from management.

In years of examining the type of hotel where all, or at least a high proportion of staff appear to sell more easily, naturally and effortlessly than other hotels, it has always appeared to me that the successful hotels have a certain mood or atmosphere which is only partially related to incentives and earnings. And this marketing atmosphere can only originate from one source – the highest executive in the hotel or company. If the general manager of the hotel (or chief executive of a group) doesn't understand marketing, and doesn't create the right atmosphere, all the efforts of the team of management under him (or her) will be dissipated. This will result in a high proportion of the hotel's staff not really wishing to sell.

The marketing atmosphere is created by leadership, a full understanding of marketing, communication of objectives to all staff, and a sense of positive enthusiasm which spreads to the whole team.

When I was very young my father told me that Britain won the first battle in the Second World War because of 'atmosphere'. I didn't know what he was talking about. Now I do. The battle was won at Alamein in North Africa in 1942 because of a new atmosphere. We had fought a series of 'successful retreats' until they appointed Montgomery in charge. I make no apology for including a part of the speech in this book, as it has lessons for every manager. It typifies Monty:

> 'I want first of all to introduce myself to you. You do not know me. I do not know you. But we have got to work together – therefore we must understand each other and we must have confidence in each other. I have only been here a few hours. But from what I have seen and heard since I arrived I am prepared to say, here and now, that I have confidence in you. We will then work together as a team – and together we will gain the confidence of this great army and go forward to final victory in Africa.

'I believe that one of the first duties of a commander is to create what I call "atmosphere" and in that atmosphere, his staff, subordinate commanders, and troops will live and work and fight. I do not like the general atmosphere I find here. It is an atmosphere of doubt, of looking back to select the next place to which to withdraw, of loss of confidence in our ability to defeat Rommel, of desperate defence measures by reserves in preparing positions in Cairo and the Delta.

'All that must cease. Let us have a new atmosphere.

'The defence of Egypt lies here in Alamein and on the Ruweisat Ridge. What is the use of digging trenches in the Delta? It is quite useless; if we lose this position we lose Egypt; all the fighting troops now in the delta must come here at once, and will. Here we will stand and fight; there will be no further withdrawal. I have ordered that all plans and instructions dealing with further withdrawal are to be burnt, and at once. We will stand and fight here. If we can't stay here alive, then let us stay here dead.

'Now I understand that Rommel is expected to attack at any moment. Excellent. Let him attack. I would sooner it didn't come for a week, just give me time to sort things out. If we have two weeks to prepare we will be sitting pretty; Rommel can attack as soon as he likes after that, and I hope he does. Meanwhile, we ourselves will start to plan a great offensive; it will be the beginning of a campaign which will hit Rommel and his army for six right out of Africa.

'I have no intention of launching our great attack until we are completely ready. There will be pressure from many quarters to attack soon; I will not attack until we are ready, and you can rest assured on that point. Meanwhile, if Rommel attacks while we are preparing, let him do so with pleasure; we will merely continue with our own preparations and we will attack when we are ready, and not before.

'I have little more to say just at present. And some of you may think it is quite enough and may wonder if I am mad. I assure you I am quite sane. I understand there are people who often think I am slightly mad; so often that I now regard it as rather a compliment. All I have to say to that is that if I am slightly mad, there are a large number of people I could name who are raving lunatics.

'What I have done is to get over to you the "atmosphere" in which we will now work and fight; you must see that atmosphere permeates right down through the Eighth Army to the most junior private soldier. All the soldiers must know what is wanted; when

> they see it coming to pass there will be a surge of confidence throughout the army.
>
> 'I ask you to give me your confidence and to have faith that what I have said will come to pass. The chief of staff will be issuing orders on many points very shortly, and I am always available to be consulted by the senior officers of the staff. The great point to remember is that we are going to finish with this chap Rommel once and for all. It will be quite easy. There is no doubt about it. He is definitely a nuisance. Therefore we will hit him a crack and finish with him.'

You will notice that Monty communicates, he has a plan and he is totally positive. Above all he creates a certain atmosphere. All these are relevant to the hotel industry. We are in a total people-and-atmosphere situation in hotels. Some people say we face a decade of recession and problems. I say that we face a decade of opportunities. If we can create the right atmosphere related to marketing and selling, the future will be very bright.

*   *   *   *   *

10

SALES ACTION PLANS

DEFINING BUSY AND QUIET PERIODS

After markets have been defined, or in the case of most hotels regularly redefined, it is essential to prepare a plan of action on how increased sales (and increased profits) are going to be achieved from the market objectives. There has to be a well thought out action plan if sales are to be maximized. If the hotel is large with many different departments, the plan would cover action to sustain and increase sales for *every* source of business and market segment.

Thus a large hotel's action plans might cover virtually every source of business, e.g. business visitors, local tourists, foreign tourists, overnight conventions, day meetings, exhibitions, management seminars, etc. In fact a very large hotel might have a special executive, or a separate executive in charge of selling for each source. However, it is vital to avoid selling 'a mile wide and an inch deep'.

Most hotels are not very large and have a limited source of executive time and energy to devote to selling. Therefore it is vital to concentrate this money and energy on the sources of business which are most vulnerable to a decline in sales, or will produce the most significant increase in net profits. Only a thorough knowledge of the hotel's sales activity, guest profiles, etc. will enable you to define the correct aspects to concentrate money and energy on.

As elaborated later there is a danger that a considerable proportion of the various sales techniques used to reach a prospective customer (e.g. paid advertising, mailing shots, sales letters. etc.) produce business when the hotel is already busy. Most hotels have a part of the year, or week, or seasons, when they seem to fill up automatically. Some business hotels in industrial or commercial areas turn away business Monday to Thursday nights and are then much quieter at weekends. Or the business hotel might be full Monday through to

Wednesday, but always have empty rooms on Thursday night as businessmen head home for the weekend.

Some hotels near a tourist attraction may have a reverse pattern of being full weekends but experiencing a lower occupancy midweek. Business hotels will often show a decline in occupancies in summer months when more businessmen take holidays. Many hotels will always be full, or very busy, in the function rooms, bars and restaurants in the run-up period to Christmas. Some successful function hotels will always be busy, but are actually much quieter on a Sunday, or Tuesday night, and very rarely have a function on a Monday night.

In no way should you be complacent or neglect the busy periods. But if they appear to fill up automatically then they are kept full to a large extent by making sure the product is right, i.e. giving them the best service possible, and by a planned systematic follow up. Most readers will see this pattern in their own hotel and be able to define the periods in the year, months, days or meal periods which:

1 fill up without a lot of marketing and sales promotion
2 are 'soft' periods i.e. there is some business but the period could achieve higher sales
3 are quiet periods without much business at all

The first market requires servicing and planned follow ups. The second usually requires a steady systematic sales campaign and quite often just a small increase in sales for these 'soft' periods produces a large increase in bottom line net profit. The third period is what I call 'dead periods'. Most hotels have some, but hopefully not too many. Sometimes it just isn't worth bothering with them. As an example, in some seaside resorts it pays to shut down in the 'dead months' when the whole resort is like a ghost town. But the solution is usually to redefine markets and change market direction. Some resort hotels have filled the quiet months by marketing to senior citizens. Very often thinking like spacemen (see earlier chapter) can fill a quiet period. Who would have thought that so many well known hotels like Grosvenor House, Park Lane, Hilton Park Lane, London, and Piccadilly, Manchester, England would turn a complete 'dead' Monday evening in their function rooms into high-income evenings by having two sweaty, blood-soaked men boxing in a ring at Sportsmens' Clubs?

Therefore before producing the detail of how you are going to reach the new and increased business an overall strategy has to be agreed. A checklist is shown on the following pages which should help in the preparation of your own action plan. You will see that this is sub-divided into two parts. (Checklists 10.1 and 10.2)

CHECKLIST 10.1

SALES ACTION PLAN – BROAD STRATEGY

1 An overall strategy and policy for the whole hotel and the different income producing areas. This strategy must cover:

Marketing policy
Busy and quiet periods and areas
Profit forecasts
Marketing costs
Capital expenditure plans (if required)

2 The local marketing strategy must be analysed into a plan for each different area which produces, or could produce, sales by source of business:

Rooms
Restaurant(s)
Bars
Function areas
Meeting rooms
Etc.

3 The strategy should define which aspects are going to be tackled in the immediate future and which will be left until later, i.e. management by exception, sell an inch wide and a mile deep.
4 Targets of increased sales and increased profits must be prepared.
5 A monetary budget must be prepared, analysed into how, where and when the money is going to be spent, and the total.
6 A time budget must be prepared – who is going to spend time on gathering information, key names, research, etc. – who is going to sell, and how much time is going to be spent on 'outside' selling – who is going to organize and sustain in-house selling.

The first deals with overall strategy, targets, defining busy and quiet periods, etc. The second covers how to reach potential customers, i.e. the various methods one might use to make them ask for more information, visit your hotel, and try you out. In order to help elaborate the checklists on a Sales Action Plan, two other Schedules have been shown on separate pages. Both are actual indices, one on a Marketing Plan, the other on a Sales Action Plan. (Schedules A and B).

CHECKLIST 10.2

HOW TO REACH THE POTENTIAL CUSTOMERS

1 Explain whole plan of action to all staff.
2 'Outside' Selling

(a) Letters
(b) Mailing shot/promotional literature
(c) Telephone selling
(d) Face to face selling
(e) Paid advertising – national and local newspapers, magazines, commercial radio, commercial television, etc.
(f) Unpaid publicity
(g) Word of mouth publicity

3 In house selling
4 Subdivide action points into

(a) Past
(b) Present
(c) Potential customers

5 Periodic checking of expenditure against budget
6 Monitoring sales results
7 Revision of plan bearing in mind 5 and 6

These checklists and indices are fairly self-explanatory but some elaboration is required.

ACTION PLANS

During the last ten years I have worked on the preparation of marketing and sales action plans with clients on three large hotel groups and about twenty individual hotels. All the plans were different. During the last decade I must have run eighty of our marketing courses with an average of eighteen delegates on each course, or nearly 1,500 delegates, although some hoteliers deliberately came on the course twice. In these courses the delegates, in working parties of three to five people, had to produce a sales action

SCHEDULE A

SAMPLE INDEX – MARKETING PLAN

Part I

1 The problem
2 Objectives (main markets to aim at – quiet periods, targets, etc.)
3 Special comments
4 General background: location, communications, industry, special selling features of the area
5 Advantage/limitation list (A/L list) of your hotel
6 Competition: competitive hotels according to type of business and A/L list on competition by source of business
7 Quantification of existing market (where appropriate) and analysis of size of the problem
8 Research: external, internal
9 Changes required to the product (hotel or restaurant) – subdivided between: rooms, public areas, back of the house, exterior.

plan. Often they were all different. Very often the difference may have been on emphasis. But I would not say because many of them were different that they were wrong. Everyone must make their own business judgment of priorities, and how they are going to reach the potential market. Ten hoteliers might all tackle the same hotel in ten slightly different ways. Providing the pitfalls mentioned in the previous chapter are avoided, and the checklists are used, all ten hoteliers would produce results, and this is what counts.

What period should the action cover? Should it be a year, six months, a season? Again this will vary depending on the broad marketing strategy. In fact all the plans I have worked on cover different time periods for different sources of business. One plan I prepared had action over the following periods

Restaurant – 2 months
Functions – 6 months
Business Incentive Market – 2 years
Conferences – 2 years
Midweek bedrooms – 2 months
Weekend Tourist Market – 3 years.

Naturally, in breaking into a new market over a three year period like the weekend tourist market the strategy was to become really

SCHEDULE B

SAMPLE INDEX – SALES ACTION PLAN

Part II

1 Plan of action and timetable of action.
2 Midweek: potential guests, past guests, mail shot plan, telephone sales plan, face-to-face selling.
3 Weekend: packaging for weekend sales, advertising and distribution of literature.
4 Function rooms: (past and potential markets): meetings and conferences, functions, other uses of function rooms, room sales from functions.
5 Exhibitions: interior, exterior.
6 Additional selling points: printing, staff, signposting, etc.
7 Plan for staff training.
8 Internal selling.
10 Special promotional ideas.

profitable from this source *within* three years, and the action points were far more detailed in the first year than the second and third years.

In one case the client had large food and beverage areas with good car parking. The catchment area was large – and there was considerable eating (and drinking) out in the area. This client had spent some years systematically and successfully selling bedrooms and was now turning his attention to the food and beverage areas which were not doing too well. We devised a sales action plan which did not just promote or advertise the superb function room, or fine restaurant. Instead we linked the promotion of these areas to five special days of the year, in addition to the entertaining period up to and over Christmas and New Year's Day. There are numerous days in the year which lend themselves to a simple, special promotion with a spin off during the rest of the year. Some examples are:

Chinese New Year
St Valentine's Day
Shrove Tuesday
Mother's Day
Father's Day
First Day of Spring
Midsummer's Day

Bastille Day
American Independence Day
Halloween
Guy Fawkes
Derby Day and Other Sporting Occasions

The foregoing list is not exhaustive and we only chose five for that client, plus Christmas. They all lend themselves to a fun theme (massacre on Valentine's Day), the most saleable commodity in the world 'love' (Valentine's, Mother's Days), or special dishes – pancakes on Shrove Tuesday, Chinese, French or American style special menus. The plan was very effective for this client and the special day promotions are done every year with certain standard days (e.g. Valentine's, Mother's and Father's Days) and the other special days varying each year.

I see a situation where not only individual hotels organize a special day, or week, on their own but where every hotel and restaurant in a town or city combines to create special events with an emphasis on food. At present these special occasions are organized, although not necessarily with a food theme, e.g. Blackpool Lights, the Edinburgh Festival. If a food theme could be organized in the 'quieter' times of the year, the combined impact of all the hotels and restaurants promoting the occasion would be considerable. An example is Chicago, where an entire area declared Bastille Day a kind of holiday. Thousands walked the streets until late at night (near Michigan Avenue) eating at special open-air booths and – of prime importance – filling up all the restaurants and bars in and around the festivities. Why couldn't the hotels, restaurants and public houses organize a series of theme events in a whole town, or an area of a larger city, in the quieter periods and shoulders of the season?

Which comes first – do you fix a budget and then the action plan, or do you prepare the action plan, cost it, and come up with a budget? This is the chicken and the egg situation. Many companies do fix a budget first. I find it is useful to have a rough guideline of the budget first, then produce the detailed action, cost it, and go back and rethink the total budget. The budget might be increased at this point, or reduced. I remember one case where the action plan was over three months and the marketing budget was reduced considerably because it was decided to concentrate virtually everyone's time on a follow-up campaign by telephone sales calls, personalized sales letters, and visits to previous customers.

The action plan does not have to be very lengthy although it should contain quite a lot of detail, particularly in the sections on:

1 How to retain existing business
2 In-house selling
3 How one reaches new sources of business.

The last two have to include specific plans on the various techniques in reaching the targets which must have been researched beforehand (e.g. target list of conference organisers, names, etc.) As set out in the checklist on the Sales Action Plan there are probably less than ten methods of reaching a potential market, i.e.:

1 Sales letters
2 Mailing shots/promotional literature
3 Telephone calls
4 Face to face sales situations which may be firstly in the prospective customer's premises and/or in your own hotel.
5 Paid advertising.
6 Unpaid publicity.
7 Word of mouth publicity.

I have used telegrams and cables in a sales action plan and some people are using telexes to sell or to follow up. In a sense these are part of the techniques of sales letters and mailing shots. Later chapters in this book contain checklists with explanations to assist readers in deciding which of these techniques to use, and how to obtain a more effective response from the various techniques. Naturally, in your own plan it is not essential to use every one of these techniques. But whichever you choose the detail of how often, timing, content, objectives, must be defined for the action plan, even if you vary an aspect as the plan goes into action.

STAFF INVOLVEMENT

Therefore the plan must be detailed but could be fairly simple and does not have to be a lengthy document. A simple plan can be presented to every member of the staff. The explanation of the plan to the *whole* team is strongly recommended and this is listed as the very first point on the checklist. This may seem obvious but there are still many hotel managers who feel it is only necessary to show the plan of action to their deputies, the sales executive and certain departmental heads. Naturally you might not show the plan to a *casual* kitchen porter but I would show the plan – and give a verbal explanation – to all permanent staff *and* regular casuals including staff who have no apparent contact with guests and customers, e.g.

the storeman and the hotel engineer. There may be aspects of the plan, like the profit forecasts and financial targets which the hotel owner may not wish to disclose. If there is any chance that regular casuals may also work for your competitors then, naturally, I would not show the plan to them.

Wherever I have seen the plan presented to the whole team, as against a few people at the top, the results from the plan have always been better. I can well remember one situation of a client employing around 200 staff where business had steadily deteriorated. We were asked to prepare a detailed marketing and sales action plan. Eventually when the plan was completed and agreed by the board of directors we decided that the first thing to do was to present the whole plan to all the staff in two separate meetings away from the main busy periods. The employees had seen business decline for two years. They knew independent management consultants had been called in, and they heard there had been a series of board meetings. Then they were called together to meet the directors and consultants, and two large staff meetings took place. Apparently rumours had spread that the meetings were to announce redundancies. I watched the faces of the staff who all looked stern and worried. The managing director gave a short dynamic speech, not about redundancies, but that we were all going to solve the problem by *selling*. He then introduced me and I began to go through the action plan. The change in the mood was electrifying. When we began that assignment we were also asked to look at costs, so it was agreed that employees would not be told about the directors' intentions until a final decision was made. Ever since then I have always tried to involve all employees from the very beginning, and staff can also contribute many ideas on selling, particularly on in-house selling.

We have to get across to all staff that *no* hotel building ever made a profit. All a hotel *building* does is incur costs – heat, light, power, property taxes, property rates, and the payroll of employees in them. It is only when customers start to cross the hotel threshold and spend money that the hotel *might* make a profit, if there are sufficient customers who spend money *and* come back again.

THE SIZE OF THE PROBLEM

The degree of complexity of the action plan will depend on a number of factors, e.g. the time management have available, the amount of money which can be spent (invested) in the plan and what I call the size of the problem. If the hotel is new with a lot of existing competition, or if the hotel is not achieving high sales in any income producing areas, then a whole series of detailed action points may be required for every income producing area, and aimed at a series of different sources of business.

But usually this is not the case and the action plan may cover one or two 'quiet' or 'soft' income producing areas in detail, with a simple series of actions to sustain income in the busy times, or areas. For instance, in practice I have seen plans which just covered one or two of the following:

1. Thursday nights – room sales
2. Weekend room sales
3. Function rooms July and August
4. Weddings during the day on Saturdays
5. Sundays – functions
6. Restaurant lunch on Sundays
7. Restaurant lunch every day
8. Attracting more overnight stays from people attending dinners or dinner dances
9. Increasing average spend on rooms
10. Shoulder months of season for seaside seasonal holiday hotel with objective of staying open nine months rather than eight months each year.

Where a hotel has a major problem of low sales in virtually every department or is a brand new hotel just about to open, then the sales action plans should be more detailed with many more action points for each income producing area and the total amount of money to be spent in the budget may be high. Behind the specific action points to specific targets (e.g. a company or a travel agent) there might be the overall objective of making the hotel better known or launching it for the first time. This might be costly.

But this need not be the case. As you will read in the chapter on paid advertising, which is often the most costly form of promotion, paid advertising is only recommended in specific situations. Even with an opening of a new hotel nowadays I often wonder whether so much extensive paid advertising is necessary.

After all, many people can see the hotel being built and watch it through its various stages. There are numerous opportunities to obtain free media publicity throughout the building contract, e.g.:

Award of building contract
Topping out ceremony

Employment of key staff – manager, chef, housekeeper
Publicity on furniture and furnishings being installed
Countdown signs to opening days
Handing over keys ceremony

All of these provide opportunities for free press publicity in the local press, travel press, conference magazines and, if well organized, can get into the national press and television. In many countries hotels create jobs and this could well be 'news' over the next few years.

With the opening of a new hotel, new bedroom extension, new restaurant or a new conference room, this is one situation where marketing and promotion should be low key. It is essential that the new operation settles down and begins to work as a team and that the 'bugs are ironed out' on the new building or new convention room. Most people use the word 'new' as a promotional feature and as an obvious advantage over their competition. I usually recommend very strongly that the advantages of the new convention room are stressed, and there should be many, and that the word 'new' is not used.

Using empathy, many people associate the promotion of *new* as really meaning brand new. Experienced buyers and users of hotels avoid brand new hotels until they have settled down. If you were organizing a convention would you book it into a brand new hotel? I know of a number of people who organize large conventions who never use a new hotel until the second year. Surely it is better for the staff and for long term bookings not to show travel agents, local companies, local secretaties, etc. around the hotel anywhere near opening day. I usually recommend two opening days. A low key official opening with a small gathering of people, followed by another opening day three to six months later. And the sales literature and face to face selling should not say new, but that 'we opened recently, or last year (which is still very new) but we deliberately waited to sell to you until things had settled down.' I am sure customers and prospective customers appreciate this.

KEEP THE PLAN SIMPLE

Generally with most established hotels it is not necessary to 'put the hotel on the map' and the Sales Action Plan may cover one objective or, say, just these three things as an example:

1 To increase Thursday night room sales from 70 per cent to 90 per cent at the same average room rate as Monday to Wednesday nights

2 To increase covers in the restaurant by an average of ten covers per day at evenings
3 Increase double (and multiple) occupancy at weekends from 40 per cent to 70 per cent double occupancy

The action required might be a simple series of action points over the next six months, and sometimes one action. As examples, there are a number of business hotels which are full four nights a week, but one night, quite often Monday or Thursday, is 'soft' and does not achieve 100 per cent room occupancy although business is turned away on the other three full nights. In one case Thursday night was on average 20 rooms empty in a 150 room hotel. A considerable amount of business was being turned away other nights. All we did was to change receptionists' wording from 'I am very sorry we are full . . . Monday to Wednesday . . .' to 'but we do have some rooms available on Thursday.' Now we know that not all businessmen can change the night they visit a town or city. But a proportion can, particularly if the other hotels are full as well. This simple change in wording increased Thursday bookings by an average of twelve rooms per night and occupancy from 86.7 per cent to 95 per cent which was the average occupancy Monday to Wednesday nights. You can still telephone many hotels to find that they are fully booked and no attempt is made to suggest another night.

I have seen covers increase immediately the restaurant manager started a simple soft-sell telephone follow-up call to local companies on the lines '. . . I thought I would give you a call . . . hope to see you again soon'. This restaurant manager had forty key users. All he did was telephone them once, every year, or before a special event and he sent them a Christmas card. As soon as he started to do this his average lunchtime covers jumped from 50 to 75 and dinner covers from 80 to 100 covers, an increase of 45 covers per day on average for six days a week. This amounted to $270,000 higher sales and an increase in restaurant profits by $130,000 per year, after higher food and operating costs.

In another case we just decided to put a brochure on the hotel's weekend break holiday in the envelope sent confirming a booking to every businessman staying in the hotel on Thursday night with the usual message 'Why not extend to a weekend break?' Weekend bookings increased from this one action point. So we included a brochure for everyone who had booked on Monday night. Again a proportion booked a weekend break. So we tried doing this for every booking midweek and more weekend bookings came in.

One businessman with wife and friends would often result in a weekend booking for two, three, sometimes four rooms and this hotel with eighty rooms was experiencing an average of seventy rooms sold every weekend as compared to only thirty previously after four months of putting brochures in with confirmation slips. We then adopted a special free gift for guests staying more than three times in any two year period, and an extremely good free gift for guests staying more than six times in any two year period. One guest has taken five weekend breaks so far in just over a year, with a different woman each time, and we are thinking of giving him a special award.

This inset mailing shot cost no extra postage but we did resist the temptation to include other promotional items in the envelope, particularly on the hotel's two small conference rooms. This would have been fatal. So often I receive an envelope with the hotel brochure, a weekend brochure, a conference sheet, particulars of the restaurant, a booking form, etc. Who has the time to read them? I am sure that the success of the previous promotion was for two reasons. Firstly, the guest was familiar with the hotel already, so there was no Threshold Barrier. And we only put one piece of promotional literature in each envelope.

So the action points do not have to be numerous. The key to success is not to overwhelm potential customers with saturation bombing so that the sheer weight of bombs might hit *one* target.

Over the years of studying this I am quite sure that the only successful approach is a 'steady drip drip' to remind customers you are there. If you have researched your targets correctly, a planned systematic steady approach produces results, even if the message, sales letter, or sales literature is not very sophisticated. With, say, organizers of functions or local companies booking rooms, all you need do is to contact them perhaps three or four times a year. It may be a letter, followed by a telephone call, followed by a face-to-face situation, followed by a mailing shot. A well-thought-out, steady approach will produce more business.

The whole planning of the approach, action, words and selling should be subdivided between:

1 Past users who have not used you lately
2 Present guests and users of the hotel
3 Potential new additional customers

Why should the approach vary? Firstly, as I have said before, present users need the best servicing as they are with you now, and a follow-up. The first two groups have seen the inside of your hotel and so it is usually pointless 'burdening' them with your very attractive literature on the hotel. A contact must be made with past users as to why they no longer use you, perhaps something went wrong in your hotel before, or they have not held another conference for years but are thinking of one now. Maybe they have moved to one of your competitors but are dissatisfied and thinking of a change. The initial objective is to find out why they no longer use you.

Potential new additional customers are a totally different sales situation. The objective behind any first approach should be research, i.e. find out as much about them and enter it on an index card. A second early objective must be to get them to see the product, i.e. get them into the hotel so that they can see what they are actually buying rather than words on a sheet, or photographs. However, in order to get them to be receptive to an invitation to view the hotel or try it out once, attractive brochures and literature are essential. With potential customers it is a systematic approach of research first, personal visit, letter, telephone call, visit to hotel. Then steady, low key follow-up to the first visit. Finally, regular follow-up.

Here I would like to make a statement about Sales Action Plans which will be elaborated later in the sections on the different sales techniques required to reach the markets. It is as easy to complicate marketing – and selling – as it is to over-simplify it. The objective of all selling is to sustain and increase sales. This is obvious and true: but there are earlier objectives to sales action points.

> 'All sales action points should be aimed at two objectives. To get people face-to-face and get the prospective buyer to visit the hotel and view its facilities.'

All mailing shots, sales letters, paid and unpaid advertising must have these objectives in mind. At some point they must create an actual contact between people, i.e. the prospective customer and some member of the hotel's staff. Advertising agents often talk as if placing paid advertising is an end in itself. Some sales people 'hide' behind sending out the most attractive, expensive literature. But the real selling starts when two people meet, even though initially it may follow an incoming telephone call from the prospective buyer or an outgoing telephone call from you, or one of your staff. And the vast majority of buyers will want to see the product first.

WORD OF MOUTH PUBLICITY

There was a time in Europe when selling was not quite respectable, although I never encountered this attitude when I worked in the States. In Europe they will boast that 'my son is a doctor' or 'a lawyer' but keep quiet if he is a salesman. This attitude has nearly changed in Europe. I found no inhibition about selling when I was in India, but a decided feeling in some African countries that top executives should not have to sell.

I think it was Robert Louis Stevenson who said 'everyone lives by selling something'.

Although most hoteliers in the world are totally committed to marketing and selling, there are significant numbers who still say, 'The best form of selling is word of mouth'.

This is correct. But the trouble with it is that it is too slow. You cannot rely on it in these times of inflation, rising costs, and weaker markets, particularly if your competitor hotels are quietly out there selling to your present customers. Word of mouth is vitally important. Conversely one bad meal will often do more damage by word of mouth than fifty good meals. People take a good meal for granted but complain like mad to their friends about a bad meal. It wouldn't be so bad if they complained to the hotelier, or restaurateur, because a complaint is one of the best forms of market research you can get. But too often they leave close-mouthed and stiff-lipped to spread the news of that disastrous meal, like Moses descending from Mount Sinai to spread the news of the Ten Commandments.

I know of one famous hotelier who ran a fairly average hotel which was famous for its superb functions. I asked him one day what was the main cause of his high reputation for functions.

He looked at me, smiled and said that he went and sat in the toilets!

This manager was convinced that when he asked the function organizers whether everything was satisfactory he never really got a true answer. His theory was that it is a series of small points which make the difference between an average function and a superb one. He felt if it was something major like cold food, or slow service, he or his banqueting manager would spot it. So about ten years earlier he started to sit in the toilet, with a pen and notepad, at the point after every meal when a lot of men went to the toilet. He found that a lot of men asked each other 'What did you think of the meal?' And he picked up so many useful tips and ideas that he began to do this on a sample basis of one out of every five functions. He also got an assistant manageress to do the same in the ladies toilet where she dressed the same as guests at the banquet. Now you may think this true story is funny or perhaps frivolous, but this manager swears it was the key to his success in curing negative comments.

Where you rely on positive word of mouth publicity how can you encourage this and expand the potential? One way is to make sure that people know and *remember* your name, address and telephone number. All hotels use word of mouth publicity even if they are very active in other kinds of selling or they do no other forms of selling, except possibly subconsciously.

What I have found is that a significant number of people cannot remember the name of the hotel or restaurant. There are many well known hotels where people will never forget the name. And the same applies to many well known restaurants. But there are many more hotels and restaurants which are very good, but not household names. I am sure that a significant proportion of their guests and customers forget the name the second they leave. If what I am saying is true, then a large proportion of word of mouth publicity is lost.

People have often said to me that they have just been on their annual package tour holiday to Spain, Jamaica or Paris and the hotel was great. And I ask the name but they cannot remember, although they can always tell you the name of the tour operator. My wife's parents go on a series of short break coach holidays in Britain which they thoroughly enjoy. I always ask them what was the hotel and food like. In many cases they rarely know if the hotel is part of a national group, which invariably it is.

A number of times people say they had 'a superb meal in that Italian restaurant in St. Martin's Lane' or 'a really good Chinese meal in Soho'. And recently a man and his wife said they thought the best steaks were at the Berni Inn they go to in the Aldwych, or was it a Schooner Inn, they asked each other? No, it must have been a Garners Steak House, they said. Eventually it turned out to be the Angus Steak House in the Aldwych.

How can one really 'exploit' the potential of word of mouth publicity if the unpaid publicist for your hotel and restaurant may forget the name? Basically I find only three situations where a person can remember a name *for some time* and therefore talk about it for some time, and I am including world famous names like The Plaza, New York, or international chains like Trust House Forte or Travelodge.

Firstly people remember a name if it is the name of a person, e.g. Joe Allen in Covent Garden. Secondly, they remember a name if it is associated with the theme of the decor of the location, e.g. The

Greenhouse in Mayfair, or The Swan at Thames Ditton. But if these two points do not apply, a much higher proportion of word of mouth publicists are going to name your hotel and restaurant to their friends or business colleagues if you give them something to take away with the name on it, or follow them up with some message in the post. It could be the hotel brochure, book matches (although these have a limited life), sewing kits, shower caps, promotion on the forthcoming Christmas activities, or just a follow up letter thanking them and 'hope to see you again.' It doesn't matter what it is as long as they have something to remind them of you which is useful and has your name (and telephone number) on it.

By doing this you are going to obtain much better results from your word of mouth publicity. You have them in your own hotel or you have seen them in other hotels. There are masses of simple ideas which do not cost a lot of money. I favour giving people a copy of your menu, if they want one, to take away. Menus are often expensive because the print run is short. Why not use menus for promotional purposes outside the restaurant by having a large print run and giving them away?

But two 'original' long lasting ideas I would like to tell you about must help word of mouth publicity. At the Konover Hotel in Miami Beach I met a man with one of the most unique life stories I have ever heard, the owner, Harold Konover. But his life is another story. He gave me, not the usual pen with the hotel's name on it, but a pen you fix to the side of your telephone. It is still there after three years. Every time I need a pen when I am on the telephone, I pick up Harold Konover's pen and see the hotel name and telephone number.

One of the most successful independent British hotel owners and operators is, in my opinion, David Levin of The Capital Hotel, Basil Street, Knightsbridge. When he opened another restaurant, The Greenhouse in Mayfair, he gave away a packet with a seed and instructions on how to plant it in a pot. It grew into a long lasting attractive plant. And all the time stuck in the earth was a small sign with the plant's Latin name and The Greenhouse telephone number. People ask about the plant and it promotes the restaurant. I have recommended numerous people to that restaurant by word of mouth when people started talking about the plant first.

To sum up, word of mouth publicity is essential but should be one part of the total action plan, should never be relied on solely, and even word of mouth benefits can be increased with the right kind of marketing. The real, essential message is shown in Figure 10.1.

Figure 10.1

TARGETS

The checklists on Sales Action Plans include fixing targets and monitoring actual results against targets. An overall target, or budget Profit and Loss Account as an overall yardstick of results is essential not just for marketing purposes but also for cost control and forecasting cash flow – which is absolutely essential nowadays.

However, I have found that the overall generalized targets of increased sales do *not* really work effectively in helping to build an effective sales action plan. As an example, a target to increase sales overall by 5 per cent, or a target increase of 10 per cent on room sales and 15 per cent on food and beverage sales, may be fine as a broad yardstick but it does not really help the team of staff measure exactly how they are achieving results in the terms they can identify with. Therefore it is far better to break the targets down into actual number of rooms and covers. Once again, the set of targets need not be complicated and could be quite simple. Some examples are as follows. A seasonal hotel had this pattern of occupancy with 102 rooms:

	Room occupancy %	*Target* %
January	Closed	Closed
February	Closed	Closed
March	Closed	30
April	60	70
May	60	70
June	70	90
July	100	100
August	100	100
September	70	80
October	50	60
November	Closed	Closed
December	Closed	Closed
Average	42.5%	50%

If you say to a sales executive, some operating managers and most staff that the target is to increase occupany by 'x' per cent per night, on average they will agree but not be able to come to grips with it. But if you say, we must sell ten more rooms every night in June, no more in July, just maintain full occupancy, then this is far easier to understand.

The target in this case was not given to staff as increasing the occupancy by 7.5% to 50 per cent, but was (a) to open two weeks earlier in March and (b) close at the end of October rather than the third week in October and (c) to sell the following additional rooms *more* than last year:

	Extra no. of rooms
March (open 2 weeks)	60
April	10
May	10
June	20
July	—
August	—
September	10
October (open 4 weeks)	—

Other indications of targets might be as follows:

1 Sell four more rooms every Monday to Wednesday night at $70 per room

2 Sell ten more rooms every Thursday night at $70 per night

3 Increase midweek double occupancy from present average of 30 per cent to 40 per cent by selling six more rooms per night with double occupancy at an extra income of $15 per night as room sales

4 Sell twenty more rooms per night over the three weekend nights at double occupancy at $55 per night

5 Sell thirty more conferences per year gathering together on Sunday night for five nights leaving Friday at an average size of sixty delegates.

The foregoing are illustrations of how a target can be set for selling extra rooms which create a calculable amount of extra sales, but are not initially set as target *amounts*. With extra rooms sold, some at single and others at double occupancy, it is not difficult to estimate the additional food and beverage sales resulting therefrom. Virtually all of the bedroom guests will have breakfast, the conference delegates probably two meals a day, and the weekenders one or two meals depending on how inclusive the terms are. Past average spends on drinks will provide an indication of target bar and wine sales arising from the additional bedroom guests.

Then other targets might be set for Food and Beverage Sales:

1 Sell ten extra covers at lunch at an average spend of $20 on food and $5 on drinks

2 Sell fifteen extra covers in the evening at an average spend of $25 on food and $10 on drinks

3 Attract fifteen weddings on Saturdays more than last year, bring total to thirty-five weddings with sixty people at each, average spend $20 on food and $15 on drinks

4 Sell forty-five more functions at an average size of 100 covers at $26 per cover food and $14 on drinks

I have seen overall targets for every aspect of a hotel and for every period of the year. Others just cover two or three key aspects which they are going to concentrate on in the coming sales period. Naturally, in practice no one ever achieves these targets exactly. But it does create a greater sense of urgency, and provides a better sense of direction to break targets down into rooms, covers, desserts, brandies, bottles of wine sold, etc., rather than an overall target sales increase. This type of target setting is more easily understood by heads of departments and staff – and therefore more easily achievable.

The main techniques in reaching potential target customers are covered in later sections of this book. Other aspects which are really part of a sales action plan but for convenience's sake are included in separate chapters are:

In-house Selling
Management Reporting for Marketing.

* * * * *

11

INCREASING IN-HOUSE SALES

Part of every Sales Action Plan should be a systematic set of actions required to increase income from *existing* guests and customers using the hotel. I must emphasize that I am not talking about a hard-sell situation where the customer is virtually forced to spend more money with you than he is inclined to, but about increasing sales quite honestly and legitimately because the customer genuinely wants to spend money.

However bad business is and even where *average* occupancies are low, there are still many nights in a year when a hotel is full and business is being turned away. On these peak 100 per cent occupancy nights the only way the hotelier can increase sales is by selling more to existing guests. When a hotel or restaurant is not fully booked it is possible to increase sales by selling outside the hotel and selling within the hotel. There are primarily two aspects of selling which should concern hoteliers:

1 Selling *outside* the hotel to past, present and potential customers by mailing shot, letter, advertising, telephone call and personal visit
2 Selling *within* the hotel to existing overnight guests, restaurant customers, bar customers and people attending functions, i.e. in-house selling.

The two aspects are inter-related. This chapter deals with the second, namely in-house selling, although many of the techniques mentioned in following chapters are applicable to both, e.g. on face-to-face selling, being consumer orientated, etc. Increasing in-house sales is probably one of the easiest methods to tackle and could produce very quick results. You may agree as you read this, because you have seen so many missed opportunities to sell in *other* hotels, but some readers may think it does not apply to their own hotel.

Quite often if you say to a hotel owner or hotel general manager that he could improve sales within the hotel he takes offence. This applies to other people's hotels, not their own. The higher you climb in the organization, the more you find this attitude applies, particularly to directors and managing directors of a group of hotels.

It is most important that directors and senior executives of hotels and hotel groups realize that they get special service even if they do not ask for it. It happens when they eat in the restaurant, pick up the telephone, use room service. I have never had a meal with a client in his hotel when we have not been offered a brandy or liqueur after the meal. But I have sometimes had a meal in the same restaurant on my own (usually the night before) and not been offered a drink at the end of the meal.

Many hotels nowadays have a plan of action for selling *outside* the hotel. There is usually a considerable concentration of time, thought, energy and action on this. But often there is less of a planned approach and activity in selling in-house. I once worked in one of the largest American hotel groups who had systemized every aspect of the hotel in a very dynamic fashion. Everything had been thought through, planned and systemized. They had covered everything – sales, food control, hygiene, cleaning bedrooms – you name it, they had covered it. They even had systemized the recovery of cutlery from swill bins where they did not have industrial waste disposal. But there was one gap in the total system. There was no planned system for in-house selling, and we were asked to produce one.

We have to ask ourselves a number of questions, e.g.

1 Why is it that so many hotel guests (who are not on inclusive terms) eat outside the hotel?
2 How often does a waiter come up to you (in someone else's hotel) and ask 'Would you like a dessert?' or 'Would you like to see the dessert trolley?'
3 Why are the sales on anything displayed visually in the restaurant higher than other very exciting dishes written as words on a menu?
4 Why do many visitors to a hotel for the first (and sometimes the second) time experience difficulty in finding their way around?
5 Why is it that so few people attending evening functions stay the night in the hotel when they are tired and may have had a fair amount to drink?
6 How many times have you felt like another drink but did not have one because the barman or waiter did not ask you?

Often the answers are because we haven't thought out and planned our in-house selling systematically. But is it worth it? After all, why bother to try to increase in-house sales when there are so many other pressing problems. Is it really that significant? If a moderately sized hotel with sales of $2 million per annum was to sell $4 extra goods or services to each of its residents (approximately 40,000) it could expect to make an increased net profit contribution of about $60,000 to $80,000. These extra sales have a high profit proportion as they only incur material costs but very little other direct or indirect costs.

Although at first sight the objective of $4 extra sales *per* resident might appear high it can be achieved by a multitude of methods, for example:

- a large brandy
- a third of a bottle of wine
- 10 per cent increase in residents eating in the restaurant
- one resident in twenty making a repeat or referral booking
- one resident in ten booking a room for double occupancy
- a combination of these and many others

And this ignores additional sales (and profit) by persuading more restaurant customers to have an aperitif, or a dessert from the trolley, or an extra vegetable. If one moderately sized hotel can increase net profit by $80,000, a group of twenty-five hotels could achieve $2 million *increased net profits*. But how can these extra sales objectives be realized?

HOW DO WE ACHIEVE IT?

There are two inter-related methods of increasing sales to customers and obtaining repeat or referrral business (both for rooms and beverage sales)

- In-house selling
- Customer satisfaction

Customer satisfaction can arise not only from the quality of the products but also from the customer's knowledge that the product is available if he so desires – for example, leisure facilities or room service, which are considered a 'plus' for a hotel even if that customer does not use them. Customer satisfaction and consequent repeat/referral business can be aided by imparting a knowledge of all the products and services available in the unit. In-house selling may be defined as promoting a sale by informing the consumer of the variety of products and services available and the benefits and advantages of using these products and services.

This tends to exclude any forms of 'hard' selling.

Unfortunately – but if you think about it, naturally – it is difficult for hotel operators and staff to achieve maximum efficiency with in-house selling. They have *complete* knowledge of their services and products, so consequently often overestimate the knowledge of their customers. Traditionally, in-house selling has been considered on an area by area basis – bars, restaurants, rooms, etc.; but because the customer is not fixed in any one area – a bar customer may also become a restaurant customer – it is more logical to plan in-house selling by looking at it from the customer's point of view, i.e. to have empathy.

In order to monitor the effectiveness of selling techniques and materials, and logically plan ways of making improvements, the first step is to view the unit as a first time potential customer – and better still to enlist help in identifying in-house selling problems from someone who is not familiar with the unit. Look at the unit as a whole and ask the questions; to *Whom* can be sold *What* and *Where* – the three W's.

For example, residents checking in can be sold use of the restaurant at reception. When all the possible sales opportunities have been identified, the sales methods can be devised – the question *How*? For example, how can use of the restaurants be sold at reception to residents – by the receptionist enquiring whether she can make a table reservation, by having a copy of the menu at reception, by having a special promotion poster on the reception wall, etc.

After some work a complete list of sales opportunities and methods of maximizing them will appear in the form:

To Whom	• for example, potential customers, inside/outside the hotel, residents, bar customers, etc.
What	• the various products/services offered
Where	• the location of the sales opportunities, e.g. reception, bedrooms, car parks, etc.
How	• the method and technique of achieving the sale.

From this list it is now practical to break the methods and techniques down into sales handbooks or action checklists for each department/area under the headings:

PHYSICAL

Informative Signs – the products and services available (including photographs and other visual aids)

Directional Signs – to where the various products and services are located in that area and to where other facilities in the unit are located

Displays – (i) Menus, tariffs, etc.
(ii) Brochures, etc.
(iii) Physical displays – food, drinks, etc.

Posters and other temporary promotional material

Tent cards and other small promotional material

Giveaways

Hotel Information Packs and Service Directories

Miscellaneous – including guests bills, advance reservations, etc.

and the absolutely vital:

PERSONAL

Sales techniques, face-to-face selling and relevant sales aids.

Action check lists may be produced for all the 'physical' methods and specific responsibility delegated to various members of the staff to monitor their effectiveness, on a regular basis. Action points can be agreed for each day, or meal period. The 'personal' methods are the responsibility of all staff in customer contact positions. These staff can be motivated to sell in a variety of ways, amongst them a mixture of:

- Financial incentive: linked to the achievement of sales targets
- Training: which should be continuous
- Job responsibility
- And, of course management leadership and the right 'atmosphere'.

In improving personal selling we are not necessarily talking about the same thing as improving social skills. If one achieved both this would be great. But it is possible to train staff to sell more without a high level of social skills.

There are some main points to avoid and main success points if you are to obtain steady, sustained improvements from in-house selling. These are as follows:

1 Firstly, many hoteliers try to increase in-house sales in one department only, or in one at a time. This is usually a mistake. Every employee can influence sales in most other departments in an indirect, if not a direct, way.
2 Some hoteliers carry out an initial 'blitz' approach. Obviously any planned systematic approach requires a 'launch'. But the action programme must make a steady continuous impact on staff firstly, and through them on to customers.
3 A detailed systematic plan of action has to be prepared first subdivided into sections, clearly showing who does what and when.

In preparing a simple but systematic action plan on in-house selling it is vital to obtain ideas and suggestions from staff and involve them from the very commencement of preparing the action plan. When the action points are listed, employees will require training and motivating to ensure that they actually do carry out the various points.

It is important not to 'overburden' staff by expecting them to remember too much. Highly skilled waiters or receptionists may be able to remember a series of sales points and in fact many of them will do so by training or instinct. But we are tending to employ more and more people in hotels who are keen and motivated, but not necessarily highly skilled. My experience is that if the number of sales points are too ambitious, either staff will do nothing, or they will rattle them off like a robot.

It is far better to motivate and train staff to cover one or two sales points successfully. Thus, a young receptionist may just try to sell a seat in the restaurant as a guest is checking in, or just ask whether the guest will be coming back to the area shortly and whether they can reserve a room as the guest is checking out. In one hotel (where reception and cash desk were combined) management, in an excess of enthusiasm, tried to get the receptionist to book guests in for their next trip if they were going to another area where they had a hotel, to hand them the weekend holiday brochure, as well as dealing with the settlement of the account. Obviously this was too much, and it is far better to stick to one point at a time. Similarly with waiters and waitresses it is far more effective if the action plans set them the objective of selling one thing at the start of the meal and one nearer the end, rather than a whole series of points throughout the meal.

All that is necessary is to sit down with a small team in each department, get everyone to think of themselves as a customer and list the sales opportunities on paper. You will find there is quite a formidable list and you will have to concentrate them into a manageable shorter priority list of action points. Start outside the hotel as customers and slowly walk into the hotel noting the opportunities to sell and whether you are missing them.

Bad signposting annoys people and creates an additional threshold barrier. You know your way round the hotel and therefore cannot notice if signposting is confusing. This animal (the customer) is entering a strange cave for the first time. On the exterior he appears confident. But deep down he is in strange territory where he is going to eat and sleep. He is away from home (his own cave) and entering someone else's cave. He is slightly tense and in some hotels the concierge or head doorman just stares at him. You can always tell the first time visitor by his posture (which is often slightly aggressive) and because his head will move from side to side. I am not exaggerating the situation. Bad signposting will make your first time visitor feel more insecure, more aggressive and quite understandably annoyed with this ******!! hotel. I spent a week in one hotel in Scotland which had a number of bars but I could not find the cocktail bar. I refused to ask where it was, convinced I would find it by using logic. On the last evening I gave in and asked the manager. He explained that as you walked down the stairs (there was no lift) a large pillar blocked the entrance to the bar and the sign. He said he would show me where it was and buy me a drink. We entered the cocktail bar at 7 p.m. and there was only one other person in there – the barman. All the other bars were busy.

This is not an isolated situation. If you raise this topic with a group of hotel users they will confirm this. The thing to do is take a first time visitor who has booked into the hotel and offer him a free meal, or something, if he will do a critique on your signposting. Then do the same with a first time visitor to the restaurant and then one attending a function for the first time. Ask them a short series of questions as they leave (e.g. did you know we had meeting rooms?) and you will have many of the answers to improve your signposting.

Many hoteliers have really attractive signs, tent cards and posters. But sometimes they are in the wrong place. All you need is empathy and watching your guests. Where do they wait, stand, what do they look at? There are still many hotel bedrooms where the sales literature, restaurant menu, etc. is in an expensive attractive folder – but placed out of sight in a drawer. Where should a key sales message be placed? Possibly just a simple message, not with the whole restaurant menu, but just a mouthwatering speciality of the house – where should you put it? There are a number of places but here are just three:

1 Designed to fit over the telephone dial
2 On the television top, but also visible if a guest in lying on the bed
3 On the bathroom mirror.

These are three areas where people will look. Keep the message simple like 'We have lobster on the menu tonight, dial 108 to reserve a table'.

Follow this procedure through other areas. Most hotels have lifts (elevators). People stand and wait outside them. And they wait inside them. So most hotels have photographs of the restaurant(s) and menus in the lifts. But where are they in most lifts? At the back and sides. And where do most people face when they stand in the lift with other people? They tend to look forward. And what do they stare at? Usually the floor numbers. So why not design the promotional message to go just underneath or alongside the floor numbers.

The first client who took this point up was Peter Catesby, the dynamic managing director of Swallow Hotels in Britain and the then general manager Alan Blenkinsop of The Swallow Hotel, Newcastle upon Tyne, who put a simple message alongside the lift numbers promoting their fish speciality. Alan told me it was very successful.

Previously I have mentioned the need to remove little things that irritate customers. Here is another small but significant problem-solving idea where you do not have a full announcement system or pageboys. Nothing is more annoying than returning from a restaurant or pool area to find you have missed an important telephone call. Figure 11.1 shows an idea that John Xydas, General Manager of the Palm Beach Hotel in Lanarca, Cyprus, has introduced for guests.

It is self-explanatory. A simple idea which shows guests you have thought about *their* problems. I saw this card when I spoke at a conference at the hotel of the Cyprus Hotel Association in 1986. Often success is a series of small points like this.

The car park is one of the least utilized areas for in-house selling – if you can call a car park 'in-house'. This point is discussed further in Chapter 12. In Britain where the hotel does not have its own car park it is usually possible to pin-point where visitors to the hotel park their cars. Promotional literature can be placed under the windscreen wiper and a very high proportion of drivers will read it.

On improving guest satisfaction for a number of my clients with a car-driving market, the hotelier arranges for a member of staff to clean the front and back windows so that a guest notices this after breakfast. Usually a small sticker is put on the windscreen saying:

> In order to help you have a safe journey we have cleaned your front and rear windows. See you again soon.
>
> The Caring Motor Hotel

In other hotels the night porter listened to the early travel news and the night receptionist or night auditor typed out a summary, duplicated it, and copies were placed on guests' tables at breakfast with details of road blackspots, train and plane delays, if any.

These ideas always result in considerable goodwill without enormous investment in money.

The most effective kind of in-house selling is face to face – 'Would you like a brandy or liqueur?'. But face to face selling is not always

WHERE ARE YOU?

Expecting a telephone call or a visitor? By filling in this form we will know where to locate you.
Please deposit it at the Reception.
Thank you

Name ________________

Room Number ________

Palm Beach Bar ☐
Swimming Pool ☐
Beach Bar ☐
On the Beach ☐
Coffee Shop ☐
Restaurant ☐
Lounge ☐
Out of Hotel
Returning at: ________

PALM BEACH HOTEL

Figure 11.1

possible, i.e. when the guest is in his/her bedroom. I have tried a soft sell telephone call shortly after a guest checks in (which in many business hotels is between 5 p.m. and 7 p.m.) welcoming them and suggesting the restaurant for dinner. This can be very effective but requires training – in telephone selling. Some hoteliers feel this is too much like a hard sell.

One of the most effective in-house selling ideas I have used is an envelope under the door. It just has to be read. It should always be short, personalized, with a number to dial to book a table, or reserve for a special evening. I have known nearly a 100 per cent response to a simple sales message in an envelope under the guest's bedroom door.

As mentioned earlier in this chapter, it is far easier to produce a plan on in-house selling and put it into action, than action on selling outside the hotel. All that is required is a little time, a logical approach and empathy. The plan should create an awareness amongst your customers of the benefits and advantages of the various services and products you have available, and give them the maximum opportunity to buy. It does not have to be a hard sell. A planned systematic approach to increasing in-house sales could really provide the opportunity for increases in your profit levels *and* improve customer satisfaction at the same time.

* * * * *

12

INCREASING RESTAURANT SALES

TEN COMMANDMENTS

Various sections in this book cover improving sales in restaurants with points on preparing sales action plans, improving food and alcohol sales, in-house selling and comments on pricing structures. Since the first edition was published a considerable number of people have asked for a specific chapter on restaurant sales, particularly for restaurants which are not part of an hotel. This chapter has been included covering the subject. It should not be read in isolation from the rest of the book if a restaurateur wishes to obtain maximum advantage.

It is emphasized that the points are generally equally applicable to restaurants within hotels, except perhaps hotels where there is no 'outside' trade and the restaurant is there purely to service guests spending the night in the hotel. Where the rate charged to guests basically includes all meals, then some aspects of this chapter would not be appropriate. However, the trend is more towards a bed and breakfast situation even in many tourist resorts. In 1985 I was asked to run a top management course for the Dan Hotel Group which is one of the finest hotel groups in Israel. The group includes certain famous hotels like the Dan Hotel in Tel Aviv and the King David Hotel in Jerusalem. The course was for Head Office Executives, Hotel General Managers and Sales Executives and included a number of sessions on preparing sales action plans and on sales techniques. Mr Ami Federman, the General Manager of the hotel group, asked me whether I would include a short session specifically on restaurants. Because of pressure for time I had to basically cover what was a very extensive subject in one hour.

I realized that I could summarize most of the key points on increasing restaurant sales in a kind of Ten Commandments. If every restaurant could follow these Ten Commandments, or the majority of them, sales would definitely increase and so would profits. The Ten Commandments are set out in Figure 12.1

TEN COMMANDMENTS FOR INCREASING RESTAURANT SALES

1 Define catchment areas for different meal periods – lunch, dinner, midweek, weekend.

2 Write down quiet, medium and busy periods.

3 Improve in-house selling.

4 Build up mailing lists within catchment areas – visiting cards, local firms.

5 Periodically remind them you are there and you want their business.

6 Produce newsletter/mailing shot.

7 Prepare action plan for quieter periods – try selling something very expensive first.

8 Pay particular attention to first time visitors and regulars' guests.

9 Use names.

10 Say something when they leave.

Figure 12.1

It would be very easy to start writing a complete new book on this one subject, but this is not the intention. Rather, the aim is to make key points so that time-sensitive hotel and restaurant owners and executives can read them and start to act fairly immediately. An elaboration on the various points is as follows:

1 *Catchment areas and customer profiles*
Very few restaurants think sufficiently about the catchment area where their customers come from and that this can differ substantially between lunch, dinner, midweek, and weekend, and sometimes days of the weekend. Knowing the catchment area, how far customers have come, how they came, the time it took them to get there, are all critical factors in deciding where to send your future mailing shots or choosing the right media for your advertising.

It is vitally important for the restaurant owner and his regular staff to sit down periodically and think about their guest profile. Who spends money in their restaurant, age group, sex, executives, etc. Again this can differ between the different meal periods, days of the week and time of the year.

I used to think that an essential quality for hotel and restaurant management is 'to like people'. I now no longer think this is the case, although if hotel and restaurant managers dislike people generally they will never be successful. The quality I feel people need more is 'curiosity'. Every time a 'strange' new customer arrives in the restaurant, the restaurant manager should have his curiosity aroused in order to find out much more about them. You do not have to interrogate them, but it is quite easy to welcome them, find out why they chose the restaurant, perhaps they have just moved their company to the area, and a series of other important things which could help in future marketing. Even if the restaurateur does not live in the catchment area it is vital that he/she purchases local newspaper(s) in order to gather clues on who is moving to the area, expanding etc.

2 *Quiet, medium and busy periods*

The various activity periods should be thought about and discussed. It is very useful to write these periods down and even to do so for each meal period. Some restaurants have a pattern in each meal period which has a plateau effect, others more a triangular mountain. Some are busy all the time but others are surprisingly quiet up until a peak busy time. So the restaurant can always look busy and yet may have a period of, say, 45 minutes when very little is going on.

Defining these quiet and busy periods is essential in sales promotion. The busy periods should not be neglected, but normally there is less of a need to promote the periods which automatically tend to get busy. Promoting the quiet periods can also be a waste of time, effort and money *unless* the product is changed completely in some way. Usually the most cost effective periods to promote are the medium periods.

3 *Improve in-house selling*

This is dealt with quite separately in Chapter 11. Often there is not a systematic plan for in-house selling and training staff. In an hotel restaurant this does not have the same significance because the hotel restaurant's profit is not a very high proportion of the total hotel's profits. This is not to say that in-house selling in hotel restaurants should not be carried out, but only that in a completely separate restaurant divorced from a hotel, improved in-house selling can literally double or treble bottom line profits.

4 *Building up mailing lists*

Experience has shown me that promotion through mailing lists to past customers and potential customers within a defined catchment area is absolutely essential. Some restaurateurs with up-market restaurants have said to me that this lowers the tone. I do not believe that this is the case and will depend very much on the mailing shot used in my Sixth Commandment. The mailing list can be produced from existing City and Sales Ledger Accounts and people and companies who have a credit facility, and by researching the area to pin-point the names of key potential customers and their companies and organizations. Remember that in many organizations there are two people to include on the mailing list. There is the person who actually makes the booking and the person who comes along to eat, as they may not be the same person.

One very successful method of building up a mailing list is to put tent cards on the tables and the cocktail bar area running a kind of competition. The idea is to suggest to visitors that if they want to be included for future news, special evenings etc., would they like to drop their visiting card into the box near the exit. I have seen many restaurants build up a sizeable mailing list in this way. But I have seen an even larger list develop when a kind of draw is held once a week or month from the visiting cards and the lucky person gets a free bottle of champagne or some other complimentary gift. The mailing list does not have to be extensive and, in fact, I have seen a well thought out list of only 50 names which is used regularly for promotions in the future. Even this low number can produce very successful results, although usually the list should include over 100 names for a more expensive restaurant and thousands for a lower-priced restaurant.

5 *Remind them that you are there and you want their business*

There is no doubt in my own mind that customers do not look upon the right kind of mailing shot as a hard sell situation. They want to know that you are doing things differently. They want to be warned (or reminded) that they should book early for the Christmas entertaining period or some other busy time of the year. They like to be told about special evenings. But above all my experience is that by sending these mailing shots you are showing that you want their business. I am convinced that psychologically everyone however important likes to be liked, and likes to feel wanted.

6 *Produce a newsletter/mailing shot*
The way you remind customers that you want their business can vary. Sometimes it could be a straightforward letter. But, if it is, the letter should always be personalized with the full correct name and title of the recipient. It could be that you just use the mailing list for a Christmas Card. There are two most effective forms of mailing. Firstly, one which gives advance knowledge of some change in menu or special week (a French week) or Mother's Day. Secondly, a chatty type newsletter which also has some news about food, wines or something related to the restaurant business. My experience, time and time again, is that a well thought out and presented newsletter sent to a mailing list about three times a year can be instrumental in obtaining extra business.

Promotional literature about restaurants (and hotels) tend to be read more extensively and kept longer than promotional literature about other consumer products like a new copier or a computer. Nowadays everyone seems to be interested in food and wine. My research shows that a higher proportion of people read a newsletter from a local restaurant than many other forms of sales literature. I have found that after a mailing of approximately 100 local business executives carried out three times a year that about 40 per cent read every page of a four-page newsletter, around 60 per cent read parts of it but nearly 90 per cent of recipients remembered receiving it one month after it had been distributed.

Often secretaries are told to throw away promotional literature, but asked to keep anything considered to be 'personal'. Research over a number of years has shown that the secretary will often show her boss a newsletter from a restaurant when she has thrown away all the other sales promotional literature.

7 *Prepare action plan for quieter periods*
Chapter 10 of this book sets out fairly detailed procedures for preparing sales action plans covering every department in an hotel. These action plans are equally applicable to a commercial restaurant, which is not part of an hotel. The preparation of an action plan is outlined later in this chapter.

Restaurants tend to have peaks and troughs with some very busy times of the year and other quiet parts of the year. Often there are certain days or periods in the week which are really quiet, others which are fairly busy and certain days and meal periods which tend to peak. A considerable amount of advertising and promotion just brings in business when the restaurant would be full anyhow, so the sales action plan should be clearly divided between the very quiet times of the day, week or year, the quieter periods (what I call the shoulder periods) and the peak periods. What often happens is that in order to fill the very quiet periods, restaurateurs try to put on something which is reduced in price or a special kind of offer. I have tried this and often it does not make a lot of difference. If people are not going to go out and eat on a Monday night they are still not going to go out just because the price is reduced. The only major exception I would make to this comment is where you can attract larger groups of people like families, rather than one person or a couple going out to eat (Sunday lunch or brunch is often a family affair with four or more people going out to eat).

What I have often found can be successful is to go to the other extreme and produce something (say on a dead Monday night) which is very up-market or unusual at a higher price, but still very good value for money. People will go out to eat even on a 'dead' night of the week if there is something special on and this does not have to be something which is cheap. A special gourmet evening, or an ethnic evening will often be more successful. If the size of the problem is that on a quiet evening an attempt is going to be made to sell 50 covers at say $15, it is often easier to sell only 25 covers at $30. So my advice is always to test selling something more expensive *first* over a period. Do not try it for just one week but over a period because it will take some four to six weeks to test the reaction to a new idea.

8 *Pay particular attention to first time visitors and regulars' guests*
It is very natural for restaurant staff to be friendly and pay particular attention to their regular customer who is entertaining someone else, because they know him (or her), that person is going to sign the check (bill) and leave the tip. But on the other hand why is it that the regular is entertaining someone? It is usually in order to please them in some way either in a social or very often from a business point of view.

In Chapter 22 I elaborate this point. Basically without neglecting the regular, more attention should be paid to the regular's guest because he/she could well be a major buyer of the regular's products or services, or someone who is socially important.

9 *Use names*
This is so important I have included a separate chapter on this point (Chapter 13). Its significance can never be underrated and therefore it is definitely one of my Ten Commandments.

10 *Say something when they leave*
When someone arrives in a restaurant there is bound to be some kind of verbal communication even if it is just to ask whether they have reserved a table. This opening question can strike a negative tone because there should be a greeting first followed by the question, but often the question is asked first. Normally the person is shown to a table, seated, asked whether he/she wants an aperitif, given the menu and generally fussed over.

When customers have paid their bill they often leave and nothing is said to them. People will often stay for quite some time after settling the bill (when obviously they are thanked). In analysing why restaurants are very successful when others are not there are obviously a whole host of reasons apart from the food and wines being good and value for money. As well as this there are whole series of other small points which make people come back to a restaurant again or make them feel they will never return. One common factor I have found in a series of successful and profitable restaurants is that when a customer leaves, someone from the restaurant staff will say goodbye to them properly at the door or exit.

I can name restaurant after restaurant where this rarely happens. Often the reason is because the kitchen and service area is on the other side of the restaurant away from the entrance and staff, including restaurant management, tend to be drawn towards the kitchen and to other guests. But I can name a number of successful restaurants where whatever happens the owner or restaurant manager will excuse him or herself from a table and go over to the exit when people are leaving in order to help them on with their coats or just to say thank you and goodbye even if they have said this when the bill was being paid. In my favourite Greek restaurant in Britain, the Kouzina in Kingston upon Thames, Surrey, the owner Mr Panos Tsentides or one of his staff will always make sure they say goodbye. And his restaurant is a continuous success story year after year. In many restaurants they pay a lot of attention to you – then take your money and ignore you.

☆ ☆ ☆ ☆ ☆

The Ten Commandments could be extended by many other points which would help to increase restaurant sales and some of them are set out in the following pages.

It is important to obtain free press and media publicity on a continuous planned systematic basis. Many restaurants obtain some 'free' press publicity in their local newspaper if they join in a special wine and dine feature and pay for an advert as well. All the other competitive restaurants obtain a good write-up at the same time. These features are often prepared when all the restaurants are going to be full anyhow, even without any paid advertising, e.g. there is always one in my local paper just before the Christmas entertaining period.

SALES ACTION PLAN

Before producing a Sales Action Plan research is necessary. The type of information which is required in order to make your action plan more effective is as follows:

CHECKLIST 12.1

Profile of customers divided between appropriate times of the year and week

Midweek	–	Lunch
Midweek	–	Dinner
Saturday	–	Lunch
Saturday	–	Dinner
Sunday		

Pattern of activity per meal
(time stamping order dockets and then shuffling them into quarter of an hour periods can help show a pattern)

Length of eating

Seat turnover ratio

Total spend per customer in price brackets

Total spend per bill in price bracket

If hotel divide between outside/resident

Catchment area of present users

Catchment area of potential users

How did they arrive there

How did they hear of you

First time or repeat business

How do they pay (cheque, credit card, cash)

Popularity indices

These various points are elaborated in other chapters. Competition analysis is vital. Many working proprietors of restaurants say they just do not have the time to study competition. If so they are running a business with 'one arm tied behind their back'. Many people tell me the cause of failure in restaurants is lack of capital, rents too high or 'low sales'! But you can trace many failures back to a total ignorance of what is happening within their own catchment area, and very little knowledge of competition. Chefs who run their own restaurants can be the worst offenders. If you cannot visit your competition from time to time then get someone else who is objective to do it – even if you have to pay them. The type of information you should seek is:

CHECKLIST 12.2

List all possible competition and argue about who really is and who is not

Re-do list by
- Price
- Style
- Ethnic
- etc.

Price league tables – total bill (including drinks, service, i.e. everything)

List advantage and limitations of your restaurant compared with them by meal period

Write down main advantages

Examine their pattern of activity. If it varies – why?

Compare menus for style, sales appeal, etc.

People will often avoid launching into even a simple sales action plan because they are overwhelmed by the size of the problem. How do you fill a 60-seat restaurant, or double a seat turnover ratio? A 60-seat restaurant may already be selling 30 covers. You do not have to 'sell' sixty seats but thirty more than you are achieving now. And 30 covers may only mean reaching fifteen decision makers. Improving a seat turnover ratio from 1 to 1.1 could make a difference at the end of the year of $100,000 sales and maybe $60,000 net profit. It could be that the objective is not to increase covers at all but to increase average spends following an in-house sales plan. The target might be to have no increase in food spends but an increase in spends through more beverage sales. Therefore an example of the targets could be:

Increase average spend by:
Food 10 per cent from $20 to $22
Drink 30 per cent from $10 to $13
Total 16.7 per cent from $30 to $35

Increase covers by:

	Covers	*Decisions*
Sunday lunch	18	6
Monday evening	20	10
Lunch midweek 10 per day × 5	50	25
	88	41

The column marked 'Decisions' is basically the number of decision makers. Monday evening and lunch midweek, every decision maker produces two covers on average. Sunday lunch, every decision maker produces an average of three covers each. In this set of objectives the aim is to produce only 41 extra decision makers per week – not a very ambitious target. And yet 41 decision makers going to eat in the restaurant per week could produce an extra $80,000 gross profit. As payroll is often fixed in restaurants, this could equate to an increased net profit of around $60,000. This target increase should be related to the advertising and promotional budgeted expenditure.

A summary of the main aspects of the Sales Action Plan is therefore shown in Checklist 12.3

CLOSED

Restaurants worry me. It concerns me that for many hours in a day restaurants are closed, earning no money, but paying rent and property rates all the time. There is no way in which a restaurant owner can assess how much business he loses when he is closed. My belief is that in many restaurants the loss is much more significant than management imagines. Moreover, by not making the most of hours when a restaurant is open, further opportunities for sales are lost.

CHECKLIST 12.3

SUMMARY OF SALES ACTION PLAN

Periods to promote
Competition for these periods
Financial objectives analysed into covers and average spend
Promotional activity
- Methods of reaching the market
  - paid advertising
  - unpaid publicity
  - mailing shots
  - in-house (tent cards, etc.)
  - telephone

Budget
Timing – of sales activity – short and long term
Who is going to do what
Write down outline of draft plan
Meeting with staff to explain, motivate and obtain their ideas
Use of incentives
Revise and finalize plan

I recently took ten high street restaurants at random when they were closed. Five out of ten had no indication of the time they would be open. My pet hate is the sign 'CLOSED'. That is a negative word. Why can't restaurants say 'Sorry we are closed, but we reopen at 7 p.m.' and add that the speciality tonight is lobster or whatever it happens to be. How much more inviting!

I also checked on that occasion ten restaurants within hotels and found that four had no indication when they opened, although I did find out after reading through the guest literature (which an outside potential customer could not see) that last order times were marked more clearly than opening times!

Apart from avoiding, wherever possible, the use of the word 'closed', particularly when it is unqualified, I recommend a further sales aid to replace yet another deterrent for customers. A small investment of around $250 in a telephone-answering machine would increase sales immediately. I am emphatic about the benefit because I have seen the improvement after one had been installed.

This may sound like random research but recently I decided to take my wife out to eat in Central London on a Sunday. Because a number of restaurants are shut on Sundays, I decided to telephone first. Obviously some were open, but out of the eight which were closed only two had answering machines. When people telephone your restaurant and there is no reply, you don't just lose one booking you create badwill. People get irritated and feel rejected.

All you need is an answerphone machine capable of asking callers to leave their name and telephone number. The recording should state when you are open. Whatever you do don't choose your answering machine just because it is cheap. Buy one which has plenty of time for each incoming message, and preferably with two tapes, so that you can change your pre-recorded message simply and in a matter of seconds.

In the morning you might wish to say when you are opening for lunch. On Saturday night you may wish to change the message to say you are not open on Sunday but will be open on Monday – please don't use that horrible word 'closed'. Nowadays, if you wish, you can buy a machine to transfer an incoming call to another number – another restaurant in a group that is open, or to an hotel reception desk, or a manager's private address.

And now for the evidence. When telephone-answering machines first 'arrived' in Britain, I persuaded a client to use one. He measured an average increase in covers of around 20 per cent. I then spent time thinking about this machine and whether we could 'exploit' its use further. The problem with most advertising and sales promotion is that it often produces business when you are busy already. The key is to sell the quiet meal periods. The restaurant in question was very busy except for the evenings of Monday, Tuesday and Wednesday. My client and I decided not to cut prices. That was the easy way out. A series of specialities were introduced on these three quiet nights and promoted within the restaurant with tent cards and on the answering machine. In fact these specialities were priced higher than existing dishes. There was no paid advertising.

Steadily, within a month, average covers in this 60-seat restaurant, on the three evenings, increased from 32 to 50 covers, without any apparent drop on other evenings. We then included the higher priced specialities at other meal periods and tried further new ideas on the 'quiet' evenings.

In restaurants and hotels you never stop working on sales ideas. Installing a telephone-answering machine could repay the investment within weeks and create an increase in goodwill as well.

BUSINESS ENTERTAINING

Some years ago business entertaining was disallowed in Britain for tax purposes. As a result, a major growth market segment in the hotel and restaurant industry began to decline. For many restaurants this decline was obscured in the evening because of the growth in eating out of private individuals and foreign tourists. But the decline was more marked and much more obvious at midweek lunchtimes, particularly in hotels. There has been a major decline over the past decade, especially when compared with the growth in many other market segments. There is potential for a massive increase in the total size of this market, and therefore in the profits of restaurants and hotels which actively decide to go after it. Here are some thoughts on the market generally.

First, it is wrong to assume that this market is as price sensitive as many people think. The vast majority of executives who are entertaining a potential buyer, or existing customer, are not paying the bill out of their own pockets. They are unlikely to risk ruining a relationship with a customer by saving the odd $5–10.

But this business market is generally very time sensitive. One of the significant social changes in the past decade is that we are short of time, or think we are. We certainly create more pressures. This time sensitivity has led to a growth in fast food, but business executives do not wish to entertain clients or customers in the typical high street fast food operation. Any restaurant which recognizes that business executives may be short of time, and actively does something about it, could greatly increase the covers sold at lunchtime.

One approach would be to explain on the menu that 'in no way do we wish to rush you, but if you are in a hurry, we have prepared a menu where it is possible to provide you with a very good meal – and you can leave the restaurant within an hour, including the time spent paying the bill'. One major problem is that when business executives decide to end the meal and return to their office or factory, they actually wish to leave then, but it can sometimes take 10 minutes or more to obtain the bill, sign it and receive any change or the credit card slip.

I am sure that most restaurateurs could quite easily produce a time sensitive menu – with a choice of, say, three items for each course which in no way lowers standards. It is often reported that executives are no longer eating desserts. I believe that a significant reason for this is not because they do not wish to have a dessert, but because they feel this might take too long – they cannot afford another 15 minutes.

There are many reasons for the success of the carving style

operation. One important reason for its popularity is that the customer can dictate the speed of serving and eating the meal, not some hidden person in the kitchen. I am not advocating that everyone should introduce the carving style operation, but I do believe there is a case for a menu called something like 'A one-hour menu'.

Naturally, there are many other ways of improving the sales from this important market segment. One of them is to remember that most executives who are entertaining a customer are selling. They are certainly creating goodwill and in many cases they are using the meal period to actually sell or put across some major advantages of their product or service. Any restaurant owner who pinpoints his/her major potential spenders and encourages them to use the restaurant staff as, in a sense, part of the salesforce, will find a major increase in his/her business.

As an example, why not suggest to the main big spenders in the restaurant – and the people who have a facility to sign – that if they have a very important client or they are in the middle of a particularly significant negotiation, they should let you know in advance so that you can put yourself out by setting aside the best table for the particular circumstances. It could be that the table with the best view is not what is required, but a quiet table somewhere, so that business can be discussed without the conversation being overheard by customers at tables nearby.

Sometimes you can over emphasize the degree of service to the executive business luncheon. Many executives wait until the coffee and liqueur stage, in order to talk business and make a few key sales points. Unfortunately, at this stage many restaurants keep interrupting the customer by asking repeatedly whether more coffee, brandy, or cigars are required.

I have known some business executives to ask the restaurant specifically to leave them alone for 15 minutes after the coffee has been poured. The customer has been 'softened' up by the meal and the wine and although it is unlikely an executive can actually clinch a deal and get a customer to sign over lunch, this is a very good period to stress the advantages of whatever the executive is selling.

Some of these comments indicate a different emphasis in thinking about this market which could help to improve your sales and profits quite considerably. The main point is that business entertaining is very different to social entertaining and the restaurateur's marketing efforts should reflect this difference.

FIXED-PRICE MENUS

Many people ask me about fixed-price menus – whether to introduce them, should they replace an à la carte menu, should they include both. Here are my thoughts on the subject.

There has been considerable publicity stating the case for fixed-price menus during the last few years. Often, the term prix fixé is used to advocate them as though the French were the inventors of the idea. Many tourist associations have called for their adoption by more restaurants and have described them as 'tourist menus'. And many trade magazines often extolled the virtue of the fixed-price menu. Rarely has there been any debate or discussion on whether they are a good or a bad thing, except by people who advocate them. Those who disagree, or are unsure, have been strangely quiet.

Quite often, the discussion on this subject has been linked to the need for lower-price menus (particularly by tourist boards). Whether to have a fixed-price menu or a more price-sensitive menu, are really two separate subjects. Officially a fixed-price menu is a set meal made up of dishes from the à la carte which prices dishes separately. Some restaurants include half a bottle of wine per person in these menus.

If you have an à la carte menu, even a limited à la carte menu, and you are very successful, there is little point in introducing a fixed-price menu too. It could well have major disadvantages. You could find your average spend per bill decreases and profit declines. You might also find that you are mixing markets, which can sometimes be disastrous in a restaurant. A lot would depend on the size of the restaurant.

I can think of many restaurants with à la carte menus which are extremely successful. By successful I mean looking at the net profit. If there is no indication of a decline in the number of covers, and any down trend in net profit, it seems pointless to introduce a fixed-price menu where the restaurant is full and not very large. Some of the most simple promotional ideas and basic selling will often fill a smaller restaurant.

But, with a larger restaurant which is not full most of the time, there could be advantages in thinking about a fixed-price menu.

As stated before, the first thing a restaurant owner has to do is to analyse his quiet and busy periods. Most restaurants can really subdivide their markets into four or six totally different situations. There is usually a market and business activity midweek at lunch which is different from midweek at dinner, and therefore thinking has to take into account these different markets. You will often find weekends completely different from midweek, and Saturday, again, is different from Sunday. Some restaurants in certain towns have a major change in their market on the day where there is half-day closing. I have seen situations in towns where there is half-day closing, where the restaurant is always packed on this day, and others where it is much quieter.

Where you are extremely busy in these different time periods there is a case for leaving well alone. But if any of these periods are quiet or showing a downward trend, the introduction of a sensibly priced fixed-menu could well have many advantages. The new menu could be for just one of the quieter periods, for example, midweek lunch. It will often attract entirely new business which has never tried the restaurant before.

Although some people think fixed-price menus are always low-price menus, this need not be the case. If you introduce both types of menu, you may well find that your food cost percentage jumps on the introduction of a fixed-price menu, because actual prices are low for portion sizes, and there is a tendency to pre-prepare and have more wastage. Very careful consideration must be given to the food cost of the particular dishes included in the menu.

In periods when there are fewer business executives around, and entertaining is done more on a social basis (for example, Saturday shoppers) the case for a fixed-price menu is fairly overwhelming. If you have a high proportion of executive business, it may be disastrous to go over completely to fixed-price menus. Many business executives trying to sell a major deal or contract aim to flatter their potential customer's ego. When they entertain in a restaurant they do not wish to look 'cheap'. If this is a large market for your restaurant you should keep the à la carte menu, together with the fixed-price menu. After the introduction of the fixed-price menu, a new additional market should be attracted consisting of people who come in for the fixed-price menu, but then choose from the à la carte menu, increasing the average spend above the level of the fixed-price menu.

With a busy restaurateur one major danger is not changing the fixed-price menu regularly. If restaurateurs do not change the fixed-price menus regularly enough, or offer only a very limited choice, executives who eat out with you on a regular basis will suffer 'menu fatigue'. Gradually your market may disappear. Some restaurateurs have a fixed-price menu with a fixed menu which varies every day of the week but is the same main course on the same day every week. This may offer less variety than appears because many executives put aside set days each week to entertain on a regular basis.

Basically the decision to adopt fixed-price menus should not be made because they appear to be 'fashionable' at present, but only if market, food and payroll cost justify their introduction. And remember if you decide to introduce a fixed-price menu you could always try two – one competitively priced and the other higher priced for an anniversary, birthday, celebratory lunch, or that special occasion.

CONCLUSION

> 'Show me a high level of customer conversation and I will show you a successful restaurant.'

When you talk to hoteliers and restaurateurs about increasing restaurant sales and profits, they will place enormous emphasis on food and wines. They will discuss price at length and sometimes portion sizes but always the emphasis is primarily on food. Because most restaurateurs are experts on wine a considerable proportion of the conversation will also be about wines. This is very understandable. But if you talk to the general public on why they go to a particular restaurant they often mention other points. Frequently they hardly mention the food. They rarely mention if there is an extensive wine list.

People often go to a restaurant to see and be seen. Others choose a restaurant because it is private and discreet and they will not be seen. I have heard people say that they like a restaurant where tables are close together. Others prefer tables well spaced out. Many like background music. Others hate it. The best background noise is people talking. Show me a high level of customer conversation and I will show you a successful restaurant.

Time and time again I have heard people say they go to a restaurant because 'they always recognize me'. Many say, 'I like going there because they do not rush me'. Others say it is good because you can get in and out quickly. Many complain about waiting ages for the bill.

Very often people say, 'I go there because there is no annoying cover charge'. Overwhelmingly I find the general public are infuriated by cover charges, except where there is a floor show or music. And yet many restaurants still have them on menus.

In Europe in the summer people will often say 'I go there because they have air conditioning', or because 'we can sit outside'.

Many people say, 'It is good value for money'. But a significant number say, 'I go there because it is expensive!'. It impresses the girlfriend, client or customer. If people talk about price they often say, 'The wines are not terribly expensive'.

In my research I found that more and more women executives said that they go to a particular restaurant because staff treat them the way they would a normal business executive and not automatically assume that they are a wife or a girlfriend when they are entertaining a man.

Many business executives say that they like a restaurant with a lounge area so that they can discuss business beforehand and relax more over the actual meal.

People who are not in our business will comment about the food. But many do not. If they do it is often, 'They have some unusual dishes.'

I am not trying to downgrade the role of food and wine in a restaurant because obviously this would be ludicrous. What I am emphasizing is that in order to promote restaurants more effectively it is necessary to promote and sell other things as well as food and wine. Successful restaurants really sell atmosphere or ambience. About 20 years ago when I was working in America I was told the success of a restaurant was related to the height of the ceiling. A well known food service expert who had personally made a fortune out of restaurants said 'low ceilings mean high profits'. Over the years I have only found this to be correct in certain market conditions and primarily in the evening. I have seen many very successful profitable restaurants in Europe and other countries where there are high ceilings and an air of spaciousness even though, quite obviously, energy and maintenance costs are going to be higher.

In Europe we totally underestimate the need for good car parking on the basis that this is always a problem so why bother. If the customer is really keen he will park somehow even if this is on a yellow line. And yet many restaurants in the United Kingdom could increase the number of cars in their parking areas with just the expenditure of some white paint for the car parking spaces. I have seen the number of cars increase by up to 30 per cent where a restaurant has drawn white parking lines in their car park.

There is one idea that I guarantee will make your restaurant's profits increase and yet I have only ever known one client doing it. If one of your big spenders or regular customers telephones in order to reserve a table why not reserve a car parking space for him at the same time. So often this would really save him an enormous amount of hassle. In Europe very often the number of your own car parking spaces is very limited. Why not reserve a proportion for regulars just as you would keep best tables for regulars.

Even where there is adequate car parking why not set aside a space for VIPs and regulars, the way most office blocks mark spaces for directors with their own numbers. So you can say 'Yes, Mr Greene, your usual table – for four, and we will keep car park space number 26 aside for you personally'. Why only stroke their ego at the table? The points apply to hotels and not just restaurants. Think of the impact on course/conference meeting organizers if you pre-allocated them their own reserved car space.

And when are we going to introduce valet parking in Europe when it is practically a standard service in the States?

Assuming you have your own car park it is probably one of the most under-utilized methods of reaching the market and promoting future events and activities in restaurants (and hotels). A simple mailing shot under the windscreen wiper of a car is more likely to be read than many other kinds of mailing shot. In a test run recently of 200 promotional slips under the windscreen wiper of cars only three were thrown away. All the others were read immediately or kept for future reference.

Everything in life is finding a simple 'edge over your competitors'.

An example is what is new about steak restaurants? They are very popular but really very similar in Britain. One restaurant introduces a salad bar, or a new starter and they all follow if it seems successful. But one steak restaurant in Edinburgh just has 'that edge'. They offer twenty varieties of mustard, not just two French or English. I have never seen it offered anywhere else and the restaurant has become famous because of this.

I could go on giving you ideas like this, but primarily this book is about principles and about an attitude of mind so that you will search out the ideas yourself. But you will also need a systematic planned Sales Action Plan. The sad thing is, in my experience, the vast majority of restaurateurs do not have one. Many restaurateurs tell me that this is not necessary because if your prices are reasonable and the food is extremely good then the public will beat a path to your door. That isn't true, particularly in the 'quieter' periods.

What I would like to see is a greater emphasis placed on the food *plus* some of the other points mentioned beforehand, *together* with the use of a systematic sales action plan. There is no doubt that many restaurateurs can increase their profits substantially if they had such a plan.

☆ ☆ ☆ ☆ ☆

13

USING NAMES

I would like to ask you a very 'deep' question which may require a very simple but profound answer. Why do some people return to a particular hotel time and time again even if it is no cheaper than its competitors and may *sometimes* have facilities which are not superior.

Many American visitors always stay at Browns Hotel in London. I know many people from the North of England who always stay at the Cumberland or Strand Palace hotels because their parents first brought them to stay in London in these hotels. There are many people who always stay at the Midland when they visit Manchester. All are excellent hotels, but why do they have 'a following'?

What is it about some hotels that makes people feel more comfortable, more at home? There are many people who choose a hotel because of price or location. There are other people who choose a hotel purely out of status. There are many more people who visit a place regularly who always choose the same hotel and this appears to be unrelated to price or status, and even unrelated to location. And if you ask these people why they return time and time again they have a vague answer or do not appear to know. Is it convenient to say to your secretary 'Book me into the same hotel as usual'? Is it sheer inertia? Does a following arise because many people are totally unadventurous and dislike change? Surely this is only a small part of the answer.

After years of studying this situation I am convinced that many people return to a hotel not because the facilities are superior – in fact they may be inferior – but because of one overriding factor. This factor is nothing to do with the physical advantages of the hotel property itself but because of *people* and a two way kind of recognition – recognition by the staff of guests and vice versa. There is nothing nicer than walking into a hotel and seeing a familiar face amongst the staff. And there is only one thing nicer than them recognizing you – it is when they remember your name and say 'Nice to see you again, Mr. Greene'.

This does not happen too often but when it does it is a very pleasant experience. It is far nicer than 'Nice to see you again, sir'. It is said you come into this world with nothing and you leave with nothing. But shortly after you are born you are given a name and you leave with a name which may be on your headstone for centuries after you die. Everyone loves to hear their own name used in a hotel or restaurant even if it isn't used the moment you walk in. After years of studying the reason for repeat business in locations where there is competition, I have found no common factor or link amongst the hotels who have a higher repeat ratio of guests – except one. This one factor is recognition and a greater use of names than their competitors.

How can you increase the degree of recognition and use of names and therefore your 'following' in your own hotel? There is no doubt that the more you use a person's name the more you will remember the name and the greater the chance of recognizing their face when they return even if the name is forgotten as they walk in.

Any hotel that sets out to use people's names more often than in the past and more often than their competitors, will find that their repeat business and occupancy will steadily increase.

Basically this can only be done by training staff in the technique and altering paperwork a little. It is no use just instructing staff that from next Monday we are going to use our customers' names wherever possible. It is necessary to show them how to do it. There is no chance of this being overdone because there is no way you can achieve even 50 per cent success except in a very small hotel. But in a larger hotel if you can train and motivate staff to remember guests' names once out of every five points of contact, this would be a very successful ratio. Just a short time ago I stayed in a 4 Star provincial City hotel. I deliberately concentrated through check-in, porters, restaurant for dinner, breakfast, and checking out, and not once was my name used, even when I had just used it. Let me summarize some situations and amendments to the system which will assist staff and encourage them to use guests' names. Some are obvious, others less obvious, but many represent lost opportunities to use the guest's name or, to be more positive, provide opportunities to use customers' names.

When you check in you have to provide your name. But so often the reception staff do not use it, although they are given it. Using a name is much better than the formal old fashioned 'sir' or 'madam'. But so often they do not even use these titles. Watch many hotels and they will call the bell boy and say 'Room 723' instead of 'Will you take Mr. Greene to room 723'. Even the doorman, linkman or porter who carries your case to the reception desk (if this happens) can often spot your name on a suitcase label and say 'Welcome to the XYZ Hotel, Mr. Greene'. The bellboy should ask whether you have been to the hotel before as he takes you to the room. If the answer is 'no' then he should point out two or three aspects of the hotel as you go to your room (where the restaurant(s) is, that there is a sauna, etc.) and if the answer is 'yes' he should be trained to get across one sales message 'Did you know we had a Mexican week in the restaurant?' or 'Our grill room on the top floor has a superb view over the City, Mr. Greene'.

And when you are in your room and telephone the grill room for a booking we must avoid this situation. Frequently I telephone to make a booking and they say 'Certainly, sir, for 7.30 p.m. and what is your room number?' And when I arrive at the entrance to the grill room the restaurant manager will ask 'Have you a reservation? Yes, what is your room number? 723, certainly, this way please'.

I hate being a room number.

Many hotel restaurants and restaurants generally have quiet and busy periods. In the busy periods people have to wait in a lounge and bar area, or they will wait in line in America. This waiting period could be a pleasant anticipating experience or a potential explosive 'walk out' situation. Let me quote from the management of the Hickory House Motor Inn, Huron, S.D., on their tactics to overcome the waiting problem. Note the three minutes:

> 'Quick recognition is the best technique. People don't mind waiting if they are recognized. What upsets them is being ignored. We have a policy of recognizing a person within three minutes, either by name or with a greeting. If our dining area is full, we will direct them to a comfortable chair in the lounge.'

The second you book a table, the restaurant staff have plenty of time to check that the name of the guest in room 723 is M. Greene and use it from that point on. The key to success is to adapt the paperwork so that there are a series of Whitney racks or listings of today's overnight guests with, say, a list of arrivals at each point usually listed by floors and room numbers rather than alphabetically. These listings should be in the different restaurant outlets, concierge, bars and even the hotel swimming pool. I have seen the delighted reaction at certain points where people carry a key around and sometimes leave them on view (e.g. as they sit at a bar) and put their key in front, when the barman comes back with the drink after glancing at the key number and says 'A gin dry martini, straight up, with a twist for you Mr. Greene' or 'Can I get you another Mr. Greene?'

This could happen all over the hotel. All you need is a slight change in the system. In a number of hotels we fixed the guests name at the bottom of every room key box so that as you asked the porter for 723 he would collect your key, hand it to you and say 'Key 723 for you, Mr. Greene.' And where a hotel has an early morning telephone call for guests, what can be nicer than being woken up in a strange city with 'Good Morning Mr. Greene, this is your 7 a.m. wake up call'. All you need is an extra line on the early morning call sheet for the name as well as the time and room number.

As I have said earlier, there is no chance of a guest hearing his name so often that it drives him crazy. In fact I believe most people would love it if it happened all the time. In practice, it is possible to motivate and train staff to use names maybe one third of the available opportunities, and this would have a sensational impact. Have you noticed that where staff have name tags on their uniforms a lot of people who stay in a hotel more than a day or two begin to use them? And the staff like this. What we need is more of a system to *help* staff use guests' names more often.

This section on using names has been included as a separate chapter, although strictly speaking it could have been included in with Sales Action Plan, and certainly in with the previous chapter, In-House Selling. But I felt it was so important that it warranted a separate short chapter on its own.

* * * * *

14

MANAGEMENT INFORMATION – MARKETING

Most management accounting systems are based on the American Uniform System of Accounts or a version of this accounting system. Primarily these accounting and management reporting systems are designed for *control* reasons – control of income from its various sources and control of the different types of costs – rather than being designed for marketing purposes.

It is recommended that much more marketing information is produced, systematically and regularly, which enables management to be more effective in their marketing and sales efforts. This can be achieved by altering and expanding present systems, or as an 'add on' of additional information.

An example of the difference between control and marketing information is on room sales. In order to control room sales we need information on room occupancy percentages and room sales by amount. But in the case of marketing information we need to know numbers and types of *unsold* rooms rather than rooms sold, and the amount of revenue lost from unsold rooms rather than revenue earned from rooms sold.

Any management reporting system, whether it is designed for marketing and/or control purposes, must be designed for the needs and requirements of every individual hotel. There is a hard core of basic information which all hotel management require whatever the style and circumstances of the hotel. But different hotels may require more, or less, information depending on the circumstances. The following pages provide an illustration of the marketing information which management might require, together with management information for income and cost control purposes (the latter on control is not covered in this book). The illustrations of marketing information shown cover:

Rooms
Restaurant(s)
Function room(s).

These lists are fairly self-explanatory but various explanations are felt necessary, although there are comments in earlier chapters on average spends particularly the chapters dealing with Pricing Strategies.

ROOMS

CHECKLIST 14.1

MARKETING INFORMATION – ROOMS

- Unoccupied room statistics by type of room
- Average room rate by type of room
- Lost room revenue (number of rooms not sold multiplied by average room rate achieved)
- Dollar occupancy percentage
- Occupancy forecasts
- Occupancy by major source
- Guest profile
- Average length of stay
- Sources of business by country
- Sources of business – conferences
  – businessmen
  – tourists
  – etc.
- Business turned away
- Percentage of 'no shows'

Unoccupied rooms really put the sales effort required into perspective. If you had a 100 room hotel and occupancy averaged 70 per cent as a fairly steady average, this is interesting as an economic measurement on the hotel but fairly useless in marketing and sales terms. It is far more useful to know that we must sell thirty more rooms which tend on average to be unoccupied. Or if the average room occupancy was 90 per cent midweek and 60 per cent on average at weekends, it provides a better sense of direction to say we must try to sell:

Ten more rooms Monday to Thursday nights and
Forty more rooms Friday to Sunday nights

And in hotels with different types of rooms (singles, twins, suites) or rooms with, say, a seaview and other rooms over the car park, the objective on unsold rooms may be specific on types of rooms which require a marketing strategy and a sales effort.

Average rates per room and per guest are important but again they have the disadvantage of being 'average' unless all the rooms are a standard size and there is no noisy side, or rooms with a view. In many parts of Europe there are still many older, attractive hotels, and some not so attractive, with only a proportion of the rooms with private bathrooms and private toilets. Wherever these are with or without private bathrooms, single and twin rooms, noisy or quiet rooms, or rooms with a view and some without, the average rate statistics must be analysed between types of rooms so that the information can be interpreted and management action can be taken.

Lost Room Revenue is a vital amount to know every night because it creates a greater sense of urgency. Everyone I know looks at their nightly occupancy statistics. If they are 80 per cent as against a target of 75 per cent everyone relaxes. But a 100 room hotel might have a Lost Room Revenue of $2,000 in one night. If I was given one wish by a fairy godmother to help the future of the hotel industry and this one wish would come true I would ask for a law to ban the use of occupancy averages and a law that hoteliers could *only* use unoccupied rooms and Lost Room Revenue. This could well change the face of the hotel world by making everyone much more sales conscious.

I remember an hotel about five years ago which was family owned, making a fairly good but not very high profit. The owners appointed a new general manager with a flair for marketing. He produced a plan of action which had a total budget of $100,000 including employing a sales executive to concentrate on attracting conventions, seminars and meetings, sales literature, mailing shots and advertising. The plan was to spend this amount in each of the first two years. The owners threw the plan out in horror. '$100,000 per year on marketing, you must be crazy.' The general manager came to me and we re-wrote the plan with a revised budget of $95,000 in the first year and $85,000 in the second year. The revised plan was virtually the same except that we included more targets and showed that this hotel, which the owners felt was doing all right, had an annual Lost Room Revenue of nearly $1 million! The plan was accepted *in total.*

The Chairman of the Board said that a reduction of Lost Room Revenue of $150,000 (with some increase in operating costs) looked easily achievable when you read the action plan and this would cover the increased marketing costs. In fact the target was to increase room sales, *reduce* Lost Room Revenue primarily from the third year onwards as follows:

	Improvement	*Lost Room Revenue*
Year 1	$150,000	$850,000
Year 2	$200,000	$800,000
Year 3	$300,000	$700,000

The Chairman said that they could easily reduce Lost Room Revenue from $1 million to $700,000 and then he added 'Of course, you can never reduce this to nil'. Well, I did not feel that that was the time to argue with him because we still had not produced any results. But when readers have read this entire book and in particular the last Chapter, they will see why I believe that a nil Lost Room Revenue should be everyone's aim in the hotel world.

Lost Room Revenue is obviously the amount of money lost by having unsold rooms and unsold beds. Another useful percentage which helps to interpret other information is the Dollar (or Pound Sterling) Occupancy Percentage. This is Actual Room Sales as a percentage of the Total Room Sales if every room was sold at full occupancy, and full rack (non-discounted) room rate. This percentage, read in conjuction with numbers of unoccupied rooms, discloses the degree of discounting, i.e. the hotel could be full but show a low Dollar Occupancy Percentage if rooms have been sold at a large discount.

Other statistics on the checklist are self-explanatory or have been dealt with previously, e.g. guest profiles, average length of stay, sources of business, etc. Source of business deals with income from conferences, businessmen, tourists, etc. and the proportions compared against the target proportions (see earlier chapter on Economic Criteria for Successful Marketing). Occupancy by major source should disclose whether your major source of business arises from tour operators, local companies, national companies, travel agents, individuals who have pre-booked, individuals who have not pre-booked.

Business Turned Away is a vital statistic which few people collate. There are many nights and periods in the year when hotels turn away business because they are fully booked, even though the average annual occupancy may not be too high. It helps enormously in fixing a pricing strategy, which may involve an increase, to know in these peak periods whether you were *just* 100 per cent full. Assuming you only had 100 rooms, did you just sell 100 rooms? Or assuming you had more rooms in this 100 room hotel, could you have filled 105 rooms or 102 or perhaps 200 rooms?

Many hotels could expand by building an extra wing or floor of bedrooms. Keeping statistics of Business Turned Away is invaluable in carrying out a feasibility study for a bedroom extension. It just requires the design of a special form to be available at reception or advance reservations to tick off this information. It can never be completely accurate because it is often difficult to find the average length of stay but it can provide a useful indicator.

Percentage of 'no shows' is an important statistic if your policy is to overbook. Overbooking, even if you call it something else, is a controversial subject and illegal in some countries. My own feeling is that other than in the top Five Star hotels some degree of overbooking is essential because of 'no shows', unless you are prepared to accept lower profit levels. Where you do overbook, the problem is of degree. How much should you overbook by? By what percentage should it be – say 5 per cent normally but 15 per cent when there is a major exhibition in town? You can only really judge this effectively if you build up a past record of 'no shows'.

Hotels will often find that on many nights the hotel is full, turning away business, but the following day the Early Bird Report, or the Daily Income Report will not show 100 per cent room occupancy. This arises in many hotels where the guests have a varied average length of stay with a small proportion of one night guests and where there is a degree of 'no shows'.

The problem cannot be solved completely, but it can be solved partially by:

1 A sensible degree of overbooking
2 Not pre-allocating guests to an actual room number until the latest possible moment. Where all rooms are identical there is no real need to pre-allocate until the night before arrival
3 Basic motivation, training and selling.

As soon as there are no more rooms to be sold the reception or reservations in many hotels nicely and politely tell people who telephone or call in that they are fully booked. My experience of deciding on a particular hotel, and then finding that it is fully booked, is an initial aggression towards the hotel. I do not blame myself for leaving it to the last moment, but rather I blame the hotel initially. So the way employees say you are fully booked has to be very tactful.

The other procedure that never happens to me and I only know of two hotel companies who do it, is to follow this procedure. Firstly, re-examine all your literature very carefully to make sure that the time you can re-sell a room is marked very clearly. Secondly take the telephone number of the person who is being 'refused a room' because you are full, and tell them you will telephone if rooms become available in case they have been unsuccessful elsewhere. If it is not possible because they are travelling, ask them to telephone back after a certain time. And if you have rooms available on other nights, try and sell them as the prospective guest may not be 'fixed' on the actual date of his trip.

There are a mass of other sales ideas that a good team will use but the most effective in filling the 'no shows' is to have a series of telephone numbers to follow up. If you are full, other hotels may be full. You may well not only sell a room to that 'desperate' person that night, but solve his problem so that he stays with you on every other trip.

RESTAURANTS

CHECKLIST 14.2

MARKETING INFORMATION – RESTAURANTS

- Covers per meal period
- Covers analysed into residents/'chance' for each meal period
- Average spends per cover (food)
- Average spends per cover (drinks)
- Total average spends per bill (check)
- Total average spends per cover
- Average spends analysed into price brackets
- Customer profiles
- Seat turnover ratios per meal period
- Table turnover ratios per meal period
- Popularity indices per meal period for food, wines and other drinks

There are various aims and objectives behind the checklist on marketing information on restaurants. Most of these points have been covered in a previous chapter on Pricing Strategy. Primarily these statistics are aimed at

1 assisting in pricing policies
2 helping to define market opportunities
3 isolating quiet and busy periods
4 to assist in menu planning and pricing

and therefore to increase sales and profits.

Covers sold per day and cumulatively per week, month and year, are useful in comparing with covers sold in the previous year, the overall target covers for the current year, or where there is a menu change. In fact they are vital before and after even a minor alteration in menus, and certainly critically important when menu prices are changed even if the dishes on the menu are exactly the same.

These statistics become more meaningful in taking immediate corrective action and planning future marketing strategy when they are analysed into meal periods and days of the week. It can often be invaluable to analyse a busy meal period into time zones, because even a busy period can have quiet periods.

Periodically it pays to time stamp waiters' order dockets and then sort them into fifteen minute intervals. By counting the covers in the quarter-hour period it is possible to draw a graph or chart of the activity pattern in a meal period. They will vary from day to day, but experience shows that most *busy* restaurants have a distinct pattern. Some have a mountain type of business, a steady build up from opening time to a peak, then a steady decline till close. Others have a step up pattern or a plateau pattern. A restaurant may open at noon, be fairly quiet till 12.45 p.m. and then very busy to 2.15 p.m. followed by a quiet period to 3 p.m. Even two very similar restaurants may have a different pattern because the pattern of eating in local offices and commerce is different. I have seen two identical restaurants in slightly different locations. One was consistently busy in a plateau affect from 12.15 p.m. to 2.15 p.m. The other was consistently busy from 1 p.m. to 3 p.m.

Whatever the pattern, the hotelier and restaurateur should know about it. It can help in setting staff standards and rotas. And it can certainly help in pricing strategies and selling. Let me give you one example. In one city centre restaurant with a mix of business executives and shoppers we found business executives were not primarily entertaining, and a fairly high proportion were eating on their own. The restaurant was highly successful. Every day from about 1 p.m. onwards throughout the afternoon every seat was normally sold. But the restaurant had a quiet period from 11 a.m. opening, to 1 p.m. A special business executive meal (it was not called lunch) was introduced and the restaurant promoted a scheme where if you paid for your meal by 12.45 p.m. there was a special 'early bird price'. It was very successful and the restaurant was then very busy from 11.45 a.m. to 12.45 p.m., which gave staff a chance to clear tables for the 1 p.m. rush.

This kind of analysis will not produce results in every area. But if the local offices are working flexitime or on shifts, there often is a demand from a lot of people for an early meal.

FUNCTION ROOMS

CHECKLIST 14.3

MARKETING INFORMATION – FUNCTION ROOMS

- Utilization ratio of function rooms
- Type of function – profile of customers
- Number of times function room fully utilized
- Average size per function
- Numbers attending into groupings related to total size
- Average spend (food, drinks, total)
- Average spend per square foot or metre (food, liquor, sub-total: catering, rental, total)
- Menu popularity (food, wines, and other drinks)
- Pattern of unutilized days
- Numbers staying overnight
- Estimated benefits for other areas (e.g. bars, coffee shop, etc.)

The aims of the marketing statistics on functions are very similar to the marketing information on restaurants and on bedrooms. The idea is to isolate the 'real' activity of the rooms, and the quiet periods when they are not being sold or, what is just as common, being *undersold*.

Average per square foot is another useful statistic in comparing the real success of different size function rooms in the same hotel. This is a very useful statistic in comparing one hotel with others in a group where the function rooms are all different sizes.

One of the other key aspects to monitor on the function side of an hotel is the 'spin off' of benefit in other areas of the hotel and to actively promote this. If you examine the organizational structure of many hotels, other than quite small hotels, it is apparent that hotels are very departmentalized and compartmentalized. In larger hotels many restaurant and function staff have never really been shown round the rest of the hotel, and certainly a surprising number have never seen a bedroom. I believe it is this compartmentalization which inhibits many hotel staff from selling other departments in the hotel. It is absolutely essential in any plan for increasing in-house sales that all staff are shown round the whole hotel at an appropriate time. It is also essential that all reception and reservation staff should sleep in the bedrooms so that they have a real idea what they are selling.

The function side of an hotel can produce a lot of business for other areas of the hotel. Many people want to meet before the function. They want to meet their partner or friends. Where do they meet? Usually in the hotel lobby or in the special lobby area outside the banqueting rooms. Why not promote through literature sent to people who are attending a function that they can meet their friends in the XYZ bar, or in a special bar area set up to sell before the reception part of the function starts? Not everyone will want, or have the time, to attend. But a significant proportion will.

It is also possible to persuade a proportion of the people who are attending an evening function that they should not drive home when they have been drinking and they are tired. What can be nicer than staying the night at the hotel? Function staff can help promote this and the management reporting system should help monitor the success of their efforts.

INTERPRETATION

The foregoing is an illustration of the kind of management information a hotelier and restaurateur should have in order to help improve marketing decisions, rather than information and management statistics provided for control purposes. Of course, however good the information is, it still needs to be interpreted correctly and this does depend on experience and willingness to act. Surprisingly, I have often found it is easier to interpret information and obtain action where the trends and results are not too significant, than when they are extremely bad. In one situation in a group of restaurants, head office found one of their restaurants suddenly beginning to show bad results. The first reaction was to check the figures in order to see they were correct. The second reaction was that 'they must improve next month'. Everyone seemed stunned into inaction because the figures were so bad.

I am reminded of a story Alistair Cooke used to tell about an old farmer in the mid-West of America who ordered a barometer from a mailing-house in Chicago. When he went to collect it a few days later from the local rail station he found the needle was stuck at the lowest reading and would not move, no matter how much he tapped it. Assuming it had been damaged in transit he packed it up again and then mailed it back before leaving the station. Turning his horse and buggy round he began the long trip back to his farm and within half an hour found himself right in the middle of the worst cyclone ever known in the state.

The moral of this story is that management information is of no use if it is just interesting: it must be interpreted sensibly and must result in positive action.

* * * * *

15

IMPROVING SALES TECHNIQUE – GENERAL COMMENTS

Readers will notice that this book follows a fairly logical pattern – Planning Ahead, Marketing, Redefining Markets, Pricing Strategy – through What Motivates People to Sales Action Plans. We have gone through the stages to the point where we actually have to 'reach out' and contact certain potential customers. We have done our research and found the name of a person in a company or organization who uses hotels at present. And we now have to persuade this person to make a decision, or advise the person who makes the decision, to come and see our hotel's excellent facilities and try us out.

Apart from in-house selling, most selling has one primary objective and this is to persuade the prospective customer to try your hotel, restaurant or function room *once*. This may appear an over-simplification but nevertheless it is true applied to new customers. Assuming he tries it once, it lives up to his expectations and he considers it, not cheap, or expensive, but value for money, the sales effort from this point takes on a new emphasis. From that point on selling has to remind him that you are there, and that you want his business. Operationally your service must be so good and such value for money that he is not tempted by another hotelier (who has also read this book) to try his hotel once.

Should you accept this point that the whole aim is to persuade the prospective customer to try you once, extra sales begin to appear more easily obtainable.

Jumping ahead a little to the situation where one is trying to close a sale, I have often helped a hotelier or hotel sales executive who is getting on very well with a prospective customer but cannot clinch a booking by advising him to adopt this tactic:

> 'Mr. Jones, we have discussed your series of ten management courses which you hold each year and you have seen our facilities

and how suitable they are for your courses'.

'Well, Mr. Jones, I don't want you to book the next series with us. If you said you wanted to book all ten of the next year's courses I would probably not take the booking. All I ask is that you try one course with us so that we can prove how well we can service your size and type of course. Why not just try one?'

Surely the answer to this question must be 'Well, why not?' He is wary of the big decision of switching a number, or all of his courses to a different venue. You know you are good but he only has your word for it. But with this change of emphasis he can try you out.

Getting a 'new' customer to try you once can often take time and patience and it requires a well-thought-out strategy. Naturally, the first thing is research so that you know it is worthwhile devoting time and patience to obtaining the business. If you ask many buyers of hotel facilities (whether they organize training sessions or just book rooms regularly for visitors) whether they are happy with their present venue they will invariably say 'yes' but mean 'no'. If they list all the problems encountered they make themselves look foolish. In most cases you have to watch how they say 'yes'. After all, you have got in to see them, which is a good sign. Many buyers are happy with their present facilities. But a significant proportion are not, usually because the hotel management may have taken them for granted. When you ask them whether they are happy they will not say 'yes' but 'ye-e-s-s' and their eyes may glaze slightly as they remember coffee being late and how the hotel staff forgot to empty the ashtrays.

When you sense that they are not as satisfied as they would be in your hotel you must then find out who they are using now, or used last time. At an appropriate moment, leave the prospective customer, after fixing a date to come and see him again or to show him round your hotel. Before you meet again go and visit the present hotel he is using in order to draw up an Advantage/Limitation List on that hotel compared to your own. The next time you meet you will be armed with at least one major advantage, and hopefully more than one, over the competitor hotel. At times it seems as if the competition is overwhelming but if you analyse their strengths and weaknesses you will often find that you have many advantages over them and this helps your self-condidence in attracting business away from them.

The various methods of reaching the market are elaborated later in this chapter. Primarily they are

Paid Advertising
Unpaid Advertising

Sales Letters and Mailing Shots
Telephone Selling
New Forms of Selling in Next Decade
Face-to-Face Selling.

These are not in any order of significance except that Face-to-Face Selling, what I often call 'eyeball-to-eyeball selling', has been deliberately left to last. As mentioned right at the start, every one of these techniques deserves a separate book, and some excellent books have already been written on advertising, letters that sell, etc. What I have attempted to do is to keep this book from becoming a huge volume by providing a series of proven checklists on the various techniques, and by writing two or three pages elaborating the points in the Checklist. Face-to-Face Selling has been left till last as I consider it of prime importance.

There are certain pitfalls which anyone selling must avoid and certain aspects which a salesperson should concentrate on. Before moving on to actual sales techniques it is necessary to comment on these. The most important ones are:

Avoid selling a mile wide and an inch deep
Non-verbal communication(NVC)
Be knowledgeable
Be consumer orientated rather than product orientated
Be Jack (or Jill) the problem solver rather than Jack (or Jill) the product seller.

Selling a mile wide and an inch deep has been fully covered in an earlier section. Some people try to cover as many prospects as possible when they are out selling. Or they send out thousands of mailing shots to all and sundry under the mistaken belief that the larger the mailing the bigger the response. It is far better, and more cost effective in time and money, to choose a careful selection of thirty to forty 'warm' or 'hot' prospects and spend time, thought and energy getting to really know them, and doing a thoroughly effective sales job. In other words sell 'an inch wide and a mile deep'.

Non-verbal communcation is elaborated under Face-to-Face Selling as it is critically important. Some people call it 'body language' or 'body signs'. I also associate it with the way people sometimes say 'yes' when they really mean 'no'. You can learn a lot from what a person says. But he often does not say what he really means. You can often learn more from what he does not say. NVC can help enormously in most sales situations, in particular in any face-to-face sales situation.

Should you say to a group of hoteliers that it is important to have knowledge of four things in order to be successful in selling, they will usually mention 'knowledge of the product' first. This is important; but in selling (as compared with, say, running) a hotel, knowledge of other things is just as important. A good hotelier/salesperson requires four attributes:

1 Knowledge of the product
2 Knowledge of the client – finding out as much as possible about him, his needs and requirements
3 Knowledge of how to sell
4 Knowledge of the benefits of the product to the client.

All of these are important. I have already mentioned in an earlier chapter the recommendation that any sales executive who is employed from outside the hotel industry should spend some time working in various departments of the hotel (including the kitchen), even if this sales executive is obviously superb at selling. Similarly, any hotel manager who developed through the craft side of the business should spend some time learning about selling and sales techniques. Your success ratio will be very low if you do not spend time obtaining knowledge of the client. And everyone can learn how to constantly improve their sales ability. These first three 'knowledges' are all important.

But the most significant of these in achieving higher sales is the last – knowledge of the benefits of the product or service to the client. This is what you really sell. This is what produces the best results. But before you can reach this stage and be successful at it, it is necessary to learn the first three.

In this sophisticated world we do not just sell the basic necessities of life. We do not just sell a product or a service – we sell the benefits of them to the consumer. Some car manufacturers, like Volvo, have not just sold cars, but safety. Some others like Jaguar sell 'proof that you have achieved a certain position in life'. Companies manufacturing drills for use at home do not sell drills. They sell the ability to drill holes and build things – the chance to save money by doing it yourself. Manufacturers of cosmetics do not just sell cosmetics, but the chance to feel good, lift your spirits, feel younger, be more successful in your social life.

Similarly, hotels should not just sell a superb bedroom and excellent food. This is being too product orientated. If the exercise in

Chapter 8, What Motivates People to Buy, is only partially correct any hoteliers who sell the benefits rather than the product (rooms, food, drinks) must be more successful. Therefore hoteliers should sell:

a good night's sleep
relaxation
escape from pressure
a feeling of contentment
let other people do the cooking and washing up
impress your friends
impress your customers
impress your girlfriend
it really is a good investment
put your customer in a more receptive mood
atmosphere and ambiance
feel better when you return to work.

Why does the mass of people drink alcohol in your bars? A small proportion may be alcoholics. But the vast majority have a drink to relax, to unwind at the end of the day, to celebrate a social event or a business success. They are not just buying a Manhattan or a gin and tonic, but they are buying the benefit this has on them when they have consumed the drink. It is the benefits which we must sell and this makes us more consumer orientated than product orientated.

You will notice a key point about many of the sales points and this is that you do not just sell to your immediate buyer but past him to your buyer's own customer, i.e. put your customer in a more receptive mood. This is why it is important in your early research and digging for information to ask your customer who *his* customers are. This is obvious on exhibitions, but just as vital on conferences, training seminars or where a local company books regular visitors into your hotel.

Two further important points which improve every sales technique are where the person selling is firstly Jack the Problem Solver rather than Jack the Product Seller and secondly consumer orientated rather than product orientated. In a sense the two are inter-related. If you are consumer orientated it leads you to become Jack the Problem Solver. Everyone who uses hotels, or thinks of using an hotel, has some kind of problem, or some niggling worry. It is difficult to put this into words exactly. But if you can find out what the problem is and help solve it you will have gained a new customer.

It could be the young up-and-coming executive mentioned earlier, who is given the 'simple' assignment of organizing the company's annual Christmas party. Quite often the problem or worry is because of lack of product knowledge by the customer about hotels which he feels inhibited about declaring in case he looks foolish. He often knows little about wines and certainly has no knowledge of French menus. Even if none of your menus are in French he may not understand some menu terms or the jargon of our business. If he is thinking of booking a wedding he may be worried about the order of speeches, or wedding etiquette generally.

It might be that the problem is transporting his equipment to the conference. Most of his delegates are coming by plane and he worries about how they will travel from the airport to the hotel. Or most of his delegates are arriving by car and he has a niggling feeling that your car-park looks small. Conference or seminar rooms never seem to be the perfect shape for the organizer's numbers and he knows he requires more space from the overhead projector to the screen. It might surprise you if I said that most convention and seminar organizers consider food and accommodation important but not their top priority. They worry about whether the hotel has an extension lead, what happens if the fuse or the bulb blows. Can all the delegates see? Will they be drowsy after a heavy lunch? Can you really feed them and clean up the room so that all the delegates are back in their chairs by 2.15 p.m. exactly?

Most conferences and management seminars are carefully timed and whenever possible a good speech or case study ends just before the natural breaks in the day at a high point. Just before coffee, lunch and tea most people running seminars try to close with a vital point, a key illustration or a high point which will make the delegate want to return after the break. And the total time is planned and monitored carefully. What sometimes happens is the conference, or seminar reaches a high point, or ends a fascinating case study, just before coffee. But the coffee is just coming!! So the organizer, realizing he is going to lose a valuable fifteen minutes, says 'Let's continue with the opening of the next session for 10 or 15 minutes.'

You can become Jack the Problem Solver by having empathy allied to experience of the hotel business and selling. It is possible to cover all the foregoing points and bring them up when you are selling. A small pamphlet on wedding etiquette will solve a problem. If his conference is for fifty people and your room takes fifty people the only way you will keep your credibility and remove his worry is to show him the room actually being used for a conference with fifty people. If you do not have one in the near future to show him, bring in chairs and tables and set the room up so that he can see for himself, preferably with all his equipment in place. If he wants a 'U' or 'V' shaped table for a seminar – and many smaller management courses use this shape so that delegates can talk to each other as well as the course organiser – set up the room with the organizer sitting at the head which is usually at the opening of the 'V' or 'U' with a screen behind him. Put a slide on the screen. Then move him to the point of the 'V' so that he can see that all the delegates have a good view. Get him used to the table and the room. Show him you have thought of the problems, and you have a booking.

I like the advertisement for a convention hotel which said 'We always tape (attach) a spare bulb to the side of your projectors'. Fantastic! The worse thing that can happen at a seminar or convention is where the microphone breaks down, or the projector bulb blows. And it is bound to happen sometime. Every customer knows it can happen and worries about it. But the hotel that always straps a spare bulb to the side of the projector *and* promotes the point is being consumer orientated and is a classic illustration of what I mean by being Jack the Problem Solver.

Some other examples are as follows. A Thistle hotel without air-conditioning (the vast majority of hotels in Europe do not have it) said to me once 'When you are having lunch we clean the whole room, put in fresh water jugs with lemon slices, and open all the windows for half an hour so that delegates feel fresh, in a fresh room after lunch.'

In many Indian hotels they have *two* early morning calls. At first I thought it was a mistake. But they do it as part of the system. We all know that early morning calls may be missed occasionally. But what happens more often is that the guest turns over and thinks 'I will just close my eyes for a minute more'. He oversleeps and is late for his plane, tour or conference. And they very often blame the hotel for not giving them an early call. In India many hotels solve this very real problem with a polite second reminder call as an automatic part of the system.

In a motor hotel in Harlow New Town I saw a sign at reception saying 'Jump leads are available if your battery is flat'. There was a similar large sign near the function room cloakrooms. A proportion of guests are bound to use your car-park and forget to switch off their lights. And who has the problem when they cannot get started the following morning or after a function – you do! Very often this sign will remind guests that they left their lights on. But it shows you care about them, and you are Jack the Problem Solver.

Saying 'we have a beautiful heated swimming pool' is good, but product orientated. What is the problem in many business areas? Many guests have forgotten to bring their swimming costumes. So put a note in the bedroom saying 'Don't worry if you have forgotten your swimming costume – we will lend residents a costume at no charge'.

The foregoing are illustrations of being consumer orientated and a problem solver, rather than a product seller. A product seller says 'Our rooms have views over the beautiful landscaped gardens'. How can a room see? It is people who have eyes. The emphasis should be more 'When you look out of your bedroom window you will see beautiful landscaped gardens'. Bedrooms should not just be described as 'large' but as large enough to spread out – large enough to pace up and down and unwind after a busy day'.

Sometimes the very nature of the hotel industry can make hoteliers product orientated. It has happened to me when I have worked (and slept) in a large hotel. One tends to forget there is another world outside. We sponsored a fascinating study by Dr. Boas Shamir a few years ago into the impact of hotel management and staff living in hotels. He found a tendency to become product orientated in attitude and in the written and spoken word. I remember wanting to book a seminar in a new hotel and asking to be shown around. The manager was obviously thrilled and proud of his new hotel and showed me around with considerable enthusiasm *for the product.* At the end he thanked me for my time and was absolutely charming. But he never asked me about my problems or my needs (even the size of the conference). His sales approach was totally product orientated. Are you that manager? Do you sell a product, or what that product can do for people. Even if you are consumer orientated, what about your staff?

When you face a prospective customer ask yourself 'What is his problem?' Hoteliers always smile when I say this. But every prospective customer has a problem, a worry, a doubt, otherwise he would be a customer, not a prospective customer. If you can solve the problem and are consumer orientated in the way you package the words when you sell – the written or spoken words – you will be much more successful in your future selling.

* * * * *

16

ADVERTISING – PAID

There are various ways of bringing your facilities to the notice of potential buyers, and reminding past and present customers that you are there and want their business. All of them deserve a book on each technique. However, this is not my objective. All I have planned to do is write a few pages commenting on each technique backed up with useful checklists so that you can decide which techniques to use in your future action plans and to help improve your technique. Firstly, let us consider paid advertising.

The best kind of sales opportunity is when you are face to face with a person, preferably in your own hotel. The next best is a telephone sales situation where you can ask questions, put forward an invitation, communicate *two* ways. Third in line of preference is a letter which is a one-way communication, but you can personalize the contents and address it to a known, chosen target, i.e. a specific person. Way down the line in cost effectiveness is Paid Advertising.

Hang on a moment! How do I come to that conclusion when it is so simple to place an advertisement and so many millions are spent on Paid Advertising? I am not going to hide behind the old, but true, cliché, 'half of all paid advertising is ineffective – but nobody knows which half'. Suffice to say that years of experience shows me that people spend a lot of unnecessary money on paid advertising for two main reasons. Firstly, because they like reading, hearing or seeing their own advertisements. Secondly, because the advertising industry is very effective in selling its services. When that highly-trained telephone sales girl telephones a hotlier or restaurateur and says something like 'We have this special Wine and Dine Feature next week, Mr Café. I thought I would let you know you are the only one of the few really good restaurants in this area who isn't included in this feature – yet . . ..' It is very difficult to say 'No' and be left out.

They really are highly skilled at selling their services and so they should be.

Paid advertising has many advantages and, except in special situations, has many disadvantages. Firstly, it is expensive, although in certain countries like America it is cheap, particularly on television and radio compared with most European countries. It is also difficult to measure its success. And often, unless the advertisement is well thought out, it produces business when you are busy anyhow.

The whole face of paid advertising could well change by the 90s because of new technologies. Video tape recorders could revolutionize television sponsored advertising and direct paid T.V. advertising. I sense that the advertising industry is a very concerned industry, not just because of the world recession, but because of technological change. In most cases the cost of television advertising is related to numbers of listeners, with peak viewing hours being the most expensive. But video tape recorders have created a 'time warp' at least compared to traditional time. A viewer with a video tape recorder need not watch a major entertainment show, a world boxing match, Wimbledon Tennis fortnight, or a major film, at peak viewing time. The viewer may wish to go out when the 'event' is on and watch the star show on the next rainy Sunday morning or anytime. Why should an advertiser pay peak viewing rates when within five years one-third of households have the facility to change the traditional peak viewing times. And there is now technical equipment which automatically switches off when the advertisements come on or which can speed up the advert.

Cassettes in motor vehicles, the growth of portable televisions, the impact of breakfast television in countries which inevitably will follow the trend in America, will cause change and problems. The technological change in producing magazines and newspapers will be revolutionary by the end of this decade. And the growth in 'free' top quality give-away newspapers and magazines will confuse the situation. Every traditional newspaper can supply their advertisers with a social grouping of buyers, readers *and* their families. How do you do this when there are no buyers in the case of free give-away newspapers delivered to every household in my own area? How do they know who actually reads them?

However, there are various situations where a paid advertisement is the only, and the most effective, method of reaching a market. If a hotel or restaurant is new or has been renovated, probably the most effective, quick way of reaching a large number of people and getting the hotel known is through paid advertising. Whenever you are trying to reach a large number of individual decision-makers, i.e. a large number of consumers who might eat in a restaurant, or drink in a bar, paid advertising within a clearly defined catchment area is the best method. Again, where a quiet period has been identified and a specific package is produced to try and fill that period (e.g. winter weekends) then paid advertising may be required and in this kind of situation it is possible to measure the results against the cost of advertising. Hotel groups, and in particular restaurant chains with a standardized system or theme, find that paid advertising is the most cost effective method of reaching a volume market.

In the case of many holiday resort hotels, paid advertising in town and area holiday guides and in specific media is the most effective, together with sales letters and mailing shots to past guests.

Where a decision is made to spend money on paid advertising, how can you ensure that it is the most cost effective and that you earn the best return for your advertising investment, relative to the size of the problem? The last part of the previous sentence is vitally important – 'relative to the size of the problem'. You might find that the best return on your advertising cost is obtained from a two-minute advertisement on peak television, or a half page in a national newspaper, if you measure results by the size of the response. But if you are only seeking to sell, say, thirty more rooms per night, or twenty more covers per meal in the restaurant, advertising in a 'powerful' media may create an overkill situation.

This is a huge subject and therefore I have summarized ten main principles of good advertising in a checklist, Checklist 16.1. Most of the principles also apply to other forms of selling, in particular to selling letters and mailing shots. Just start thumbing through your own past advertisements, and advertisements by other hoteliers and restaurateurs. You will probably find that very few advertisements follow all these principles. (Point 10 in the list is basically for national chains). In fact, it is very difficult to achieve all the first nine principles or all ten if you are part of a chain or group.

A book that I can recommend as well worth reading is *One Hundred Great Advertisements* by Barry Day. Even these adverts often cover only five or six of the points. As an example, in real life it is very difficult to be both unique and competitive (point 4).

Some hoteliers tend to be product orientated in their wording and occasionally you see the hotel and industry's jargon creeping in to an advertisement. I studied the advertisements on the 'Eating Out' page of my own local newspaper last Friday. There were eleven advertisements for restaurants. Five used phrases which could well confuse the

CHECKLIST 16.1

TEN PRINCIPLES OF GOOD SALES PROMOTION AND ADVERTISING

1 It is consumer orientated

2 It concentrates on one selling idea

3 It concentrates on the most important and persuasive advantage available

4 It presents a unique and competitive idea

5 It involves the consumer

6 It is credible and sincere

7 It is simple, clear and complete

8 It takes full advantage of the media

9 It demands action that will lead to the sale

10 It clearly associates the selling idea with the brand name

potential customer. Examples are:

'We have 43 seats'
'Our restaurant takes 60 covers'
'We have a prix fixé menu.
'We have a car park'.

The phrasing should have been more like: 'You will have no problem parking because we have a car park'. Does it interest people that you have exactly 43 seats? And do they know what a cover is, or a prix fixé menu?

It is very easy to get point 2 wrong – concentrate on one selling idea. Advertisements cost a lot. If a hotelier decides to advertise his restaurant in the evening, it is very tempting to think perhaps we should add that we do a businessman's lunch – and what about a mention in the corner that we do weddings as well?

On point 3, most hotels or restaurants have one major advantage over the competition or one important idea that will persuade people to use the restaurant. It could be the chef or restaurant manager as a craftsman or personality, joints on a trolley, special desserts, one special main course, a range of malt whiskies, really good parking, a superb view, or lovely grounds. When I was working with one new client who had a very old hotel, he mentioned that they had a priest's bolt-hole in the restaurant and we built the advertisement around this. Everyone had to come in once and see this bolt-hole. As his food was superb and good value for money, people returned regularly after trying it once because of the priest's bolt-hole.

On point 5, somehow the advertisement must involve the consumer – make him feel he is there or wants to be there. This can only be achieved if it is consumer-orientated, using 'you' more than 'I'. In this book there is a continuous use of 'you' but, as it is based on my personal experiences, there is also an inevitable use of quite a few 'I's. Point 6 – it is credible and sincere – is something only you can decide after studying your own past advertisements and other hotelier's advertisements. I have avoided giving examples in this book in case it offends people, but let me show you one which is from a major international group. You will not recognize the group, but they will recognize it. This is the actual wording. Do you feel it is credible and sincere, or does it overdo things a little?

However good an international hotel group is, can it ever achieve these standards? You only need one thing wrong with the hotel for the whole advertising idea to collapse.

THERE'S A NEW DAWN OF LUXURY
Tomorrow's luxury. It goes beyond elegant surroundings. It means more than our seemingly endless choice of diversions. More than the most advanced facilities. Tomorrow's luxury is our dedication to anticipating your needs and meeting them with service that goes beyond expectations. It is our commitment to providing the best hotels all over the world today, and building more where you'll be headed tomorrow. It is our determination to make your stay with ******* a completely new experience of ease and comfort. This is our promise: tomorrow's luxury and service, today.

Most people do not buy newspapers and magazines to read the advertisements, so try to be simple, clear and complete. Try to get your advertisement placed at the top or bottom right-hand corner of a page and remember that a full-page advertisement does not necessarily attract twice as much business as a half page advertisement, particularly if there is news or an editorial on the other half of that half-page advertisement.

Where appropriate, cut out *coded* coupons should be used so that you can monitor the results from each advertisement medium used. Most people read the morning nationals for only a maximum of thirty minutes and a lot just spend ten minutes over breakfast, or in the train to work. Try asking a group of people who have read the morning papers to name any advertisements in them. Many will not be able to mention any, some will remember one or at the maximum two. And yet the paper was full of advertisements.

I once went to an evening soccer match with six hotel managers. The pitch was surrounded with advertisements. It was interesting that afterwards only one of us could remember any advertisements. And yet we had spent nearly two hours looking at them, or at the pitch. Local weekly newspapers are very often kept longer than the nationals and read from cover to cover.

The point I am making is that any advertisement has got to be very special and unique to literally grab someone's attention, unless he is actively seeking to spend money and buy your product and services. And somehow the advertisement has got to create such an impact and a sense of urgency that it demands action that will lead to an enquiry or booking.

Here is an advertisement which is connected with food and hygiene (which we are all interested in) as an illustration of one which although not new, is very good. This is one by Saatchi & Saatchi, U.K., for the Health Education Council, shown above. It was used as an advertisement and reproduced as posters in kitchens and where food was being used.

I guarantee that you read it from beginning to end without stopping. It is simple, clear and complete. Furthermore, it is totally true, and totally credible. It takes full advantage of the media without being too verbose, and has maximum impact using a white print on black background. And by the time you have finished, reading down to 'it's your turn' and under the plate 'Cover food. Cover eating and drinking utensils. Cover dustbins', it does not demand action (point 9 on checklist) – it screams out for action.

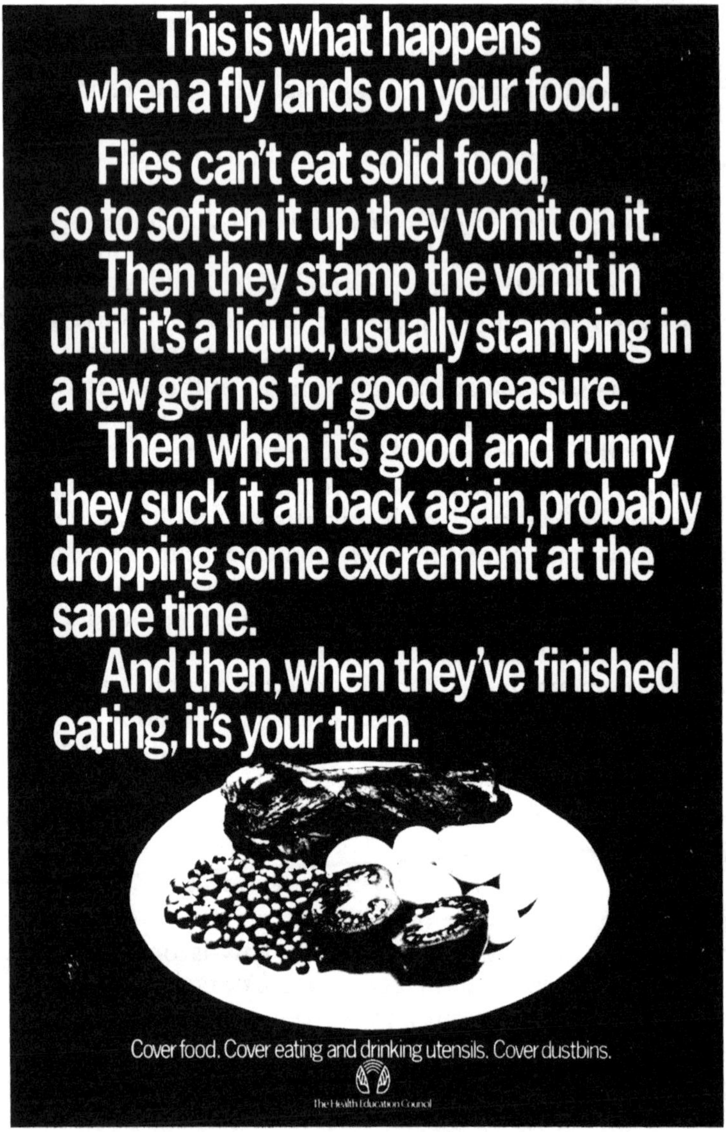

Try to avoid beautiful and elegant people in your adverts because your customers may not associate with them. Draft wording aimed at an actual person. Write to and for Mr Jones who is staying with you, Mrs Smith, the housewife who needs a break from washing up, Mr Brown who has been sent on a conference when he would rather be at home. Do not write for 'business executives' or 'tourists'. Tourists are actual people not an amorphous mass. Use everyday language, the words *they* would use.

The 10-point checklist in this chapter should help you improve your future paid advertising. There is one major 'crime' to avoid in advertising, and all forms of selling. Whatever you do try not to be *boring*.

* * * * *

17

UNPAID ADVERTISING – FREE PUBLICITY

Very few consumer industries are in quite such a position to obtain unpaid publicity as the hotel industry and yet it is one of the most under-utilized forms of publicity for many hotels, particularly in smaller towns and cities. It is no exaggeration to say that most local newspapers and local radio stations are crying out for interesting 'news'. And hotels are news.

Everyone is interested in food. Everyone reads about holidays and leisure. Well-known people stay in hotels and interesting things happen there. Unfortunately the wrong side sometimes hits the news and headlines, because bad news does not require a well-thought-out press release to obtain instant appearance in the press or media.

In everyone's sales action plan it should be possible to set a specific feasible objective of, say, obtaining a free write-up in the local newspaper every month, or six times a year. Some well-known hotels obtain this without trying because you read about a famous actress always staying at the Savoy or Grosvenor House, London.

I am reminded about a quote by the famous Hollywood producer and director, Cecil B. De Mille, who spent a fortune marketing his epic films, but was pretty good at obtaining free media coverage. His two greatest moneymaking films were 'King of Kings' and 'The Ten Commandments', both made twice. When he first thought of making a film of 'The Ten Commandments' his financial backers were very worried about whether it would be financially successful. 'You must be joking' he said, 'we've had 2,000 years of advance free publicity for this movie.'

Some exclusive hotels work hard to avoid press publicity because part of their marketing strategy is that film stars, policiticans and millionaires can stay there knowing there will be *no* publicity. And these hotels are quite correct, particularly in these days of security problems. But these exclusive hotels are few and far betwen. The vast majority of hoteliers welcome free press publicity not only because it is free, but because they know that most people buy a magazine or newspaper to read the articles, news and editorials, rather than the advertisements, unless of course they are specifically looking to buy a product, book a holiday or find a new restaurant.

Nothing in this life is easy, and obtaining free press and media publicity takes time, thought and careful planning. There are a number of events which should be 'fed' to the local press. Examples are:

1 The appointment of a new chef, his career to date and specialities
2 The appointment of a new barman with his special cocktails
3 Menus of certain functions held at the hotel
4 Particulars of special interesting conferences or exhibitions
5 Menus for special days of the year
6 Photographs of staff dressed up for special days (e.g. Valentine's Day Massacre or Pancake Day Race)
7 Well-known people staying in the hotel.

Some of these require the permission of the customer but quite often he welcomes the free press publicity. Many hotels do a lot of charitable work and help to organize charitable, fund-raising events. Nowadays sponsored events often start and finish at hotels, or are run in the hotel grounds. I have seen write-ups in the press on sponsored walks, welly-throwing competitions, sponsored car rallies. From the largest omelette to the longest sausage, hotels obtain press coverage – particularly if you can get in to the Guinness Book of Records, like the world speed record for drinking a Yard of Ale. Beaujolais races, first grouse on the restaurant table – these are all of interest to readers and therefore to journalists. Figure 17.1 shows a typical example of some press coverage providing free press publicity to hotels on the glorious twelfth'.

It is necessary to get to know journalists, in particular local journalists on newspapers, local radio and local television, if applicable. Spend time and money entertaining them even when you haven't got a story (i.e. work at establishing a personal relationship with them so that when you do have a story, there is no 'barrier' when you suddenly telephone them.) One manager I know swears he was able to persuade a television crew to move the camera six inches, as they featured a story of a robbery at a bank next door to his hotel, so that the shot included the hotel name and sign and the voice mentioned the bank was next to his hotel. This appeared on Police 5

Glorious day for the grouse race

by Neil Darbyshire

THE DAWN silence over the Yorkshire moors was broken today by the blast of 12-bore shotguns.

For this is the Glorious Twelfth, the day Britain's only true native bird pays the price for being good to eat and hard to shoot.

Unlike the witless pheasant, red grouse are the ultimate challenge to the hunter. They lie beneath the scrub until flushed out by dogs and beaters, when they fly, squawking all the way up to 70 miles an hour, ducking and weaving towards new sanctuary.

Once again this year the race is on to get the first grouse of the season on to the dining table of a London restaurant.

In previous years the Savoy, and Browns Hotel have been among the front runners, as well as a Surrey pub, the Onslow Arms, which last year had its first grace parachuted in by the Red Devils.

This year the London Hilton plans to lead the field. At 4.30 this morning a team set off for Elstree airport where a private plane was taking them to Bolton moor in Wensleydale.

On then to the grouse-rich land of Lord Bolton to pick up the first brace shot this morning, back to Battersea by helicopter and from Battersea to Park Lane by Rolls-Royce.

All being well there should be grouse on the menu for breakfast.

"The prospects for the shoot are quite good," said lord of the manor Lord Bolton. "The bad weather early in the year upset the breeding but there shouldn't be bad long-term effects.

"Eight guns will go out for the next three days and we expect the bag to be reasonable."

Grouse go first class

ON the "Glorious Twelfth" last week the first grouse of the season joined businessmen travelling to London on the early morning flight from Glasgow.

Peter Hill, general manager of Trusthouse Forte's Post House Hotel, Aviemore, was up before dawn to join a shoot organised by local landowner James Williamson. He then flew from Aviemore to Glasgow Airport by helicopter arriving with the grouse at 6.45am.

On arrival at Gatwick the grouse were taken through the airport to the station where the party boarded a train for Victoria.

A limousine whisked the party through London to the Cumberland Hotel arriving at 9.58am. Executive chef Michael Preston (left) received the grouse from Jamie Williamson, son of the laird on whose estate the grouse was shot.

The birds were escorted into the hotel's kitchens to the sound of the pipes.

Figure 17.1 Free Publicity

at peak viewing time. All he did was offer them a beer or a coke as they were working outside on a hot day.

Journalists enjoy visiting hotels. It is far nicer interviewing a hotel manager than visiting a factory or standing in the cold somewhere. But remember their problem is time and a deadline. So be Jack the Problem Solver by giving them a write-up of your story, preferably on one sheet of paper. And if it is a story where a photograph is available (e.g. the new chef or the sponsored wheelbarrow race in your grounds) always send them a photograph. Photographs cover a lot of column inches but, if they use it, this is the finest eye catching kind of free publicity.

Try not to feel inhibited about obtaining press publicity. Sometimes a 'stunt' has to be thought up to obtain a write-up. An example was the Crest Hotel next door to Wembly Stadium, London, where they arranged for a horse to check in at reception when the Horse of

This prize Aberdeen Angus bull was on parade outside the Carlton Tower Hotel, London, last week to mark the re-opening of the Rib Room. Pictured with the bull are Nick Bondonno, Rib Room Manager (left), and executive chef, Bernard Gaume (right).

Carlton Tower's Rib Room re-opens

THE RIB ROOM at London's Carlton Tower, renowned for its roast beef, re-opened last Thursday with a new menu, new decor and a new image.

The restaurant was completely gutted and interior decorator and designer Charles Hammond was given a budget of £150,000 and just four weeks to complete the refurbishment.

Aiming to appeal to a new and possibly younger clientele, the 135-cover Rib Room has a piano bar, complementing the hotel's recently launched "happy hour". Mirrored walls, intimate circular banquette seating, indirect lighting and a custom-designed carpet add to the improvements.

Other features are new tableware, illuminated wine display racks holding up to 900 bottles and a new carving bar. (See Pilgrim's Diary, page 26.) □

Figure 17.2

DAILY EXPRESS Thursday May 29 1975

Everybody's welco where the bridesm

PHOTO NEWS

...at Britain's first theatre-restaurant production

"HELLO? Booking office? I'd like two seats for *Another Bride, Another Groom.*"

"Certainly, sir. With chips or croquette potatoes?"

"What? No, you misunderstand me. I'd just like two seats in the circle."

"No circles, sir. No stalls, no boxes. I can do you a couple next to the ketchup bottle. Or would you prefer the gravy-boat?"

"Oh I don't know. Just give me two at £5·95."

"Delighted, sir. Would you care to see the wine list?"

It's a whole new concept in dinner-and-the-theatre, and it opens in London on Monday.

Remember your indigestion from rushing your pre-theatre meal? Remember your indignation at being told you mustn't smoke? Remember the times the people on-stage were boozing away like loonies; while down there in the

5

me at the wedding aid does a strip!

Comic couple . . . Sally Watts and Roderick Smith are the bride and groom

Pictures: Hilaria McCarthy **Words:** Martin White

audience you were dry as Prohibition?

"Another Bride, Another Groom," puts an end to all those upsets. You can smoke yourself to death if you like. Also eat, drink and throw bread rolls.

Knees-up

And while you're at it, you're acting in the play. They call it total theatre. Well, it's total hotel, to be accurate. The play takes place in the banqueting hall of the London Tara Hotel.

You go along and banquet on pate and veal escalope. You gurgle the wine. And the clever part is . . . it's all in the script.

"Another Bride" is a comedy about a wedding reception: Well-heeled cockney lad (Roderick Smith) marries shabby-genteel girl (Sally Watts). The wine-and-dine audience double as the wedding guests. They join in the toasts and the singsongs and it ends with a bit of a knees-up: you can have a dance with Anna Karen (Olive in "On the Buses") or Benny Lee, the comic . . . or anyone you can grab.

The idea went down like mad in Melbourne, where the play ran for two years. Now it's been translated into English: "My God," said scriptwriter Alec Myles palely yesterday. "That Australian humour. The very first line was xxx???!!!***.

"Mind you, it's still pretty boozy and ribald.

"The bridesmaid (Seretta Wilson) ends up doing a strip."

"This is Britain's first real theatre-restaurant production," says director Eleanor Fazan, the woman who choreographed the 'Food Glorious Food' number in 'Oliver' and directed the revue 'Share My Lettuce.'

"Don't know about you," said Anna Karen. "When I go to the theatre I get very uptight over the fact that I can't have a cigarette until the interval.

Tricks

"People who go to the clubs can see a variety show and have a smoke. But if you want to see a play it has to be in a terribly formal atmosphere. Well, it puts people off. What we've got here is a proper play with the club atmosphere.

"It'll be a different technique with the acting, of course. There'll be 250 people, and the front table will be as close to me as you are, luv. Well, you can't get up to the little tricks you do on a normal stage.

"I'm acting for the first time with my husband, Terry Duggan," she said. "I have to hit him over the head with a plate. Normally you'd miss, of course. Here I have to give him a right thump. Well, it's not every day you get a legitimate chance to bash your old man on the head. . . ."

Weren't they afraid the audience might overact a bit? Especially with their right elbows?

"Yes, I'm sure they'll get tight," she said. "But we think they'll get happy tight."

"Waiter! Waiter! Just a little recitation entitled 'She Was Only a Clergyman's Daughter. . . .'"

Figure 17.3 Putting a Hotel on the Map

the Year Show was on. This appeared in the magazine *Horse and Hound*. The right stunt, for the right location, in exactly the right media.

When the Carlton Tower Hotel in London re-opened its Rib Room restaurant, renowned for its roast beef, with a new menu and decor, they actually brought a prize Aberdeen Angus bull outside the hotel, and receive considerable free press publicity. (See Figure 17.2, a copy of press cutting). Again the right publicity for the right theme.

With the right creative thinking and planning it is possible to obtain free press publicity in the national and international press. David Levin who owns the Capital Hotel in Knightsbridge and The Green House Restaurant in Mayfair, London, obtains some excellent write-ups in America.

I could go on giving you examples, but everyone must try to be different and a little original, which is easier said than done. Perhaps the best example of sheer maximum exposure was something The London Tara (part of The Dunfey Group owned by Aer Lingus) did around 1975. From 1971 to 1973 literally two dozen new large hotels opened in London as the then Labour government was giving a grant of 20 per cent on new hotels opened before 31st March, 1973. During this period hotels seemed to open each week. There were eleven 4 and 5 Star new hotels and many more new 3 Star hotels. Before 1971, if a new hotel opened in London that was news and the hotel would obtain considerable coverage in the national press, London press, television and media generally. By 1973 a new hotel was not news at all. They all opened and obtained publicity but generally only if they paid for it, and some hotel owners paid out a fortune in full-page advertisements in the nationals when they could have put a hotel sales executive out in the field selling for a whole year for the cost of a single advertisement.

Like every other hotel, The London Tara, with 844 rooms, could not obtain much free publicity. Then one day they introduced a very unusual theatre show in the function room. The general manager, Oien Dillon, saw a show in Australia called 'Another Bride, Another Groom' and brought it to London. As well as obtaining free press publicity it is also a good example of being a SPACEMAN, selling a function room in a quiet period. Most people like going to a wedding. The idea was that the public bought tickets to this wedding. They arrived, sat down and were served a meal. Then the bride and groom arrived with their families, apologized for being late and sat down at the top table. They were all actors. There were funny speeches, arguments, songs and the bridesmaid got drunk and did a strip. An example of the free press coverage is shown in Figure 17.3. They had a half-page of free press publicity in The Daily Express with two large photographs. And the story was featured in nearly every London and National newspaper. Can you imagine the cost if they had to buy this coverage as paid advertising? But it was all free. They did not make a huge profit on the actual sale of tickets for the meal and show, but it certainly put the Tara 'on the map', virtually overnight.

* * * * *

18

SALES LETTERS AND MAILING SHOTS

Hotel management and hotel sales executives are constantly writing sales letters, either in answer to an incoming enquiry or in order to stimulate new business. In a sense a sales letter is a mailing shot. Many people use mailing shots to stimulate new enquiries, and letters to deal with incoming enquiries. You will see in the next chapter on telephone selling that I recommend using the telephone more often to deal with incoming enquiries whenever a significant amount of business is involved, rather than just sending a letter in reply to an enquiry.

Like every form of selling, writing a successful sales letter requires empathy. Put yourself in the seat, or shoes, of the person you are selling to with a letter. Does he sit in his office alone quietly thinking when the door opens and your letter is brought in by his secretary? It rarely happens like this. Usually he is delayed by early morning traffic so he arrives in his office late. Instead of having an hour to quietly clear his post, he only has three quarters of an hour before his first meeting of the day.

He sits down at his desk and instead of just your one letter there is a pile of letters and mailing shots in front of him. Before he can start on his post his secretary points out two urgent telephone calls from Mr. Giles and Mr. Smith. He knows Giles, a supplier, is always in a panic and asks his secretary to contact him and say he will telephone him after 3 p.m. He telephones Smith, an important customer, and spends fifteen minutes dealing with this call. At this point he realizes he must visit the toilet. Eventually he sits down again to clear his post with only about 20 minutes left before his meeting. With a groan he throws all mailing shots straight into his waste paper basket, together with all long, boring-looking sales letters. He feels better at once and concentrates fully on the five remaining letters. Four are from customers. The other is from an hotel following his enquiry about booking the company's annual sales conference. He asks his secretary to file the hotel's letter with the other ones so that he can read it when all the replies are in from the six hotels he wrote to.

Exaggerated? Not at all. This is a typical reaction of a busy executive. So the very first objective behind any sales letter and mailing shot is to 'grab' his attention so that he starts to read it. This is what the lead-in opening paragraph or heading must achieve. Often an opening point in the form of a question can help attract someone's attention.

A checklist on Selling Letters and Mailing Shots is shown in Checklist 18.1. Go through your files and take out sales letters (and mailing shots) you have sent out previously and the typical letters you have sent out in response to an enquiry for, say, a conference, function or wedding. Use the checklist against your own letters to see whether you can improve on your past sales correspondence. It is also useful to use the ten point checklist on Successful Advertising, shown in a previous chapter. Re-write the series of past letters and then ask someone else to use the two checklists and carry out a critique on your own letters. Do not be afraid of criticism or using your deputy (or boss) to help re-construct a better letter. After all, the objective is to increase your success rate in the future. There has never been a sales letter I have written which I have looked at again at a later date and felt completely happy with. So many times I see obvious faults. This is healthy. Usually there are more obvious faults when I have hurried too much.

Once you have 'grabbed' the recipient's attention he then has to read on, so try to have an inspirational lead in. Business executives are rarely very inspired but the opening sentence(s) should be interesting enough to make them read on. Keep the message to one aspect per letter, e.g. a conference, annual office party, or special event in the restaurant. Wherever the particulars are likely to be lengthy attach them to the letter rather than including in the body of the letter. Tell a success story in the sense of saying 'As we tend to be fully booked . . .' or 'the last Edwardian evening we held in the restaurant was so very successful many customers asked us to hold another one.'

A really good sales letter (like all selling) requires pre-planning and 'research' first. In this way you can personalize the letter more with the special advantages of the buyer's demands and explain the benefits of your hotel (over any competition) to the prospective customer.

It is vitally important to devise a conclusion which endeavours to

CHECKLIST 18.1

SELLING LETTERS AND MAILING SHOTS

1 Write a headline or first paragraph to evoke attention.
2 Add an inspirational lead in.
3 Give a clear definition of the product (conference, weekend attraction, Christmas activities, etc.)
4 Tell a success story.
5 Include testimonials and endorsements of satisfied consumers where applicable but show these separate to the main letter.
6 List special advantages and explain benefits to consumer.
7 Devise good *action* conclusion which will stimulate immediate response.
8 Add short postscript similar to first paragraph (could be handwritten if short and your handwriting is good).

stimulate an immediate response rather than have a generalized open ended letter. However good the letter is, should the recipient put it aside to do something at a later date there is a strong chance he will not pick it up again at a later date. So the letter should try to create an immediate reaction i.e. 'book NOW by telephoning . . .' 'complete reply paid card for further information' or 'as we usually get fully booked by the end of this month . . .' One of the most successful methods I have found in order to increase the rate of response is to add a handwritten short postscript with one of the phrases mentioned in the previous sentence or linked to the lead in headline.

Keep the letter short and unless there are very special circumstances, never more than one page. Use as many 'you's' as possible related to the number of times you use the word 'I'. Try to start the letter with the word 'you' in the opening three words. It is often more readable if you interspace each paragraph with some very short paragraphs of one or two words like:

'Well, we did.'
'You might ask why?'

Nobody has even really tried to differentiate between a sales letter and a mailing shot. The major advantage of a sales letter over a mailing shot is that you can actually start with the prospective customer's name. To me this is the major difference between the two. Whenever you have a person's actual name a specific personalized letter is the answer. A series of letters addressed to 'the managing director' and 'Dear Sir' are really the same as mailing shots.

Mailing shots are less indiscriminately used nowadays as hoteliers realize the importance of face-to-face selling, telephone calls and personalized selling. They do have the disadvantage of selling a mile wide and an inch deep. Today, with the use of word processors, it is becoming much more economical to type a series of 'original' letters to prospective buyers. They can be very useful if they cover a specific promotion, special event or a new development in a hotel like the opening of a new conference room(s) or a change in the restaurant's menu. In fact, one of the most effective mailing shots I have ever seen was the actual new menu sent through the post to major past users of the restaurant. Alternatively a miniaturized exact copy of a menu can be very successful as a mailing shot.

As mentioned earlier, a steady drip, drip impact on a major user of hotel facilities is often more effective than a hard sell. Sometimes it can take one or two years of steady, persistent selling to convert a major potential customer out of his inertia, to use your hotel. If the correct research has been carried out and you know the amount of business involved is significant, it can be well worthwhile taking one or two years of selling to obtain this man's business. Telephoning him every quarter, or a sales letter every quarter, can begin to irritate unless the message is different each time – even where you have been able to show him round your own hotel. Therefore it is recommended that the sales technique is varied as a follow-up to his visit to the hotel, or in order to persuade him to examine your facilities, namely:

a sales letter followed by
a telephone call followed by
a mailing shot
then a face to face visit followed by
a letter

Throughout this sequence the objective must be to get him to try you *once*. In this sequence of events a mailing shot in between more direct selling can help to remind him that you are there and still want his business, without running the risk of appearing too desperate or overselling.

Where it is difficult to obtain potential buyers specific names, or it is just impossible to spend the time telephoning or visiting potential customers, then mailing shots may be the most cost effective and time effective method of reaching a large number of people. This is mainly applicable on the launch of a new hotel, after the revamping of a restaurant, etc. Whenever the source of business is a smaller number of customers or companies who are likely to spend a large amount per company, then ideally selling should be face to face. Where there is a large number of people spending a lower amount per person, mailing shots may be one of the techniques to use.

Mailing shots come in literally all shapes and sizes. I am not sure if I actually invented the idea but in the 60s I noticed that we were obtaining a much better response from what I called 'the see-through mailing shot'. This is where the recipient receives a mailing shot and can see part of the message through a circle or square hole so that he just has to open it up and read the message. From this time we began to use them mainly with a question visible through the opening. We even had one designed for The Royal Scot Hotel in Edinburgh (Figure 18.1) with a series of small holes and one large one in the centre so that the recipient could just see the number – 198. When it was opened the message was promoting the hotel as a base for a golfing holiday.

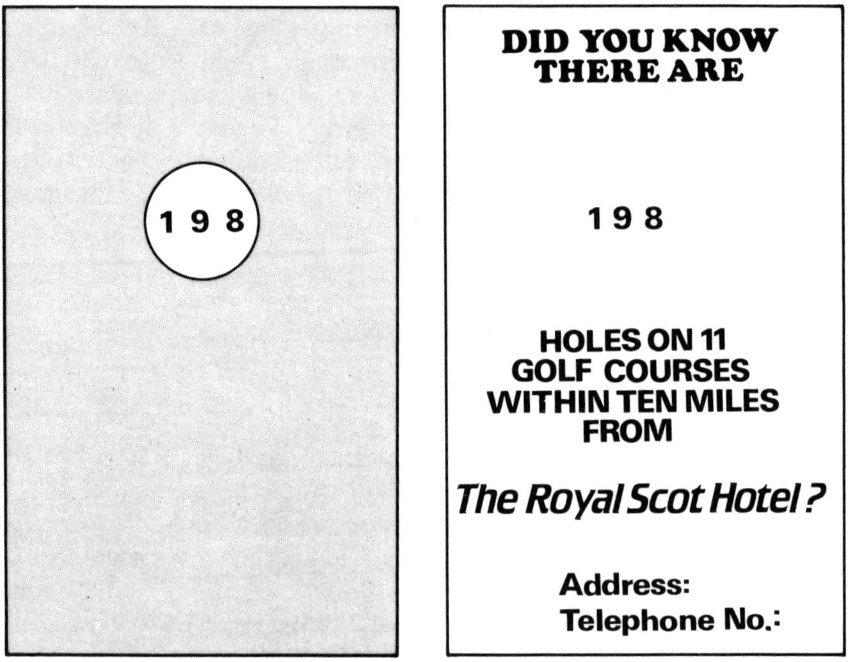

Figure 18.1 Golf Shot – Front Cover and Inside

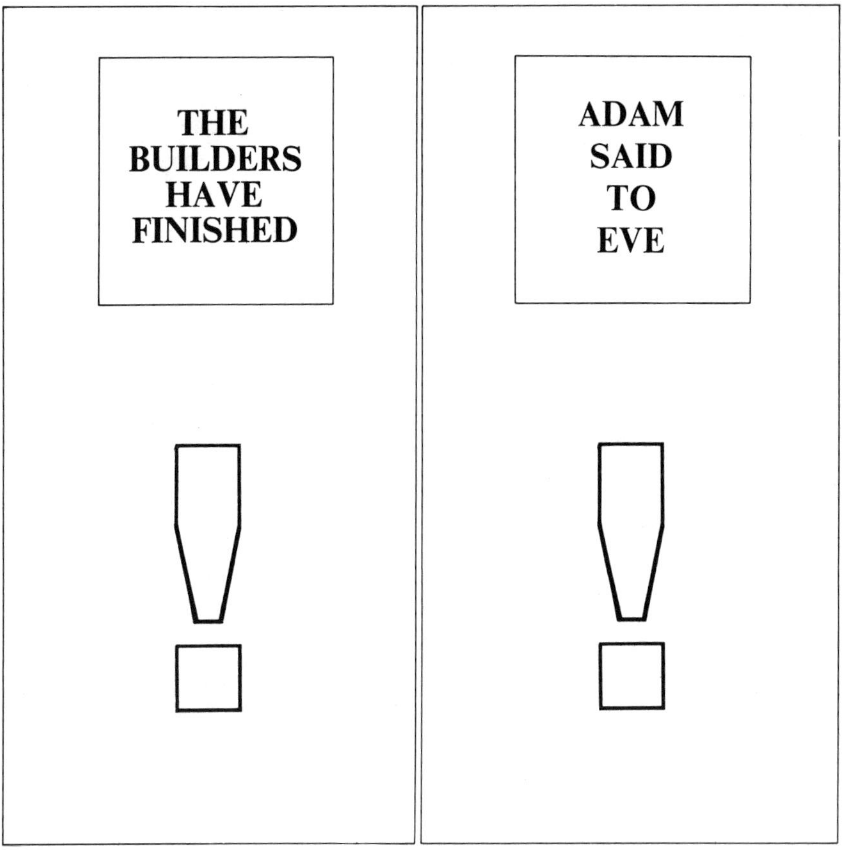

Figure 18.2 Front Covers of Two Mailing Shots

Mailing shots do not have to be expensive. Let me just show you examples of a series sent out by Paul McCoy, after he bought The Stower Grange Hotel and restaurant near Norwich, England.

The risk I take in showing Paul's mailing shots is that all my other clients and friends are going to say 'Why didn't he use ours?' So I deliberately chose an independent hotel operator rather than an illustration from a client with a group of hotels and much greater resources. These are shown in order to illustrate the 'see-through' principle where you only see a question. The reaction must be to open them and read the message. Two are shown in Figure 18.2, closed so that you only see the short statement or question. The Figures 18.3 and 18.4 show the inside of the two-page mailing shot.

THE BUILDERS HAVE FINISHED

Dear

We believe that large menus offering an extensive range of dishes are fast becoming impracticable, therefore, we have designed our three course fixed price menu with the following points in mind.

To give you a selection of dishes, some well-known, others less known which we hope you will try.

To charge a price known to you in advance (with a few exceptions) for three courses, appetiser, main course and sweet.

To use wherever possible fresh local produce, changing the range of dishes regularly to embrace the best of each season.

We look forward to welcoming you.

Yours sincerely,

PAUL McCOY

A NEW RESTAURANT FOR YOU

So when you are next entertaining Business Associates, Friends or just want a good meal in congenial surroundings, give us a call.

LUNCH
Tuesday, Wednesday, Thursday and Sunday for the family.

DINNER
Monday to Sunday

Fixed Price for Three Courses £6.95

Fixed Price for Sunday Lunch £4.75

Inclusive of VAT, plus Service Charge

The Stower Grange, Drayton

Norwich 860210

Figure 18.3 The Builders Have Finished – Inside

The first one was sent out to all local companies within ten miles of The Stower Grange just after the hotel re-opened. Paul only used a small, carefully selected mailing list, but he did find names wherever possible so he combined 'the Builders Have Finished' as a mailing shot *and* a letter so that he could personalize the message inside the left hand side of the opened mailing shot. The 'Adam Said to Eve' mailing shot is original for Britain because you rarely find spare ribs on menus outside London and some other major cities. This mailing shot is the actual menu.

Naturally the shots were in colour and every time he sent them out he used a different colour for the card and for the typeface. He steadily sends these out every few months and particularly prior to a

ADAM
SAID
TO
EVE

On **FRIDAY EVENINGS** until the end of February we will give you **FREE** a bottle of our House Wine, to enjoy with your Dinner. (Bottle between two persons).

LUNCH
Tuesday, Wednesday, Thursday and Sunday for the Family

DINNER
Monday to Saturday

Fixed Price for Three Courses £6.95

Sunday Lunch £4.75

AN IDEAL VENUE FOR WEDDING RECEPTIONS

The Stower Grange, Drayton
Norwich 860210

SPARE RIBS are back and with them you can have a choice of:-

HOME-MADE SOUP
MUSSEL TARTLET FLORENTINE
SPICED BARBEQUED SPARE RIBS
PRAWN, AVOCADO AND MUSHROOM MEDLEY
FRIED MARINATED MUSHROOMS, REMOULADE SAUCE
APPLE, SULTANA AND TURKEY APPETIZER
WITH MUSTARD MAYONNAISE
MEDITERRANEAN PRAWNS

LASSAGNE VERDI
STEAK, KIDNEY AND SMOKED OYSTER PIE
BREAST OF CHICKEN CORDON BLEU
FILLETS OF LEMON SOLE CAPRICE
TURKEY ESCALOPES WITH HAZELNUT CREAM SAUCE
NOISETTES OF LAMB, MADEIRA SAUCE (1.35p extra)
SIRLOIN STEAK (1.35p extra) or
PEPPERED SIRLOIN OF BEEF FINISHED WITH
CREAM AND BRANDY (1.65p extra)
ACCOMPANYING FRESH VEGETABLES

CHOICE OF HOME-MADE SWEETS
AND ICE CREAMS OR CHEESE
COFFEE 65p extra

£6.95 Inclusive of VAT plus 10% Service Charge

Figure 18.4 What Adam said to Eve

period where he knows business can show a seasonal decline. Paul would agree this was not an expensive exercise but it was, and still is, a very worthwhile action point in his total Sales Action Plan.

* * * * *

19

TELEPHONE SELLING

There are many occasions when we could use the telephone more often for 'outgoing' selling and in dealing with incoming enquiries. Many people write to hotels and ask for information on weddings or, say, for the convention brochure. Or they telephone and ask for this information and the hotel employee takes the message, name, address and sometimes the telephone number, saying 'Certainly we will send the information on to you'. A short call to the enquirer asking a few questions about dates, numbers, etc., followed by a letter and then a further follow-up telephone call to see if there is any additional information they require and whether they would like to visit the hotel, is bound to be far more effective than even the most attractive, dynamic letter and sales literature just on their own. And this is rarely considered a hard sell, but you will be recognized as a caring professional trying to do a good job for the customer.

If it is true that we are in a people industry, and a total people situation, then the more you can get 'closer' to an actual person, preferably in your own hotel, the more successful you will be. Often it is not practical *initially* to meet someone face-to-face and so the next best situation is where you can actually talk to each other, even if you cannot see each other. As well as dealing with incoming enquiries the telephone can be a very effective sales tool in selling to new potential customers, or to previous customers who have not used you lately.

However, people seem to be either inhibited to use the telephone for selling, or they overdo it. We are more used to the telephone when there is an incoming enquiry, so why not use it more to stimulate business? Used well, it can be the most cost-effective method of achieving a sales objective. Why cost effective? Telephone calls are expensive in some countries, but compared with the time spent on personal visits, and the lack of measurable results from paid advertising, a well-planned telephone call is one of the most effective methods of reaching a key person and achieving a specific sales objective.

One problem is that many people make a telephone call without a specific objective. A well-planned telephone sales call can be over and successful in under thirty seconds (unless the customer wants to chat). But a lot of people use the telephone to try to close a sale and make a firm booking. Too many people expect to make a booking on an *outgoing* call because they are used to making a booking from *incoming* calls. It rarely happens in practice unless you have known the customer for some time. Telephone selling is very effective for quick sales research calls, e.g. 'Have you booked your annual dinner-dance yet?' And it is probably the most effective way of setting up a face-to-face sales session, namely an appointment to see the prospective customer – or more important, an appointment within your own hotel to show him the actual 'product', namely your own facilities.

The inhibition against telephone selling can be overcome with practice. Many people feel tense in making a telephone sales call. In fact many smokers light up a cigarette immediately they start, or just before, a telephone call. This is a mistake. If the call is going to be polite and short with a limited achievable objective then it should only last a minute or two, and it is important not to smoke. Your voice and message should flow naturally. But when you are smoking, every time you breathe in smoke, your voice will pause. This could mean he will lose the thread of your message and may give him a chance to interrupt.

Use Checklist 19.1. If you have rarely made outgoing telephone sales calls before, practice on the least likely prospects whom you fell are not of primary importance. And then graduate to your primary prospects. In the checklist you will see that five of the nine points cover another of my phobias – pre-planning. They are five points *before* you have made the call.

Research calls can be carried out by many different members of the hotel staff. If you ask *one* young sales executive, or a deputy manager, to spend two or three solid weeks telephoning the 163 local companies above a certain size to find out the name and position of the person who books hotel rooms for overnight visitors to their factory/office, you may well overburden one member of the staff who may cut corners. But if you divide the work amongst four or five employees, this will create team spirit, motivate them, and they can have a laugh over their mistakes.

CHECKLIST 19.1

TELEPHONE SELLING

1 Always have prospect's indexed card and file available before you make the call and prepare new card if first call.

2 Make up your mind beforehand what message you want to put across, be it to introduce yourself and say 'hello' or to invite him for a drink and see your meeting facilities.

3 Always find out the name of the person to whom your are speaking before getting through to him – and use his name.

4 Ensure that you are not going to be interrupted.

5 Ask your telephonist/receptionist to put you through to the company, not the man, otherwise she may irritate him by getting through and then asking him to hold on while she connects with you. Better still, dial direct yourself.

6 Introduce yourself by christian and surname and state name of hotel or hotel company.

7 If it is obvious that he is in a meeting or in a totally unreceptive mood, say you will telephone back but still try to get a short message across, e.g. 'I was only going to invite you to have a look around the hotel, but as you are obviously busy, I will ring back when it is more convenient.'

8 Keep the chat short and and sharp, unless the man at the other end wishes to chat. Even then, do not go on for too long.

9 Do not forget to follow up with details and menus or a letter confirming the date of your meeting.

Once you have the key research information, the first sales call should be made by someone of authority in the hotel. Some hotel sales executives and hotel managers disagree and feel the first call could well be delegated to a more junior member of the staff, particularly as so often people are not available, or tied up at a meeting. My feeling is that the customer likes to deal with a person of authority in the hotel. Even if you establish contact with the prospective customer's secretary and learn her name this is vitally important. My own diary of clients' telephone numbers has most of their secretaries' names alongside.

Not every call will achieve the objective, in fact, you probably will only get through to the right person once out of every three calls. With outgoing calls try to set aside a specific time of the day, or week, to telephone new prospects. Avoid Monday morning or Friday afternoon. Clear your desk from eye distracting daily income reports, complaint letters, memos from head office. Turn away from this month's girl on the Unipart calendar. Try not to look out of the window and face a blank wall, or corner of the room so that you can concentrate on the call and the recipient. If you have met the recipient think of the face in front of you as you talk.

Talk down slightly into the mouthpiece rather than up to it. Do not cup the telephone under your chin when you are selling. And never use a loudspeaker hook-up because this creates a slight but disturbing echo. Your desk should be clear except for an index card, a diary, a pen and a note pad with the objective of your call written down. Smile, hum a tune, think of a funny story before you dial. Your recipient won't see it but your voice will have a more relaxed, positive tone. Then dial through yourself.

I once spent days planning to obtain free P.R. in one of Britain's top daily newspapers on our firm's annual hotel tariff studies. I found the right man, told him the results would be ready in three days, and found the exact time to telephone in order to obtain a write-up in the next morning issue. I planned, researched, prepared my message, cleared my desk and waited for just the exact time. The minutes ticked by. I dialled after days of planning. And a voice said 'I am sorry, the print room has just gone on strike'. What a disappointment. But I was successful the next time and the write-up on the hotel tariff study trends was followed by calls to be interviewed on commercial radio, BBC radio, and two television appearances.

The key to success is to set up an achievable objective, a message which can be put across in 30 seconds and to let the person receiving the call know that you 'are not going to take up much of your time'.

Naturally, if he wants to chat don't cut him short. Quite often you may feel that you are making a 'cold' call but find that he knows the hotel and has been taken out to eat there. So the ice is broken and he may wish to chat. But be careful in this situation. It is much more difficult to use body signs and non-verbal communication than in face-to-face selling. His boss may suddenly walk in and he may close the conversation suddenly before you have achieved your objective.

Telephone selling saves everyone a lot of time and can be remarkably effective. In one group of hotels we identified one of the major problems as being low food and beverage sales in the group's hotel restaurants at lunch time mid-week. Most of the hotels were 4 star with excellent restaurants. Covers had steadily declined for about a year, but only at lunchtime. A series of action points were worked out for the whole group and one of them was for the restaurant manager to make a low-key telephone call to past regulars who had not been in lately. Some had been 'cutting back', others had switched to other restaurants. But many had just slipped out of the habit. Most businessmen spend all their working lives tipping Maitre d's and restaurant managers to get the best table and good service. Can you imagine the impact this telephone sales call made on their ego? Across the range of forty hotels in this group there was an immediate increase in covers of an average of thirty per day, success in anyone's language following a simple series of low-key telephone sales calls.

One further example. I know a manager who stutters. He was always a good hotel operator, but he hated making telephone calls. He attended one of our marketing and sales promotion courses and swears it changed his life because he was forced to make telephone sales calls in front of eighteen other hotel managers. When he returned to his hotel after the course, he found a series of enquiries including three for dinners, and two for weddings. He told me that previously he would have sent them details with a letter and if he did not obtain all five bookings that was 'the luck of the draw'. But he forced himself to telephone all five, then wrote, and he followed them up with a telephone call one week after they received his letter. He obtained all five bookings.

* * * * *

20

TECHNOLOGY AND NEW FORMS OF SELLING

If they have not changed by now many industries are going to change radically, particularly in manufacturing by the 90s with the introduction of computers, robots and new technologies. I do not think that new technology is going to have the same profound impact on hotels as in, say car manufacturing or newspapers.

Many hotels over a certain size have been computerized at least in the front office for guest billing, reservations etc. We have to be very careful when we instal computers that the guest still comes first.

On a recent business trip to the Middle East, I walked into a new 5-star hotel to check in. Approaching reception I noticed that all the receptionists and cashiers had their heads bowed. I could not see what they were looking at, and at first I thought they were praying. After standing there for what seemed a long time, I coughed and they looked up. I leaned over the reception desk to see what they were looking at and found they had all been staring at VDUs.

We are told by the manufacturers and salesmen of various types of computers, that installing their equipment will release hotel management and staff to spend more time with guests, not less. I am not sure that this is true. Some hotel staff seem hypnotized by the flickering screen and spend a lot of time looking at it, rather than having eye-to-eye contact with guests.

Not long ago a businesswoman I know was staying in an hotel and I called to say 'Hello'. I knew how to pronounce her name, but I did not know how to spell it. I wasn't sure whether it was Mrs Szabo or Mrs Zcabo. I asked reception whether she was staying at the hotel. They asked me to spell the first three letters of her name and that created a problem. The head receptionist said that unless I knew the first three letters of her name they could not help. At this point I began to argue. I was convinced there must be correspondence connected with her booking. I knew the day she had arrived and I was adamant that they must not just say 'No', but seek some other method of finding whether she was staying in the hotel. I did not win and the reception staff were not prepared to do any research, other than feed into the computer a series of variations on an unusual name.

On another occasion I checked into a large hotel in New York owned by a major group. When I was shown to my room I walked into the bathroom and found that the washbasin was blocked and full of dirty water. I telephoned the housekeeping department to have this attended to and was told that the computer said it was all right for letting, and the telephone was put down. I then rang the duty manager and after a pause, he repeated: 'The computer says the room is all right for letting'.

I believe that the computer is beginning to dominate the hotel scene rather than face-to-face personal contact, which is the only reason for staying in a hotel rather than a rented apartment.

In many countries like Britain, school children are not automatically taught to touch-type. In the USA, every executive knows how to touch-type because he/she is taught at school. So when you check into an hotel with a computer in America, they will type your name to check whether you have a reservation and still be able to look at you and talk to you. When you check into an hotel in other countries, they have to look at the keyboard or the screen and therefore you lose this all-important personal contact. There is also a much greater chance of errors in typing. I strongly recommend that as an essential part of installing computers in hotels, the manufacturers teach the relevant executives to touch-type so that they do not have to read the keyboard.

I sometimes wonder what improvement for guest billing the new computers are over the previous cash registers, which did a very good job. Problems arise because people want the computer to do everything, including guest billing, advance reservations, take the place of room racks, plan staff standards, allocate bedrooms, purchase and sales ledgers, and the accounts generally. The major use of computers where the benefits are obvious is in areas such as advance reservations and taking stock checks of bars and cellars. They are also useful in producing interpretive statistics.

What I would like to see when the guest checks in is the receptionist punching the name into the keyboard and then saying: 'Well, Mr Greene, I see this is your tenth visit in the past six months. This entitles you to a free weekend for two.' (Or a free stay or a suite.)

In many small hotels I think it would be a great mistake to computerize if it stops staff looking at the guest and makes them look at VDUs. In large hotels, I accept there are many advantages, but I wonder whether we do not end up with a subtle change of emphasis where the guest has to fit in with the computer.

In fact, there is no reason why the eye-to-eye contact and personal approach which is so vital in the hotel industry should be changed on the introduction of computers. Terminals could be where the guests cannot see them. Registration can be done in the usual way and the guest information taken down by hand. Sufficient information can be gathered in order to initiate the registration in the computer when the guest's full name and length of stay have been obtained. If the guest is a regular visitor or has stayed at the hotel recently that is all the information required to complete the entire check-in process if the registration is combined with a guest history data base stored in the computer's memory.

Computers started off as an aid to guest billing and then spread to other areas, like marketing. I wish in many ways it had been the other way round. We are just seeing the benefits on marketing on areas like guest history records and word processing. It is very difficult to produce a programme for guest history records and to keep records of *every* visitor. Software is now available to produce detailed guest histories providing records are only kept for guests who stay in an hotel more than once.

A very exciting potential for selling is in word processing. In the past it has always been difficult to prepare a sudden mailing on a key point which will go stale if not sent out very quickly. Now we can send out personal letters all individually typed, and separate mailing lists into different market segments for separate mailing – i.e. conference organizers, business clients, travel agents, full rate paying guests. I have found regular promotional mailings to a listing of guests who paid the full rack rate to be very effective.

And we should use this facility for present guests as well. With the word processing aspect of computers we could help to do some personalized in-house selling as well to present guests. Figure 20.1 shows an example of a personalized letter to guests which my wife and I received on a holiday in Rome. It isn't the finest sales letter in the world, but it has charm, and is very simpatico. Many readers could well use the penultimate paragraph on 'complaints' in their own letters.

With these facilities for your own use, even smaller hotels will have the basis for an executive centre so that the service can be offered to guests. I see this being as standard by the 90s as offering in-house movies.

By then the new technologies are going to have a profound effect on the way we communicate, and as communication is instrumental in selling they are going to have a major impact on how we sell.

The technology of printing and communicating the written word is changing now, and this change will be accelerated. Businessmen in their own countries and around the world through satellites are now able to hold audio-visual conferences with a telephone and screen, although this is more costly than people imagine. As they are beginning to do now, many businessmen will carry briefcase-size computers with them when they travel and will link up with the main central computer at head office.

Within hotels, hotel owners must keep up with the new methods of quick instant communication, otherwise the business market may decrease their use of hotels. Even as I write there are still many hotels, some of them well known, which have no telex or where there are no direct dial telephones in the bedrooms.

By the 90s hotels will use the telex and fax system much more instead of sales letters. Tape-recorded messages with background noises that sell, as well as the message, will be much more widely used than mailing shots.

Video tape films and discs promoting an hotel will be sent out to prospective buyers so that they can see the actual hotel's convention facilities on their own televisions. Hotel management and hotel sales executives will be able to take with them on sales trips flat, thin, miniaturized three-dimensional televisions and show their hotel's superb facilities. There will be a mass of whole new technological developments which will enable the hotel salesperson to show the hotel's facilities much more effectively than just the present brochure with the written word and photograph. It will indeed be a Brave New World. Or will it? Will it change everything?

I do not believe it will solve many of the problems – and there is a great danger. *Every* hotel will have access to these new methods of selling. Every professional buyer knows that these sales methods always make the hotel look better than it really is. And the entire public are all becoming 'professional buyers'. They all know that the hotel swimming pool in the tour operator's brochure is not as large as it appears.

The danger is that hotel people involved in selling away from the actual hotel may begin to rely on these aids too much. There is one phrase I will never forget, said by a propsective customer to a sales executive who had sent him beautiful brochures:

MARINI STRAND HOTEL

Via del Tritone, 17

67 20 61 - MariniHotel

00187 ROMA

TELEX: 612295 MARINI I

Direzione

7th Nov. 1985

Dear Mr and Mrs Greene,

I am delighted to welcome you to our HOTEL MARINI STRAND di ROMA.

I trust your journey was not too tiring and I hope your stay in Rome will be a happy one. Rest assured that I and my staff will do everything possible to make it so.

PLEASE do not hesitate to get in touch with me at once, via the Receptionist or Hall Porter, should you need any assistance or advice. Equally I should appreciate any comments or suggestions you care to make.

You may feel a little tired after your journey. Please accept with our compliments and I trust you will enjoy this refreshment as a small token of welcome.

I should like you to feel at home in our HOTEL MARINI STRAND di ROMA, and I very much desire that your stay with us will remain as one of the fond memories of your holiday.

Finally, please remember that I would prefer your complaint now rather than go home and grumble!

Always at YOUR service!

Yours sincerely

J.L. Pagani

Direttore

Figure 20.1

'I can see and I can read. Now I want *you* to make these words come to life.'

The most advanced audio visual display will not quite achieve this. They may provide facts, figures and information, but they will never answer all the questions. At least not by the 90s. In fact, I feel there will be a kind of rebellion or backlash against these sales aids. The advent of television in the home, and then colour television, helped to stimulate growth in international tourism. And these new technological developments will help as well.

But when *all* hotels use them in selling, the buyer is going to examine the people behind the glossy presentations even more carefully. Do their words carry credibility, does the 'chemistry' create confidence that when the buyer actually uses the hotel it will be as good as the audio visual presentation claims?

We will still ultimately have to rely on people to sell and with people the most important technique will always be face-to-face selling.

☆ ☆ ☆ ☆ ☆

21

FACE-TO-FACE SELLING

Nothing I could ever write would ever do justice to the importance of this subject. I have given a series of lectures with illustrations and question and answer sessions lasting for three days to small groups of hotel executives, and still felt a profound sense of being unsuccessful in putting across this subject. I am constantly surprised when I run through a checklist on myself after a face-to-face sales situation to find just how many major mistakes I have made and how many sales opportunities I have missed. Many times very successful salesmen say to me they remember a key sales point they wanted to stress, after they have left the sales situation.

Although I qualified originally as a chartered accountant, in some respects I am prouder of having a hotel and food service qualification, namely being a Fellow of the Hotel and Catering Institutional Management Association – HCIMA. But I consider myself a marketeer and am by nature a salesman. Salesmen are supposed to be self confident. Why do I feel as the years go by that I am still learning about selling and in particular face-to-face selling? Perhaps this is the way it should be. I get rather worried when people say to me there is nothing left for them to learn about selling and they have learned everything about sales technique.

All the experts agree that in order to succeed in selling you need:

EMPATHY

I have said a lot about EMPATHY. But this is only half the picture. You can have all the empathy in the world but if you cannot put your case to people (i.e. project yourself) you will never be good at selling. So as well as empathy it is necessary to have PROJECTION, the ability to project yourself. Projection is a combination of:

TECHNIQUE – how you package the words and present the offer

and

PSYCHOLOGY – the ability to understand and deal with people

Technique is always changing and there is no way any person involved in selling can ever have a perfect sales technique. Every set of circumstances is different. Every place you sell in can be different. You could be selling an identical product in your hotel e.g. a three-day convention for 500 delegates. You may have to sell this face to face:

in the actual convention room
in the buyer's office which might be private and quiet, or an open plan noisy office
to a committee
in a foreign country
etc.

The customers may be older than you, younger, or nowadays may even be gay. You may have plenty of time to prepare or be called at a moment's notice. All these circumstances and situations require a different emphasis in sales technique. And you can never stop learning about psychology – the ability to deal with people.

The day anyone says to you they have nothing to learn about selling, or that they are good at selling, is the day you can tell them they know *nothing* about selling. Sales technique can always be improved and one can never stop learning about people – psychology. Therefore one can never stop improving sales ability.

So the first, most important point to admit to yourself is that you can always improve your ability to sell. Following an acceptance of this point one can assume that if you can improve your ability to sell, you can also improve your hotel's sales and profits.

Essentially in selling, and in particular in face-to-face selling, you have to like people. In hotels and food service we often see the worst side of people. They can be rude to us in a way they would never be to other people. We see people when they are overawed, overeating and over-drinking. But whatever one thinks about people there is no doubt they are fascinating and generally likeable. And this is why face-to-face selling is so interesting.

There are many reasons why face-to-face selling is of greater importance than any other sales technique.

Firstly, it is the only sales situation where you can really have direct *instant* communication and see reactions. You can ask questions and show examples of menus, prices, etc. The buyer can ask you questions. You can show alternatives. The face-to-face sales situation may be in your own hotel, or initially in the prospective customer's own office. Either way it is the best situation to move a prospect forward steadily to achieve your pre-set sales objectives and ultimately a booking. And through this situation you can watch them *and* they can see you.

It provides the best circumstances for establishing a personal relationship. Some people are extremely good over the telephone or at writing letters and can establish a good rapport this way. An example of a superb letter writer is David Wexler, publisher of *Restaurant* and *Institutions*. We corresponded for about two years before we finally met at the 21 Club in New York. His style of writing letters is so good I felt I knew him before we met. But in the vast majority of cases the best, and often the only, way of establishing a personal relationship is face-to-face.

However large a hotel is, the importance of customers having a relationship with someone of authority should never be underestimated. In a small to medium-size hotel this should preferably be with the hotel manager. In a large hotel this could be the head of sales, food and beverage manager, head receptionist or banquetting manager. I am not saying that the manager or general manager of every medium to large size hotel should meet all guests or customers every time they visit the hotel. But thc general manager should have met all customers who provide a significant amount of business for his hotel, or other hotels in the group.

The importance of establishing a personal relationship really lies in two 'negative' situations. *Every* hotel has one, or some, faults or disadvantages for the customer. There are few hotels that have perfect facilities for every different source of business, or every different type of buyer. I remember one hotel manager of a 150-room business hotel who argued that I was wrong and he sincerely felt his hotel had everything correct relevant to his price bracket. So one evening we politely asked five of his regular guests whether this was true. Nearly all of them complained about three points.

They said the light switches were not immediately inside the bedroom door and were not luminous. The bathroom shelf in front of the mirror was too deep so some had to wear their glasses to shave. And they all said that the two hotel elevators (lifts) were slow, and seemed much slower in the morning when they were hurrying out to work. But they all very obviously had a good personal relationship with this hotel manager and his staff and therefore were prepared to ignore these 'small' but annoying points.

There comes a time when a regular customer thinks of trying another hotel. Sometimes he is bored and looking for a change. Perhaps a series of things have gone wrong. Or his head office have reduced his total budget for hotel accommodation, his management seminars, or his entertainment budget. If there is a personal relationship there is a much greater chance he will mention this to the hotel manager so he will have an opportunity to do something about it. Where there is no personal relationship he just leaves one day and you never see him again.

NON-VERBAL COMMUNICATION

Apart from face-to-face selling having the foregoing advantages it has one other major advantage. It is the only real sales situation where you can practice non-verbal communication (NVC), a subject mentioned before with the earlier example of the way people answer 'ye . s . s'. When people are buying they do not like to commit themselves too much (at least early on in the sales situation) by saying too much – even if they agree with you. But they may nod slightly in agreement without noticing they are nodding.

It is far easier for people to control the words they say than the body movements that they make, very often, without realizing. Later on, after the various checklists, there is a section on Closing, or achieving one's objectives, where an example of how you can use NVC yourself is shown. Let me provide a few more examples.

A new prospective customer arrives in your office, or in the case of a small hotel, in a quiet corner of the hotel, and you sit him down. You may ask him whether he wants a coffee and you start selling by listening to him if he wants to talk. Perhaps you start to ask him questions. This could be before you show him your facilities, or you have already shown him the hotel. Generally experience tells you not to sell too much as soon as he is seated. So you gradually move the situation forward in a logical sequence. But when should you start to move to close the sale? He will rarely tell you, if he has never used your hotel before. So how will you know?

Very often a good clue is the way he is sitting. When they first sit down in a strange office most people do not sit on the whole chair, or armchair – they sit on the front two-thirds and they do not lean back. But at a certain point they will often shift their weight and put their whole bottom on the chair and their own back against the back of the chair, i.e. they begin to relax. When they first come in their eyes cannot help looking around for the first few minutes or longer. And then their eyes rest on you and their attention on your sales message. These non-verbal situations really mean this is the point when they are receptive to whatever you are saying.

The other advantage of face-to-face is you can sense the vibrations, or chemistry, of a meeting. No audio visual link-up will ever have this advantage. There are times when the prospective buyer is tired, hot and fed up. Perhaps he had a row with his wife that morning. And you receive bad vibrations even though you have in no way caused them yourself. But hopefully if you are conscious of them you can change the whole chemistry of the meeting because he receives the right vibrations from you.

Between 6 p.m. and 7 p.m. in the evening most hoteliers in the hotel lobby, watching their guests returning from work, can tell you which one had a good day and which had a bad day, just by the way they walk in. In a busy restaurant you can tell who is getting bad service – the swivelling head, the drumming of fingers – without asking anyone.

Like everything, face-to-face selling has degrees of success. Successful face-to-face selling arises from six aspects:

1 Carrying out as much RESEARCH as possible in advance.
2 Detailed PLANNING of the sales call/situation – including setting your objective.
3 How one COMMUNICATES with the client.
4 Being JACK THE PROBLEM SOLVER.
5 Being CONSUMER ORIENTATED.
6 The CLOSE – achieving your objective.

All of these have been dealt with previously except for point 6 on Closing, which will be covered later. A series of checklists is included in this chapter. The first one is shown in the following 16 points on a situation where the potential customer comes to you but many of them are equally applicable if you go out to visit him:

CHECKLIST 21.1

FACE TO FACE SELLING

1 Knowledge of the client before his arrival – full name, what he wants, who he works for (if applicable) and when he is arriving. Set your objectives beforehand.
2 Have his index history card in front of you – or if it is a first enquiry, prepare one ready for the meeting. Have prospectus sheet checklists available (functions, meetings, courses, exhibitions) – a separate one for the different sources of business.
3 Reception and porters should be informed that you are expecting a customer, his name, time, etc., so that they can greet him by name.
4 Be punctual at meetings and if possible receive the client at the reception desk.
5 Introduce yourself by stating christian name and surname – be friendly rather than familiar – the object being to try to break down any formal barriers. 'My name is Greene – Melvyn Greene'.
6 If you do not have an office which is quiet and suitable for your meeting, use an unobtrusive area of the hotel.
7 In order to achieve a relaxed atmosphere offer the client a coffee, drink or cold drink, and a cigarette: if he declines, resist over-indulgence yourself, particularly if he says he is a non-smoker. Beware of a first time visitor who arrives just before lunch and asks for a dry martini, when he was due earlier. He may well be a free-loader.
8 Avoid any physical or mental barriers being created, e.g. a desk between you, the customer being seated in too low a chair, too much paperwork on the table.
9 Be clear and concise about the description of the services which you offer
10 Always answer questions directly.
11 Avoid being interrupted at all costs by telephone or by staff.
12 Avoid having to search for information.
13 Do not interrupt him when he is talking but make sure you move the meeting forward.
14 Avoid rushing him and allow adequate time for the meeting.
15 At some time during the sales meeting mention price clearly – but if possible choose your own time for mentioning this.
16 Did you achieve your objectives?

Even if you follow all the points you may still lose a sale on some personal aspect. With personal aspects it is necessary to be fairly self-critical of your own personality because sometimes you don't realize you are doing some things wrong – distracting mannerisms, for example, may be difficult to recognize in yourself. Some personal aspects to avoid are:

(a) Distracting or offensive mannerisms
(b) Insincerity
(c) Disrespect
(d) Unfriendliness
(e) Creation of doubt
(f) Unreliability
(g) Too much or too little enthusiasm
(h) Lack of knowledge of the product or client
(i) Over-confidence
(j) Never run down a competitor
(k) Never tell a customer about your problems

Most of the foregoing are self-explanatory. On point (j), be careful about running down a competitor as the buyer may be using the competitor at present. If you list *all* the disadvantages of the current hotel he is using there is a danger you may alienate him because he may feel foolish. It is far more constructive selling to simply stress your advantages without overdoing all the other hotel's disadvantages.

On point (k) avoid telling a customer about your problems. He doesn't really want to know if your chef just quit or it is difficult to hire good banqueting staff nowadays. After all he may well have staff problems in his own company.

An appraisal checklist is shown in Checklist 21.2. I was given this years ago and although I amend it from time to time it is still very useful. Use this before *and* after a sales call to monitor your own performance. Many hotel and sales executives who use it have told me that it is instrumental in helping them improve their face-to-face selling. Do not worry if you constantly score below 100 per cent. Nobody scores 100 per cent. After all, you are not in complete control of the situation.

The buyer may interrupt the whole time or cut the meeting short quite suddenly. The objective of this checklist is to help you improve future ratings. A number of the twenty points in the checklist are applicable to other sales techniques, e.g. telephone sales calls.

CHECKLIST 21.2

APPRAISAL OF SELLING TECHNIQUE

You should check through this list before and after a sales call and try to judge objectively how you performed.

1 Appointment getting and planning

2 Plan pre-call – setting objectives of call

3 Punctuality

4 Greeting

5 Your appearance

6 Information seeking

7 'Yes' questions

8 Listening

9 Not interrupting – self control

10 Control of interview

11 Closing

12 Product knowledge

13 Empathy

14 Business ethics

15 Mannerisms

16 Originality

17 Handling objections

18 Logic

19 Use of alternatives

20 Ask for sale.

Be careful that you do not lose a sale because of what I call *technique expressions* which are basically:

EYES
VOICE
SPEECH
ATTITUDE
LISTENING

With EYES look the other person straight in the eyes without staring. Sometimes people look up, or look down, when they are asked a question which requires thought, or a mental calculation. And what happens if you look up at the ceiling before answering. He will look up as well – and you may lose his attention. Unless you have some kind of eye trouble do not wear tinted or photochromic glasses when you are selling.

Try to keep your VOICE varied and interesting. The three main mistakes which invariably turn people off or send them to sleep are:

1 Talking in a monotone
2 Talking in short bursts of three or four words with too many pauses
3 Dropping the voice at the end of every sentence or phrase rather than raising the last word(s) slightly.

Many preachers fall into the trap of the second two points. On SPEECH, whatever your accent of education, be natural, don't change. But make sure your speech is clear and you are articulate whether the accent is broad Cockney, Birmingham in England, or Birmingham in Alabama.

ATTITUDE is simply whether you are positive and enthusiastic, or a repetitive robot. Do you really want their business or are you just filling up another of your quota of call cards? (Fixing quotas of calls is a practice I deplore in selling for hotels).

LISTENING is of prime importance. People have often said to me 'I'm not really a salesman' or 'I'm too introverted to sell'. Many times people have said to me 'He's a born salesman – but I'm too shy'. Knowing the people involved, in some cases this is nonsense. The people who say that can usually be good at selling, but they do not look or act like the typical salesman. They are often extremely good listeners – which is half way to being a good salesman. Anyone can be trained to improve his ability to sell if he has the will and being a good listener is a good start. Listening is an art. It takes concentration and a genuine interest in people. It flatters people if you listen genuinely and intently (see Figure 21.1). Ask yourself a basic question and give an honest answer. Do you really prefer listening, or do you really prefer talking? Whatever the answer avoid overdoing what you prefer. There is a time when you have to stop listening and move to a close. And vice versa if you enjoy talking. The point about a good salesman is that you really do not notice he is selling. Selling with integrity is as 'professional' as practising law or accountancy.

Figure 21.1

Most of the twenty points on the checklist are self explanatory but some elaboration may be necessary. On point 7 it is a fact that if you ask questions which elicit the answer 'yes' or 'that's correct', the sales sequence stands more chance of moving forward to a successful conclusion. You can only do this with practice and doing some homework first.

Supposing you have found a prospective buyer who has not booked his annual Christmas office dinner dance which 200 employees normally attend. You could phrase the questions:

'Have you booked your annual dinner dance yet?'
'No.'
'Could you tell me the approximate number attending?'
'Around 200 people.'

Alternatively you could re-phrase the questions:

'I understand you have not booked your annual dance yet?'
'Yes'
'Is it correct that you usually have around 200 employees?'
'Yes, that's correct.'

Point 19 on the use of alternatives is interesting. If you give a buyer no alternatives on, say, dates, menus, prices, etc., then he may well find this a hard sell, a kind of mental straightjacket which he will resist. If you give him to many alternatives he may find it difficult to make up his mind and will never make a decision. It is generally better to offer two, or a maximum of three alternatives.

Use more 'you's' than I's in selling. Practice starting questions with

Would you . . .
Will you . . .
Could you . . .
Have you . . .
Are you . . .

These five will cover most of the situations where you want to start questions. Examples are:

'Would you like to make a (provisional) booking?'
'Will you be organizing your annual sales conference again this year?'
'Could you tell me who books hotel accommodation for your overnight visitors?'
'Have you fixed up your daughter's wedding yet?'
'Are you going to hold a further dinner party?'

Whatever you do in selling, have empathy and be consumer orientated. Twenty years ago I went on an excellent course run by The Tack Sales Organisation. I think this was the first time I saw something called 'I am a Potential Customer'. I have amended it many times for the hotel industry but it is still a classic illustration of a complete mental switch in empathy to become a prospective customer. The customer sounds rather tough but I feel it would be well worthwhile if readers thought carefully about each point.

I AM A POTENTIAL CUSTOMER

1 I dislike being called 'Mr. Er' or 'Mr. Um'. I am proud of my name and I like the hotel sales executive to use it. If he cannot discover it, worm it out of someone or ask me for it, he isn't good at selling and I'd rather he didn't waste my time.
2 Start talking about ME. I like myself, my family, my business, and my soccer team. I don't necessarily like you, your family, your business and I certainly don't think much of your soccer team.
3 Sometimes I arouse my own interest in a hotel by talking about it; give me a chance to speak and then listen to me.
4 Find out all about my needs. You may be barking up the wrong tree.
5 Never take me for granted.
6 Find out about your voice. I am a little hard of hearing, but I don't like to be shouted at. Practice voice projection so that I can understand what you are talking about.
7 Don't try to persuade me by a spate of words. I might make a booking, but I will probably think better of it later and cancel it. Convince me by facts and we shall both he happy.
8 Tell me the truth and keep your promises.
9 Be optimistic. I know all the bad news without you telling it to me.
10 Be warm and kindly, not just an unsympathetic parrot. I can get all the information I want from a brochure. I need you to make the words live.
11 Ask my advice. Make me feel important. If you talk down to me I shall kick you right out.
12 Be well mannered and friendly, but not too friendly.
13 For goodness' sake don't talk, talk, talk. Please ease up now and again.
14 I don't like buying from a grubby person. Do me a favour and look, right now, at your fingernails, hair, shoes – and don't forget to brush that suit before you visit me.

15 If it's raining I don't object to you carrying an umbrella. But don't rest it in my room so that puddles of water form on my floor. And don't rest your briefcase on my beautiful desk. It has taken me twenty years, and half my stomach, to reach the grade of this office and that desk, and you walk in and place your briefcase on *my* desk!!

16 If I am to make up my mind, I want to hear the whole story. Don't cut your sales sequence, even if I appear to be disinterested. That is my act for putting off weak hotel sales executives. I reckon that if a hotelier can be put off easily he hasn't much faith in his hotel.

17 Don't waste my time by telling me funny stories. I rarely laugh at stage comedians, and what makes you think that you are funnier than the professionals?

18 Know your sales aids. I don't appreciate fumblers and 'I'll-find-it-in-a-minute' hotel executives.

19 Remember, there is only one thing more contagious than enthusiasm and that is the lack of it.

20 Let me feel, when you leave me, that I have a friend – that you will do nothing to jeopardize the good opinion I have formed of you.

THE CLOSE

Some readers might feel that any comment on closing a sale, obtaining a booking, achieving an objective is a waste of time and quite unnecessary. After all, everyone knows that the whole objective behind any form of selling is to close and obtain some actual business. It happens all the time with incoming enquiries so why bother with a section on something as obvious as this?

Firstly, it doesn't always happen with incoming enquiries, particularly with incoming enquiries by letter, or over the telephone. Most people leave the actual decision entirely up to the customer. They do not try and move an enquiry a stage further by making a provisional booking, or offering to show the enquirer the function room or hotel. The majority of people who telephone a hotel and ask for a brochure and tariff receive just that, what they have asked for. But staff should be trained to ask at least one question (when were you thinking of coming?) and trained to try for at least a provisional booking – 'because we are normally fully booked in August' or whenever the enquirer was thinking of coming.

With an outgoing sales situation to a previous user of the hotel, or a prospective new customer, the close is one of the most difficult things to achieve.

Sometimes the nicer the prospective customer the easier it is to overlook the close and forget the objective entirely. The hotelier or sales executive walks out after a most enjoyable chat. Perhaps they both play golf and watched the Open Golf Championship on television last night. It is very easy to close the door, leave – and then remember that no objective was achieved except for a vague creation of goodwill. Alternatively, the eager sales executive repeatedly tries to close and obtain that booking only to find the buyer backs away each time. Therefore some comments and suggestions are worthwhile.

Firstly, set objective(s) which are achievable. It could be that the objective is simply fact gathering and research. Or to get the prospective buyer to see the actual bedrooms, or the convention facilities. Naturally if the buyer says he wants to book his annual dinner dance without seeing your superb function rooms with their many advantages, the hotelier will by pass his more limited objective and take the booking. But normally it pays to take it step by step if the amount of business involved is worthwhile:

Research visit
Invitation to see the hotel
Provisional booking
Actual booking (perhaps with deposit)

Sometimes the whole sales call flows logically through to a booking. But many times it seems to stall at a certain point. There are three types of people in this world as far as our customers are concerned. These are:

(a) People who make decisions
(b) People who advise the decision-makers
(c) People who carry out decisions.

The third group is the largest number of people. And who has most time to spend (waste) with sales executives? Yes, the third group. This is the trap female hotel sales executives must try to avoid because they are most vulnerable to this situation. If I was the third assistant under-buyer in a major company what more pleasant way could I think of to pass the afternoon than talking to that attractive Ms. Sheraton Hilton about her conference facilities?

Obviously it is possible to obtain an objective and a booking more easily from the first group – the decision-makers. But they are the most difficult people to get in to see, and they are usually very busy. So very often it is necessary to sell, at least initially, to the second group, the advisers to the decision-makers. This role is played by different people in every company, so some telephone research is required first. It could be a member of the personnel department, the managing director's secretary, or that young up and coming executive mentioned twice before in this book, who is still trying to fix up his company's annual office dance.

There are many times when the words being used warn you it is too early to close, as well as the NVC signs mentioned previously. Sometimes a prospective customer has not heard all the advantages and at an early stage does not wish to buy. People rarely come out and say 'I am just not interested'. What they do is say 'Yes, but . . .'. They do not mean 'yes' at all, but really 'no'. So they counter your sales point or advantage with a 'Yes, but . . .'.

'We have just installed multi-language translation in our convention room'
'Yes . . . but, the hotel I am using now already has it'.

This 'yes, but' situation is a warning signal not to try and close, and to keep on stressing more advantages.

There comes a time when the buyer stops a deadpan reaction, or a 'yes, but' and starts to use certain much more positive words. He nods and uses certain words which indicate that you can start to move to a close. Often subconsciously he will avoid the actual word 'yes' but uses words like:

Sounds fine
OK
I see
That's right
That's correct
Good
Fine

I don't know about other languages, but in the English language these words have a positive ring – words like OK, that's right, fine. And as soon as the customer starts to use them, *you* must start to use them.

'You mentioned you have around 200 delegates to your conference.'
'That's right.'

'Right, ... well the room takes 300 delegates, so there is no problem there.'

In the second example in the next section the customer says 'That's fine' and the hotelier says 'Fine' so that the whole meeting flows on until the hotelier closes and achieves his objective.

There are many ways of closing and sometimes you just come out and suggest he makes a booking if the date is known, he has inspected the facilities and appears to want to make a decison. But if there is any chance that the bold, direct approach may frighten him off here are three alternative closing approaches.

Firstly, the *summing up close*. Basically you say to the prospective buyer 'Let us just sum up to see I have everything down correctly.' The salesperson then summarizes the type of function, numbers, special equipment, hotel prices, menu, wines and date. Using this summing-up sequence the buyer should say 'yes' to all stages as you have previously agreed all these details with him. And therefore it is easier for him to say 'yes' to the actual booking.

Another method of moving the sale forward to a close is to ask 'When is the final date you have to make a decision by? Nothing consolidates the mind of an indecisive person more than the realization that time is passing, and a decision must be made soon. Obviously, this question should never be asked sarcastically to an obvious 'waffler' as he may take offence. But I have often seen this question have the desired effect in obtaining a booking.

Both of these could be used in conjunction with a *trial close*. In fact, I would recommend that this approach is used in many closing situations. This is a classic illustration of NVC. Most selling/buying situations connected with hotels have a common link and this is that there is usually a day, night, or date involved. Making an actual booking invariably means fixing a date. And dates are always connected with diaries. At a certain stage near the end of the sales situation open your briefcase if it is not open already, carry on talking, but do nothing more. After a minute or two, take out your diary and put it in front of yourself so he can see it. Carry on talking for a few more minutes. Then open the diary at the month or week when he is thinking of booking.

Certain things could have happened by then. You are sending out a clear non-verbal message that you want to book a date for him. If he is a time-wasting member of the third group – people who carry out decisions – he will suddenly look at his watch and say something like 'Good Lord, is that the time? Look, I am sorry Mr Greene (or Ms

Sheraton Hilton) but I am late for a meeting with my Chief Executive.' And he will disappear fast. At least you will not waste any more time. However, if he is a Decision Maker or an adviser to the decision maker, then he knows you are going to ask for a booking. You haven't suddenly come out and asked for one. You *have* gradually, but without saying so. A booking after a steady trial close is then far easier. In fact, I have noticed that in two out of every three situations they will actually make the booking themselves and say 'Well, I suppose I'd better make a booking' or 'I suppose I'd better fix a date' without your saying a word. If the buyer still will not make a decision, this may not arise because he does not want to, but because he has to refer to someone else before making a final decision. Do not feel any reluctance about suggesting to him that you 'pencil in a provisional booking and hold the date for a week, or to the end of the month'. Often he will agree and this usually means you are nearly there, providing you remember to follow him up if he does not contact you with a definite booking.

CREATIVE SELLING

Whenever people talk about creative selling, they often think of an exceptional advertisement, a unique eye-catching mailing shot, a brilliant slogan, or a successful gimmicky idea. Creative selling is rarely associated with face to face selling. And yet face-to-face selling can be creative, can certainly create more business, and can open up new markets.

I wanted to close this chapter with an example of creative selling and have chosen a market which has enormous growth potential for virtually every hotel. The commercial, industrial, welfare and non-commercial world suffers from a disease called 'meetingitus'. There is no know antidote. It appears to be highly infectious and expanding all the time. Attracting a proportion of this market to hold meetings in hotels rather than in their own factories and offices is an enormous growth potential market. Nearly every hotel in or near a commercial market has experienced incredible growth from this particular source of business, in particular if the hotel sets out to service and sell to this market. One hotel I know experienced a 400 per cent growth in this market in the last three years.

Here is an illustration of how to attract more of this business. Although the business source is meetings, the principles set out in this sales situation are equally applicable to selling to *every* other source of business.

Mr John Hotel (Mr H) is the manager of a hotel with 100 bedrooms, a restaurant, bar, function room seating 200 people, and three meeting/private dining rooms taking around 20 people in each. The function room and three smaller meeting rooms have just been redecorated. He is worried abut the overall sales and profits which have shown no real growth for the last two years. He is self-motivated and has decided to sell more actively to factories and offices in his local catchment area. Mr Hotel knows the hotel business thoroughly, having worked in most departments before moving into hotel management. He is very experienced at socializing and meeting people, but has had no formal training in selling.

Mr Hotel has identified a potential customer in Mr Alex Customer (Mr C) who is managing director of a new factory only three years old, and just three miles from the hotel. His research shows Mr C holds regular meetings in his factory, many of which go on all day. He has made an appointment with Mr C (at his factory) with the objective of persuading him to hold some of his longer meetings at the hotel. Mr C's secretary shows Mr H into his office.

Mr. H: Good morning Mr. C. I am Mr. H, the manager of the Regency Hotel. Thank you for sparing me some of your very valuable time.

Mr. C: Good morning, please have a seat. What can I do for you?

Mr. H: Well, Mr. C, I believe you hold a lot of meetings in your offices here.

Mr. C: Yes, we do.

Mr. H: And many of them go on all day.

Mr. C: Yes, that's correct.

Mr. H: Well, we have some meeting rooms in my hotel and I believe they would be very suitable for your meetings.

Mr. C: But we have a superb board room in our offices here which is very suitable for meetings.

Mr. H: Yes, but we have recently redecorated our meeting rooms and . . .

Mr. C: There is nothing wrong with the decor of our own room.

Mr. H: I am sure it is very nice. You see, we can lay on a really good meal and we have . . .

Mr. C: Look, I don't know if you realize this but we have an excellent chef of our own who prepares superb meals every lunchtime.

Mr. H: I am sure he is good, but we have an excellent wine list as well.

(There is a pause at this point.)

Mr. H: Could I suggest you try one of your next meetings with us?
Mr. C: Well maybe, look I am going abroad for one week on business, why don't I give you a call when I return?
Mr. H: Marvellous. I look forward to hearing from you when you return.

They shake hands and Mr. H leaves, well pleased with the meeting. What do you think of it? Was he product or consumer orientated? Was he Jack the Problem Solver or Jack the Product Seller? Did he achieve his objective, will Mr. C call him? No way.

So let us try exactly the same situation again, from the point where Mr. H is shown in.

Mr. H: Good morning Mr. C, my name is Hotel, John Hotel. I'm the manager of the Regency Hotel just two miles down the road from here.
Mr. C: Ah yes, I pass it on the way to work, please have a seat. What can I do for you?
Mr. H: Well, Mr. C., I understand you hold a lot of meetings in your boardroom here.
Mr. C: Yes, we do.
Mr. H: And many of them go on all day?
Mr. C: Yes, that's correct.
Mr. H: Could you tell me about your problems in holding these meetings?
Mr. C: (Pauses) Problems, what problems?
Mr. H: Well, as an example do you get interruptions – when there is a telephone call, or a problem in the factory?
Mr. C: (Thoughtfully) Ye . . ss, we do. In fact there is always one of the team who seems to get telephone calls every meeting.
Mr. H: I suppose this affects the whole flow and productivity of the meeting.
Mr. C: (Emphatically) It certainly does! Pretty costly interruptions even if it is just ten minutes. The salaries I pay . . . . . . !!
Mr. H: Could I ask you Mr. C whether your meetings are creative in the sense that you are looking for ways of reducing costs or increasing sales?
Mr. C: That is the idea – yes.
Mr. H: Well, Mr. C, let me tell you what I'd like to do for you. Would you try one of your next meetings in our redecorated meeting rooms and I will do two things.

Firstly, I will see that the meeting is not interrupted unless it really is urgent. This should help the whole productivity of the meeting. Secondly, I believe that by moving some of your day meetings to a new environment in the Regency Hotel they will be more productive of ideas for making or saving money. Could I suggest in your own premises there is more chance of your drawing office manager worrying about his problems along the corridor, or the works director thinking about his new automated lathe . . .

Mr. C: Well it's worth trying. But how are we all going to get there?

Mr. H: I have already thought about that problem. Most of these day meetings will be booked in advance and I would be happy to pick you all up first thing in the morning at your factory here in our hotel mini-bus.

Mr. C: Sounds fine.

Mr. H: Fine.

During the last few minutes Mr. H has moved to a trial close bringing out his diary first. Then opening it.

Mr C: How much is this all going to cost?

Mr. H: Before talking about your investment in holding some of these meetings in the Regency could I suggest you make a provisional booking for your next meeting, and you call in within the next few days to show me exactly how you want the room set up. I will set it up to show you what it looks like and show you our special executive conference package. What is the date of your next meeting Mr. C?

Mr. C: Well . . er . . (looks at his diary) Tuesday, October 19th.

Mr. H: (Looks at diary and frowns). I'm terribly sorry, Mr. C, but all three meeting rooms are already booked on that day. I gather your dates are fixed. When is the next one?

Mr. C: Yes, they are fixed – pity. Look, the next one is Tuesday, October 26th.

Mr. H: That's fine. I have booked it provisionally. I've taken up a lot of your time. All I have to do is fix a time for you to see the room and discuss how you want it set up.

Mr. C: Well, I'm busy today. What about on my way home tomorrow at, say, 6 p.m.?

Mr. H: Fine, ask for me at reception – John Hotel. Here is my card and I will leave another one with your secretary Miss Jones on the way out.

Mr. C: O.K. . . . John.

(They shake hands)

Mr. H: Thank you for your time, Mr. C, see you tomorrow.

Mr. C: Thank *you* . . . 6 p.m. then, bye.

Can you see the complete difference in the two approaches? With the second had he done his research? Yes. Had he pre-planned the call? Yes. Was he product or consumer orientated? Actually, a bit of both. Was he Jack the Problem Solver? He certainly was. And did he achieve his objective? He certainly did. He could have asked whether any of the people attending required bedroom accommodation, but that may come later. He used a lot of 'I's' but also many 'you's'.

You will notice he politely ducked the question of 'How much is this all going to cost' by talking about Mr. C's investment. This has credibility because he is trying to solve a very real problem for anyone holding meetings. There is always one executive who wishes to show how busy and indispensable he is by arranging (unwittingly sometimes) that they receive 'urgent' calls during important meetings.

John Hotel sold the investment aspect of them all being more creative of ideas for making and saving money in a different environment of his hotel. Great! Did you notice how he said October 19th was fully booked already? Were they? Probably not. But he did not want Mr. C to think he was the only potential customer around. He closed by achieving his objective which was not to obtain a definite booking at this first meeting, His objectives were:

1 to obtain a provisional booking
2 to arrange a date for Mr. C to visit the hotel, see the rooms (when the provisional booking would become definite)
3 to establish a personal relationship.

I feel he achieved all these objectives. See how he began to develop a personal relationship. Mr. C. used the word 'fine'. John picked it up and said 'fine'. At the end Mr. C began to call him John, but notice that at the first meeting John played safe by still calling the Managing Director by his surname.

* * * * *

22

CONCLUSION – THE THRESHOLD BARRIER

GENERAL

When you are writing about the next ten years a lot can change in the time it takes to write this book and have it published which can have a considerable influence on the next ten years.

As I am writing we are all experiencing difficult times. Inflation is declining but is still a problem, not just in most Western and developed countries, but is even worse in some developing countries. Energy costs have reduced recently although we are told there is bound to be a long-term fuel shortage. There is a strong likelihood that the energy producing countries will continue to create inflation in other countries through future energy price increases. When I started the dollar was a very weak currency against virtually every other currency and the pound Sterling and French franc were strong. As I finished writing the book the situation has reversed and the dollar has been strong for some time.

Who knows what the situation will be as you actually read these words? Interest rates are currently extremely high in Britain and in most other countries. I do not see a possibility of an end to the world recession unless interest rates are lowered generally. In fact, the main point of disagreement amongst economists and the people who run our lives is whether we are in a recession or a depression – pure semantics to the growing number of unemployed.

As I read back through the opening of this book, and indeed the opening of this chapter, it does appear that I have dwelt quite a lot on the problems we all face – problems of overcapacity, rising costs, rapid change, difficult pricing problems. There is an old sales maxim 'Don't tell people about their problems when you are selling'. They know all about them and don't need you to remind them. We face many problems over the next decade and it would be wrong to ignore or minimize them.

Although we face uncertain times there is no doubt that there are also great opportunities. New markets will develop and we must take every opportunity to expand them. The incentive market is in its infancy and will show steady growth over the next decade. There has been rapid growth in the short break market and this will continue as hoteliers show imagination in marketing special 'week-ends'.

You can now take pottery lessons or listen to classical music on a week-end break. You can even act out a murder, just like an Agatha Christie play.

In order to illustrate an attitude of mind in looking for new markets, let me give you another illustration. In 1983 the British Government privatized (sold) a very old and famous hotel group owned by British Rail called British Transport Hotels (BTH). This group included five famous London hotels located at five main railway stations: the Charing Cross, the Great Western Royal, the Great Eastern, the Great Northern and the Grosvenor hotels. The group had 29 hotels in total with 24 out of London, including some world famous golfing hotels – St Andrew's, Gleneagles, and Turnbury.

I worked for the group advising them on marketing in the year before it was privatized. During that year there were great hopes of a management buy out (which was not successful) and therefore all levels of management were actively trying new ideas to reduce costs and improve sales.

One problem that existed was that many of the hotels were in British provincial cities like Newcastle, Leeds, Liverpool and Manchester where there was very little opportunity to promote week-end breaks in substantial quantities or to obtain any other significant business. In walking round the catchment areas of these hotels I suddenly had an idea. There was one major activity in all of these cities and this was that they all had very significant universities. Some of these universities had up to 20,000 resident students and this meant a possible 40,000 parents. Research showed that there were over 200 universities, colleges, polytechnics and boarding schools in Britain. Because of the shortage of university places many students end up in a university a long distance from home.

We launched a marketing campaign to package what was called 'The BTH Parent Breaks Offer' at a competitive price. Our objective was to persuade a small percentage of the parents who did not live locally to visit their son or daughter for at least one overnight stay.

A complete sales action plan was prepared which included direct selling at universities, posters on student university noticeboards, free press publicity, and an advertising campaign (primarily in women's magazines). I would emphasize that the BTH Parent Break idea was only one part of a *complete* marketing and sales action plan for each hotel and the company overall.

The campaign was deliberately aimed on an emotional level with headline slogans like 'I realize now how much I miss them . . .' or just before the start of a new term we used the headline 'We hardly spoke the whole way home . . .' An illustration of the kind of advertisement is shown in Figure 22.1. As the hotels tended to be empty over the week-end the 'punch line' was that the student son or daughter could have a free separate room as well. At this time I began to realize how many parents are separated, because a high response tended to be from this market segment.

The whole promotional programme was launched about four months before privatization and the objective was to analyse results and revise the sales action plan for the following year. We missed the start of the university year, but the results were extremely encouraging. One or two cities showed a low response but the vast majority showed considerable interest and bookings. Although only twenty hotels were included in the programme, bookings rose in a significant way for some hotels left off the programme (e.g. Inverness). Everyone involved in this new idea was convinced that if given two or three years of steady marketing we would have created what appeared to be a new market in 'dead' periods of the week. Unfortunately the management buy out did not succeed and the hotels were sold to a variety of different purchasers.

Although we face many problems there is no doubt that there are also great opportunities. Many of them arise if we can break down or overcome what I call The Threshold Barrier. The foregoing illustration began to attract a new market over the threshold who had never thought of staying in a BTH hotel before.

To overcome The Threshold Barrier we firstly have to become much more conscious that it exists, and secondly we have to be very positive in our attitudes to creating new markets. I do not like using stories from other industries to illustrate a point. But there is one classic story which many of you will know in the shoe manufacturing industry.

A major shoe manufacturer decided to export to an African country. They divided the country into two halves and sent two young sales executives to the country to sell shoes. A week passed and head office received two separate telexes. One salesman sent the message: 'I am coming home. No opportunities here. Everyone walks around barefooted.' The other sales executive sent another telex on the same day saying: 'Send 10,000 pair of shoes. Incredible potential

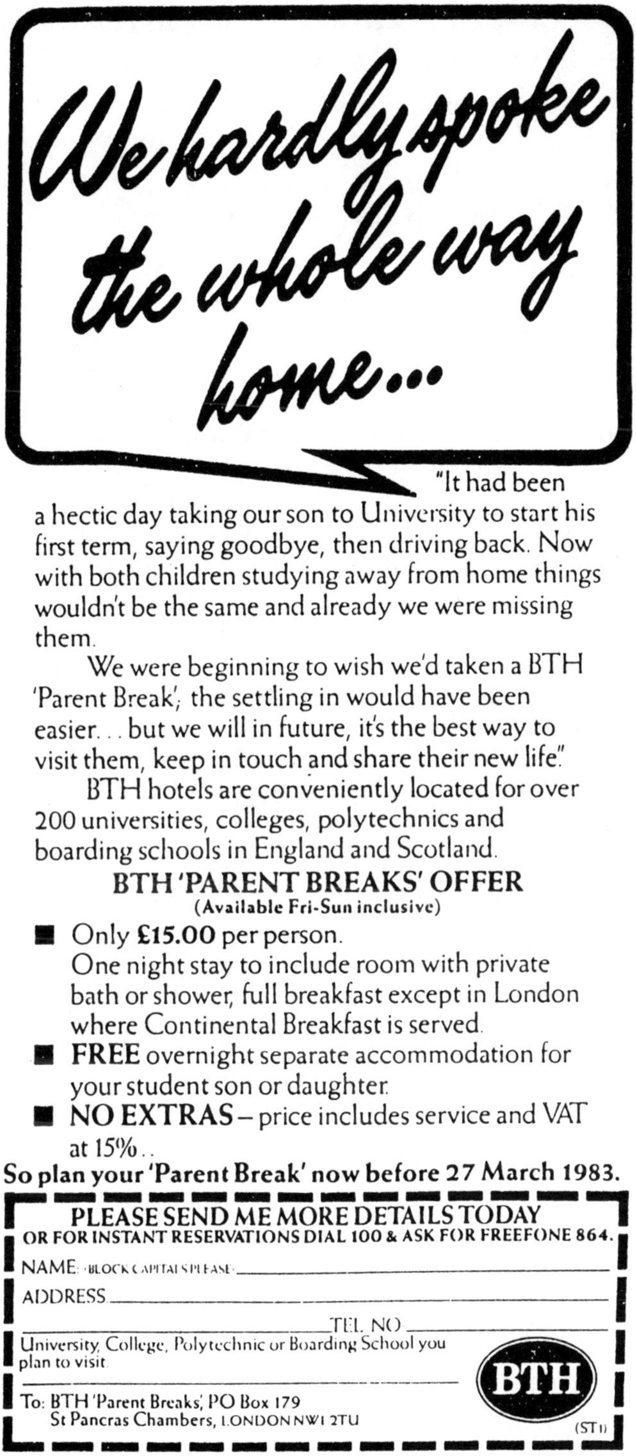
We hardly spoke the whole way home...
"It had been a hectic day taking our son to University to start his first term, saying goodbye, then driving back. Now with both children studying away from home things wouldn't be the same and already we were missing them.
We were beginning to wish we'd taken a BTH 'Parent Break'; the settling in would have been easier... but we will in future, it's the best way to visit them, keep in touch and share their new life."
BTH hotels are conveniently located for over 200 universities, colleges, polytechnics and boarding schools in England and Scotland.
BTH 'PARENT BREAKS' OFFER
(Available Fri-Sun inclusive)
Only £15.00 per person. One night stay to include room with private bath or shower, full breakfast except in London where Continental Breakfast is served.
FREE overnight separate accommodation for your student son or daughter.
NO EXTRAS – price includes service and VAT at 15%..
So plan your 'Parent Break' now before 27 March 1983.
PLEASE SEND ME MORE DETAILS TODAY
OR FOR INSTANT RESERVATIONS DIAL 100 & ASK FOR FREEFONE 864.
NAME (BLOCK CAPITALS PLEASE)
ADDRESS
TEL NO
University, College, Polytechnic or Boarding School you plan to visit
To: BTH 'Parent Breaks', PO Box 179
St Pancras Chambers, LONDON NW1 2TU
BTH
(ST1)

Figure 22.1

here. Everyone walks around barefooted.'

We, in the hotel industry, have to think like the second executive.

THE THRESHOLD BARRIER

The hotel industry attracts a large number of people at present. People who stay in bedrooms, attend functions, conferences and spend money in hotel restaurants and bars. But there is a far greater number of people who do *not* enter hotels because of The Threshold Barrier. Literally millions of people eat out in a whole range of eating places, but never eat in an hotel restaurant. The vast majority of people in many developed countries have never stayed in an hotel overnight in their own country.

The country sending the largest number of tourists abroad each year is America. And yet the vast majority of Americans have never been abroad on holiday, even if Canada is included as abroad, as of course it should be. I was told that only 7 per cent of Americans hold passports in any year, which means 93 per cent do not. There are poor or elderly and many people who may never travel abroad. But it is not over-optimistic to assume that the number of Americans travelling abroad could, in the right circumstances, double in number. The same applies to most other countries. Nearly 2 million Britons a year visit Spain on holiday. The vast proportion never step inside a hotel in their own home town. If they began to use their local hotel's bar and restaurant the impact on profits would be considerable.

Thousands of people attend functions in even the smallest hotel but for some reason never go back at a later date to eat in that same hotel's restaurant or have a drink in the bar. An hotel with a quite small function room could well have 20,000 different people attending functions in a year and research shows that a large proportion never use the hotel's other facilities. Why not? What can be done about it? Can you imagine if in a small hotel with 20,000 people attending functions only 10 per cent, or 2,000, could be persuaded to return and eat in the restaurant once . . . or twice, a year. Think of the impact on profits.

Hotels have a threshold barrier which inhibits people trying its facilities once. All hotels have it, even if the hotel's staff are very friendly. And to succeed we must become more aware of it, and then actively work to overcome it. Hoteliers do not suffer from it at all in their own hotel, and experience it far less than the general public in other people's hotels.

Take two identically designed hotel restaurants both with exactly the same menu and prices, one with its own entrance to the street, and another where you have to walk through the hotel lobby to reach the restaurant. Invariably the former will do better business, even if you covered the outside of the hotel with advertising on the latter restaurant. For some reason a large number of people do not like walking through an hotel lobby to an 'inside' restaurant.

Some hotel staff are friendly. Some doormen, porters and receptionists literally frighten people away or inhibit the potential buyer. It has happened to me even though I am so used to hotels. At times I am overawed. I was in the toilet (rest room) of a major new superb hotel in America recently when an American father said to his son, aged about 12 years, 'Why are you whispering?'

There is a successful, profitable future for the hotelier who recognizes this problem and does something about it. This is why I have included separate sections previously on In-House Selling and Using Names. Training, motivation and better in-house servicing and selling can help break down this barrier. Signposting and posters can sell other areas, e.g. the place where people hand in their coats before a function should always have a poster or sales aids on the hotel restaurant. You only have to get them to step over the threshold barrier and try it once. Social events, fashion displays, gourmet sessions, etc. for housewives can help, particularly as they are often the decision-maker in going out to eat and *where* to eat. A change in thinking and emphasis is needed. Let me give you two examples, and then the same thinking process should be applied to other parts of your own hotel.

In the restaurant the greeting, attention, recognition and fuss is usually greater for the customer who made the booking in his name, as he is usually the one who is paying. I am in no way suggesting this should change. But he has more than likely been there before and has already broken down any barrier. His guest is on new strange territory. Can we persuade his guest to cross the threshold again and return next time to entertain someone themselves. A subtle switch in emphasis should be made – welcoming them both, recognizing that the guest may need 'guidance' with the menu – and if you can find out his name and use it . . .

Recently with one client with a top level restaurant the head waiter very politely gave every 'new visitor' a card 'in case you ever need our telephone number . . .' They then monitored the bookings and covers jumped by an average of one-third more per day with 'new' faces. I would add that the restaurant was good and fairly expensive. A progress meeting was held each week and not one person seemed annoyed at being given the telephone number. This was the only action point we introduced in the first three months. There was no paid advertising or anything else. But there was a subtle change in staff attitudes when we told them what we were going to do over the whole year and they caught the fire of enthusiasm.

We must recognize that hotel employees may be more gregrarious than employees in many other industries. But it is still only natural for them to relax and feel more at ease with a customer they know rather than a stranger who enters their restaurant, bar or hotel for the first time. When you meet and greet a stranger it is always natural to feel slightly tense and wary. This is why, without realizing it, many hotel staff are friendlier and warmer in their greeting to a regular guest than a new one. If you can motivate and train staff to be equally inviting to both regular and new guests you are bound to increase sales.

Another example, which has been mentioned before, is promotions through car parks. In Britain and other European countries many hotels in major cities like London have no, or very limited, car park facilities. Outside the main cities most hotels have car parks. These are often full with customers who are attending a function, or in the bar on a busy Friday or Saturday evening. Many British hotels started as hostelries or pubs and they are treated like this by the market working and living locally.

Some public house bars in hotels are very popular. We once did a count on an hotel's popular theme bar which showed over 1,000 customers on a busy night. A check with these customers showed only three had ever eaten in the hotel's main more expensive restaurant and only thirty-seven had eaten in the hotel's medium-priced coffee shop. The same research showed that around 150 planned to go somewhere else for a take-away locally when the bar closed. Some simple poster promotion in the bar and under the windscreen wipers of the cars in the car park produced a small regular amount of extra business for the main restaurant and a significant amount of regular extra income for the coffee shop. Another 'shot' under the windscreen wiper on weddings in the hotel's function room carried out once a month for three consecutive months produced sixty-three enquiries and twenty-three definite bookings from a total distribution of around 900 leaflets in three months, at a minimal cost.

The main point I am making is that these bar customers have already crossed the threshold at least once and therefore are less likely to be inhibited about trying out the restaurant, or bringing their mother in about a forthcoming wedding, once you show them you want their custom.

Some people argue that a big factor influencing hotels and in particular eating out is going to be home entertainment. Instead of eating out on a Saturday evening, a group of people will get together in one of their homes, with wine and a pre-cooked frozen gourmet style meal and munch away as they watch the latest smash hit movie on a large screen with quadrophonic sound in their own living room.

This could have a short-term impact on the eating out market. But this need not be long-term if we *all* sell eating out as not just food and wine – but as an enjoyable experience with no clearing up afterwards. We must sell it as a pleasurable investment.

As well as selling the hotel as a pleasant investment we should all start to stress that it is an 'add on' cost. If a family of four eat Sunday brunch, or any meal in your restaurant and your charge is $15 each including service, and taxes, it does not cost them $60. The extra add on cost compared to eating Sunday lunch at home is much less than $60. Think of the cost of buying a roast, energy, etc. Similarly, most people taking a two week annual holiday or one of the short break packages staying in an hotel, save the costs of living and eating at home. This is not the case with many other consumer items. A $500 cooker actually costs the buyer $500. A $500 holiday may save the buyer $150 of stay home costs. Certainly with some of the longer term holidays promoted to retired people who live in a cold climate, the cost of taking one of these holidays is not much more than staying at home.

If the *whole* hotel industry started to put this message across steadily and systematically en masse, there would be a substantial growth in the future.

OPTIMISM IN FUTURE

There are grounds for long-term optimism providing we actively work to overcome the Threshold Barrier because there are certain social changes in our markets which could be beneficial and many of our markets could expand in the coming decade.

Break down the generations into age brackets of every five years and you will find that the younger age groups eat out far more than the older age groups ever did when they were in the younger age bracket. More youngsters I know in the 15 to 25 age group deliberately choose to eat out as a social decision than the 'older' people did when they were 15 to 25. They start with hamburgers or pizzas. They graduate to Chinese or Indian and then they become more adventurous as they get menu fatigue and obtain more spending money. The eating-out habits of the present 15 to 25 age group is cause for optimism when they are 25 to 35 years old over the next ten years. But we must recognize this age grouping and market very specifically, so that they relax easily when they first enter your restaurant and blend with all age groups. We must also introduce more ethnic dishes on hotel menus from other countries (Mexican/Indian/ Chinese) and not be so obsessed with French cuisine.

Similarly, if you sit in any main tourism holiday resort hotel and watch the families come into the restaurant it is very interesting. I was in an hotel recently watching the families. Many of the parents did not go abroad or stay in an hotel until they were in their 'twenties'. The children started staying in these hotels from 5 years onwards. The kids are far more relaxed and talk louder than their parents do in the restaurant. These youngsters have crossed the threshold barrier already. And they are our future markets.

By the 90s the population between 30 to 50 years old will be totally different to the same age group in the past decades. They will have experienced 30 years of 'conditioning' by television. In Britain they will have experienced over a decade of breakfast television, i.e. television all day. Many American decision makers have experienced six hours a day viewing for two decades. Few of them will be savers for a rainy day. They are the 'me' generation of spenders. You may think this is wrong but it is a fact of life. And it will create incredible marketing opportunities.

There is much more spending power around than is apparent. In the Southern half of England there are literally millions of people in the age bracket of 50 plus who do not earn a lot of money but who are comparatively wealthy. These are the people whose children have grown up and who own a house which they probably purchased around 25 years ago and no longer have a mortgage or the mortgage is quite low. The cheapest three bedroomed, semi-detached house is generally worth over £90,000 in the South of England.

These people are sitting on quite a lot of wealth. They are also the generation who used to save but are now beginning to change their habits. More and more you hear people saying 'I said to my children, I am not going to leave you a lot of money when I die'.

Many are developing the attitude that they have worked hard all their lifetime and wish to spend some of the wealth they have created.

In the United Kingdom, Inheritance Tax, which is more or less our equivalent of Death Duties starts at £71,000, about the price of a three bedroomed family house. Most people dislike the idea of paying this tax. You can see a number of what appear to be very ordinary people beginning to travel more on holiday – sometimes to long haul, or expensive destinations. A growing number of people are taking more than one holiday each year.

People are living longer. And people well into their 70s are much more active than earlier generations and more prepared to travel on holiday abroad, or on short break trips within their own country. The potential growth from this age bracket is extremely high. I know that we have over 3 million unemployed in Britain but the working population appears to have considerable spending power.

The business market staying in hotels may vary depending on the economy over the next decade but there is considerable indication that this will grow steadily as world trade and economies generally start to recover. There is big growth potential in business meetings of all sizes, even small working meetings in bedrooms designed for sleep at night and work during the day. In virtually every feasibility study on new hotels I have worked on in the last twenty years located in a commercial area, I and my clients have grossly underestimated the demand for the smaller meeting and seminar facilities.

Other growth areas are the 'working' conferences and conventions where someone is selling or people are learning – rather than the pure 'boozy' junket which I feel will be phased out. The exhibition market will expand. Business incentive holiday and business study tours are huge growth markets which are really just in their infancy now.

We can view the future with considerable optimism although inevitably there will be some 'casualties' over the next ten years. I have tried to show readers a number of things in this book which will not only ensure that you are not a 'casualty' but that you are very successful into the 90s. Some of the main ones are:

1 Firstly to make readers more aware of marketing and as much as we may dislike change – and most people do – that change and redefining markets constantly is vital in order to survive and maximize profits.
2 We must have empathy, which will arise if we are consumer orientated rather than product orientated. We will be very successful if we are Jack the Problem Solver rather than Jack the Product Seller.
3 That there is a systematic, more analytical approach to marketing and sales action plans which requires much more brainstorming and thinking time. This systemized selling can be combined

completely with flair and the entrepreneur's instinct.

4 We survive and expand by looking not at occupancy alone, but at average occupancies *and* average room rates. Too much discounting of room rates may lead to 'profitless prosperity'. Inevitably it will destroy a great international industry.
5 We must involve all staff in the great adventure of selling.
6 Only the man at the top can create a sense of direction and a special type of atmosphere where employees thrive and this atmosphere is communicated by the staff to the guests.

Above all, we must be positive. If we are positive in our whole outlook and communicate this to our staff and guests, there is nothing we cannot achieve.

* * * * *

APPENDIX A

PROFITABILITY BY AREA

This appendix summarizes the management reporting technique mentioned earlier in this book of periodically (perhaps half yearly or annually) analysing the management accounts in order to show an indication of the actual profit, or loss, from each significant income source. The usual Profit and Loss Account in the Uniform System of Accounts provides a specific grouping of income producing departments (e.g. rooms, food, beverage, telephone), together with cost centres for those expenses which cannot be directly related to any income-producing department and which are applicable to the hotel operation as a whole.

Whilst this form provides the means through which control can be effected, and adverse trends spotlighted, the information shown does not wholly reflect the profitability of any particular area of activity within these groupings. In order to give a clearer indication of profitability it is advisable to extend the form of Profit and Loss Statement periodically by allocating all groupings of income and expense presented in the statement to the various income areas. This will indicate not only whether food service is profitable as a whole, but whether different restaurants, function rooms and other eating areas are profitable. Unless there is a depth of knowledge over the hotel is it not possible to carry out these exercise with absolute accuracy, but it does provide a good indication of the profit, or loss, contribution which each income-producing area is making to the whole hotel profit.

In order to prepare the profitability statement it is first necessary to re-group Sales under their respective areas. Cost of Sales can be determined by reference to the Profit and Loss Statement. In the case of food costs where there is a central kitchen, consideration must be given to the policy and expected cost percentages of each outlet. With regard to liquor costs a breakdown should be available from the various bar result reports, and stocktakers report.

A detailed breakdown over the wages is available from the departmental Payroll Report. Kitchen payroll should be apportioned on the same basis as food costs unless circumstances suggest otherwise. Other expenses of the operated department would normally be distributed on the basis of sales, except where an item of expense can be specifically identified.

It is then necessary to apportion the Undistributed Operating Expenses, and the other items of expense to the various income producing areas. Naturally the basis of allocation depends on the circumstances in each hotel but normally would be allocated as shown in the following section.

Administration and General Expenses

These expenses would normally be allocated on the basis of sales, or wage costs. Normally wages provide a fairer basis than sales, since income value is not necessarily indicative of overhead or administrative burden. On the basis of payroll, the expenses should be apportioned in the ratio of the number of employees of an income producing area to the total number of employees of all income producing areas.

Advertising and Marketing

The most common method would be to allocate these expenses to the major income-producing areas on the basis of sales. Naturally should a special marketing programme have been entered into for any one particular department then the cost of such a programme should be allocated direct to that department.

Heat, Light and Water

Ideally this should be allocated on the basis of floor areas or volume space of each area.

Repairs and Maintenance

This is often a difficult expense to apportion to the income producing areas. Ideally it should be done on the basis of jobs carried out in the various areas. However, more often than not, this information is not available. The chief engineer should be able to make accurate estimates, and a study of purchases and service invoices would help. Provided the analysis suggested in the departmental schedules is being maintained then this item should not prove too difficult to allocate.

Fixed Charges

The bulk of fixed charges covers such items as rent and rates and property taxes. Therefore the most practical basis is to allocate according to floor area.

Depreciation

Depreciation should be allocated in proportion to the value of assets employed in the various departments and areas.

In order to provide an illustration, a Profit and Loss Statement has been extended on the foregoing basis into areas and the results are shown in the following pages. It will be seen that the results emanating therefrom can be very revealing. A summary Area Profitability Statement is illustrated showing the profit (or loss) of each income producing area after allocating undistributed operating expenses, fixed charges and depreciation. Apart from a Food and Beverage Area Profitability Statement an illustration is also shown of the Restaurant Profitability Statement and there would normally be further statements covering the other areas, e.g. coffee shop, banqueting, cocktail bar, public bar, etc.

The illustrations are actual results in a small hotel.

Table AI.1 Summary Area Profitability Statement

Income Producing Area	*This Year*		*Last Year*	
	$	%	$	%
ROOMS	358,000	109	362,000	84
FOOD & BEVERAGE				
Restaurant	(78,500)	(24)	(37,800)	(9)
Coffee Shop	(11,500)	(4)	300	—
Floor Service	5,000	2	8,000	2
Banquets	(10,500)	(3)	49,500	11
Cocktail Bar	18,500	6	17,500	4
Public Bar	28,000	9	16,500	4
	(49,000)	(15)	54,000	12
TELEPHONE	(27,500)	(8)	(21,500)	(5)
SHOP	12,500	4	8,500	2
OTHER INCOME	33,000	10	30,000	7
TOTAL NET PROFIT	327,000	100%	433,000	100%

Table AI.2 Rooms Area Profitability Statement

	This Year		Last Year	
	$	%	$	%
Room Sales	1,100,000	100	1,000,000	100
Payroll and Related Expenses	280,000	25	200,000	20
Other Expenses	110,000	10	100,000	10
1 DEPARTMENTAL PROFIT	710,000	65	700,000	70
Undistributed Operating Expenses	225,000	20	211,000	21
Fixed Charges	77,000	7	77,000	8
Depreciation	50,000	5	50,000	5
	352,000	32	338,000	34
2 PROFITABILITY	358,000	33%	362,000	36%
Ratio of Rooms Net Profit to Total Hotel Net Profit		109%		84%

Table AI.3 Food & Beverage Area Profitability Statement

	This Year		Last Year	
	$	%	$	%
Food	490,000	54	550,000	60
Liquor	340,000	38	300,000	33
Tobacco	70,000	8	60,000	7
Total Sales	900,000	100	910,000	100
Cost of Sales	421,500	47	372,500	41
Payroll and Related Expenses	232,000	26	213,000	23
Other Expenses	92,000	10	81,000	9
	745,500	83	666,500	73
1 DEPARTMENTAL PROFIT	154,500	17	243,500	27
Undistributed Operating Expenses	153,500	17	139,500	15
Fixed Charges	32,000	4	32,000	4
Depreciation	18,000	2	18,000	2
	203,500	23	189,500	21
2 PROFITABILITY (LOSS)	(49,000)	6%	54,000	6%
Ratio of Catering Net Profit (Loss) to Total Hotel Net Profit		(15)%		12%

Table AI.4 Restaurant Area Profitability Statement

	This year		*Last Year*	
	$	%	$	%
Sales				
Food	200,000	71.4	210,000	72.4
Liquor	60,000	21.4	60,000	20.7
Tobacco	20,000	7.2	20,000	6.9
Total Sales	280,000	100.0	290,000	100.0
Cost of Sales				
Food	108,000	54.0	96,000	45.7
Liquor	23,000	38.3	20,800	34.7
Tobacco	15,000	75.0	16,000	80.0
Total Cost of Sales	146,000	52.1	132,800	45.8
Gross Profit	134,000	47.9	157,200	54.2
Payroll and Related Expenses	102,000	36.4	94,000	32.4
Other Expenses	35,000	12.5	30,000	10.3
Departmental Profit (Loss)	(3,000)	(1.0)	33,200	11.5
Undistributed Overheads	60,500	21.6	56,000	19.3
Fixed Charges	8,000	2.9	8,000	2.8
Depreciation	7,000	2.5	7,000	2.4
Profitability (Loss)	(78,500)	(28.0%)	(37,800)	(13.0%)

APPENDIX B

SOCIAL GRADING UNITED KINGDOM

GUIDE TO GRADE 'A' HOUSEHOLDS – UPPER MIDDLE CLASS

Informants from Grade 'A' households constitute about 3 per cent of the total. The head of the household is a successful business or professional man, senior civil servant, or has considerable private means. A young man in some of these occupations who has not fully established himself may still be round in Grade 'B', though he eventually should reach Grade 'A'.

In country or suburban areas, 'A' grade households usually live in large, detached houses or in expensive flats. In towns, they may live in expensive flats or town houses in the better parts of town.

GUIDE TO GRADE 'B' HOUSEHOLDS – MIDDLE CLASS

Grade 'B' informants account for about 12 per cent of the total. In general, the heads of 'B' Grade households will be quite senior people but not at the very top of their profession or business. They are quite well-off, but their style of life is generally respectable rather than rich or luxurious. Non-earners will be living on private pensions or on fairly modest private means.

GUIDE TO GRADE 'C1' HOUSEHOLDS – LOWER MIDDLE CLASS

Grade C1 constitutes about 23 per cent of total informants. In general it is made up of the families of small tradespeople and non-manual workers who carry out less important administrative, supervisory and clerical jobs, i.e. what are sometimes called 'white-collar' workers.

GUIDE TO GRADE 'C2' HOUSEHOLDS – THE SKILLED WORKING CLASS

Grade C2 consists in the main of skilled manual workers and their families. It constitutes about 32 per cent of informants. When in doubt as to whether the head of the household is skilled or unskilled, check whether he has served an apprenticeship; this may be a guide, though not all skilled workers have served an apprenticeship.

GUIDE TO GRADE 'D' HOUSEHOLDS – THE SEMI-SKILLED AND UNSKILLED WORKING CLASS

Grade D consists entirely of manual workers, generally semi-skilled or unskilled. This grade accounts for 21 per cent of families.

GUIDE TO GRADE 'E' HOUSEHOLDS – THOSE AT LOWEST LEVELS OF SUBSISTENCE

Grade E consists of Old Age Pensioners, Widows and their families, casual workers and those who, through sickness or unemployment, are dependent on social security schemes, or have very small private means. They constitute about 9 per cent of all informants. Individual income of the head of the household (disregarding additions such as supplementary benefits) will be little, if any, above the basic flat-rate social security benefit.

Source: JICNARS – Joint Industry Committee for National Readership Surveys, 44, Belgrave Square, SW1X 8QS.

APPENDIX C

ACTIVITIES IN FUNCTION AREAS OTHER THAN FUNCTIONS

1 MANAGEMENT TRAINING SEMINARS
2 VARIOUS TYPES OF BUSINESS MEETINGS
3 CONFERENCES
4 ROTARY CLUB
5 MASONIC MEETINGS
6 EXHIBITIONS
7 FILM SHOWS
8 AUCTIONS
9 WEIGHTWATCHER CLUBS
10 CHESS, WHIST COMPETITIONS
11 LIQUIDATORS/RECEIVERS MEETINGS
12 BOXING/WRESTLING NIGHTS
13 GOURMET/COOKING EXHIBITIONS
14 FASHION SHOWS
15 ANTIQUE FAIRS
16 ART GALLERIES
17 MUSICAL RECITALS
18 OPERATIC EVENINGS
19 MEETINGS OF THE MAGIC CIRCLE

INDEX